# IN THE
# SHADOW
# OF THE
# WALL

**A TRUE STORY**

To Margaret.

Best Wishes,

# In The Shadow Of The Wall

BY
## Carsten Kaaz
WITH
### Michael J. Riemann

GUILD BINDERY PRESS
MEMPHIS, TENNESSEE

Published in Memphis, Tennessee
by Guild Bindery Press, Inc.

Library of Congress Cataloging-in-Publication Data

LC Card Catalog Number: 94-79631

Editor and Publisher: Randall Bedwell
Senior Editor: Robbin Brent
Associate Editors: Palmer Jones, Trent Booker
Consulting Editor: David Yawn
Jacket Design: Pat Patterson, Patterson Design Works
Maps and Wall diagram: Toby Lyon

Kaaz, Carsten
<u>In The Shadow Of The Wall</u>

ISBN# 1-55793-023-6

published in the United States by

GUILD BINDERY PRESS
Post Office Box 38099
Memphis, Tennessee  38183

1 2 3 4 5 6 7 8 9 10
First Edition

Distributed to the trade by
SOUTHERN PUBLISHERS GROUP
1-800-628-0903

# Dedication

I would like to dedicate this book to my firstborn son, Kyle Aaron, with the hope that he will love America and respect freedom as much as I do.

Also, to my wife Bethany, for her love and kindness; my parents Fred and Barbara Kaaz, who were always there for me; my friends Lutz Bobzien and Mike Geraghty who showed me the meaning of true friendship; and to my best friend Uwe George — without him, I would have never obtained freedom.

*— We hold these truths to be self-evident,*
*that all men are created equal,*
*that they are endowed by their Creator*
*with certain unalienable Rights,*
*that among these are Life, Liberty*
*and the pursuit of Happiness.*
*— That to secure these rights,*
*Governments are instituted among Men,*
*deriving their just powers*
*from the consent of the governed,*
*— That whenever any Form of Government*
*becomes destructive of these ends,*
*it is the Right of the People*
*to alter or to abolish it,*
*and to institute new Government,*
*laying its foundation on such principles*
*and organizing its powers in such form,*
*as to them shall seem most likely*
*to effect their Safety and Happiness.*

— from THE DECLARATION OF INDEPENDENCE

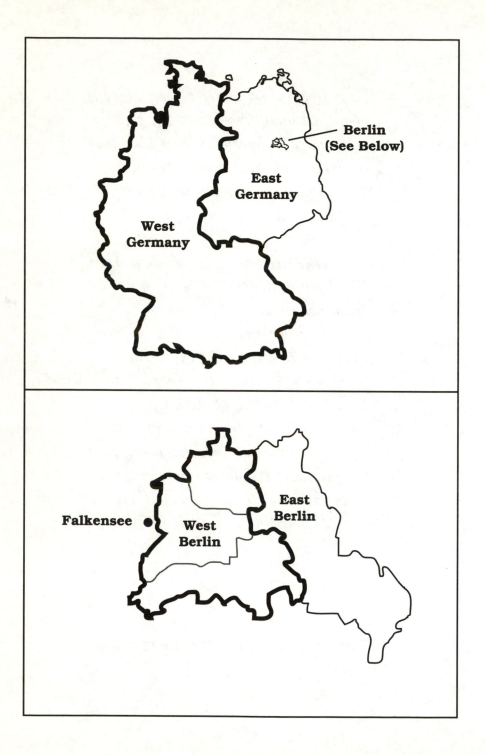

# PROLOGUE

I remember those days because I must, and I speak to remind anyone who will listen that there is no nation on earth immune to the poison that infected my country's veins. Memories of East Germany are all that remain. A cataclysm came and erased the familiar landmarks, leaving that society to find its way into tomorrow through a delirium of desperate hope.

We must journey back to the time when that old place still bloomed in its naked, threadbare strength, to the day-to-day reality that was the invisible foundation of the East German state. Oppression is not a living entity with pulse and breath, but a creeping, scaly thing born in the darkness of men's hearts. It was a relentless situation for a whole generation when hope was on holiday, reason had taken a recess, and the dumb patience of a generation was stretched to its absolute limits by those who would be masters — no matter what the cost.

Slowly, carefully, I wound the tiny paper around the shaft of the little arrow made from a hazelnut branch. A rubber band would serve to keep it in place for the short flight. Only a few meters up, then out over the neatly raked bare brown dirt. How far did it have to fly? An eleven-year-old boy isn't very good at judging distance. Perhaps 50 meters. I really had no idea. I squinted against the morning sun and breathed deeply. The sky was a deep blue and full of the promise of autumn. Newly fallen leaves crunched under every step, and the breeze was beginning to wield a sharp crisp edge. It was the kind of day when a man remembers the word carefree being spoken; it was the kind of sky where anything would be happy to fly.

On blustery afternoons I had seen them swaying against the

1

sky, darting back and forth, waving madly, celebrating freedom from the earth, tugging in their nervous haste to climb higher on the living air. The kites belonged to West German children who lived in the high-rise, beyond the Wall. From my vantage point, they were tiny figures racing across the distant high ground, pulling the colorful toys aloft. When a string broke, the kite would fall in a twisting tangle, tail over string, fighting the earth's tug in a helpless silent tantrum, sometimes drifting in a terminal dance over the Wall to be claimed by the largest and strongest boys in our neighborhood. I was small and weak, so I could only watch as the prize was re-rigged and sent aloft by its new master.

I heard the distant cries of delight at the fluttering loops and swoops; my child's hands ached to possess just one.

"We can't get that kind here. They aren't available," Mother had told me. "We can't go get one either. That's why they have the Wall, to keep us away from those people." Her gesture indicated the general direction of the high-rise.

But there were so many in the sky across the Wall, perhaps someone over there could get one for me. Perhaps the right person would find a special message. My stubby yellow pencil made carefully formed letters.

> *Dear unknown friend,*
> *I am eleven years old and my name is Carsten Kaaz. I live in Falkensee at Number Four, Zwingli Strasse. I can't get nice kites like yours where I live. Could you please send me one like you have in the mail? I'm just a little kid and I need someone to help me. Thank you very much.*

The rubber band snapped into place and the note was firmly secured to the shaft. Almost ready.

The homemade bow was strung with my father's twine; I had used it many times in our neighborhood cowboy and Indian games. It was the best one I had ever made, but as I looked through the high fence toward the outer wall, I was not sure. Would my arrow fly that far? Would anyone find it if it fell on the West side? If they did find it, would they send me a kite, or would they only laugh at the clumsy arrow with its sparrow-feather fletching and break it across their knee?

Draw back, aim upward. Higher, over the wire and higher still, because it was a long way across the distant wall. Let go with a satisfying twung sound, and see it turning, twisting in parabolic flight.

Down to the earth it fell, lying spent and failed across the neatly raked bare, beige dirt furrows in the forbidden area. No hope today for a kite from an unknown friend. I slung the bow over my shoulder and scuffed my feet home, kicking rocks and wondering if there was some other way.

The next Monday blue smoke drifted across the front yard as Herr Mowes, our district policeman, pulled up to the front gate on his Schwalbe motor scooter. His thick body hung over the seat and burdened the small machine, forcing it low on its suspension. A green Wartburg sedan crunched to a stop directly behind him. Mowes, dressed in his green Polizei uniform, entered the yard followed by two men in dark suits. They did not bother to ring the bell on the gate.

"Are your parents home?" Mowes asked. His stride never slowed as the three men pushed past me, uninvited, into the living room. They sat roughly on the couch, perching at the edge of the worn cushions, as my mother was coming out of the kitchen. A silent but questioning expression was all I could manage, not knowing what to say about how they came in. Her expression switched quickly from surprise to incredulous anger at the intruders, who had not even bothered to wipe their feet.

"Get your father," she said.

My father entered the room, surveyed the company and sat next to Mom without speaking. His eyes reflected suspicion and thinly veiled anger.

Mowes began, "I suppose you know why we are here."

Mother's face was hard as she looked at him through narrowed eyes. "Not the slightest idea." She didn't seem afraid, but I was nearly overcome with dread.

My father sat silently, assessing the situation.

"You need to pay better attention to how you are raising

your child," Mowes said. "Do you know what he did?"

I was hiding just out of sight around the corner in the short hallway.

"Carsten, come in here, please," Mom said.

I complied.

Mowes half turned and regarded me with his most stern expression of official disapproval. "Carsten, did you shoot an arrow over the fence toward the Wall?"

I nodded and looked at the floor. Who could have told anyone that I did it? Why was that so bad?

"Well it didn't reach its destination," Mowes indicated to his silent companions with a slight nod.

"You might say that it landed on their desk at headquarters in Potsdam."

I didn't understand that the place he spoke of was the district headquarters for Staatssicherheitsdienst, the State Security Service.

My father's features changed, first to disbelief, then to a furrowed-brow intensity that I had only seen just before he got really angry. He slid forward to the edge of the chair, his body tilted forward in an aggressive posture. Still silent, his dark eyes bored into Mowes.

"There was a note on the arrow asking someone on the West side to send him a kite." Mowes paused, gathering himself for the main message. "In the note, your son addressed those on the other side as unknown 'friends.'" His narrowed eyes darted back and forth from Mother to Father. "They are not our friends. They are our enemies!" The words boomed out as though they had been given to him by God.

A few seconds of silence followed. No one moved.

"What's the big deal?" Mother said.

Mowes' lips twitched. He turned his attention to my father. "Why don't you build him a kite? We often see young people go the wrong way when their family life is not good."

Father stiffened and met Mowes' stare with an iron one of his own. "You tell me where I can find some decent material within a hundred kilometers and I can do it." He made no attempt to hide his disgust. "Have you ever tried to buy anything around here? Have you ever heard the phrase, 'I'm sorry but it's not available'?" He shook his head.

I took a shallow breath. At least Mom and Dad weren't mad at me.

"Do you have any idea how serious this is?" Mowes said.

"What's so serious?" Dad said. "He's just a little kid."

Mother spoke. "I can't guarantee that he won't send another message, and there's really something wrong if you think this is some kind of crime."

The two Stasi agents were still sitting immobile, impassive, like sullen statues overshadowing us all, not reacting, not really participating, but watching, impaling us with dispassionate stares.

"Well, we have done what we came to do," Mowes said abruptly. "Just remember that this goes on his record."

The three stood as though on cue, straightened their jackets and swaggered slowly out the front door.

The Wartburg's starter whined, and Mowes kicked the Schwalbe's motor and it popped to life. Mother and Dad warmly hugged me like they did before bed every night.

"Don't worry about this sweetheart," Mom said. "Dad will find some way to get you a kite." Dad hugged me again and stalked out the front door, shutting it harder than usual, and Mom held me close again. Her fingers stroked my hair, and my heart found its normal rhythm.

Outside, our visitors' exhaust sounds grew faint and faded until they were swallowed by the silence of our peaceful neighborhood.

Soon enough, Mowes' bluster and the Stasi's predatory watching evaporated, and by supper-time other concerns eclipsed my fears.

I returned to the more immediate business of being a child.

Although comprehension of its intent was years away, I met the spirit of my country face to face that Monday afternoon as it reached out in a first embrace.

Zwinglistrasse, where author lived — 1987

# CHAPTER ONE

Life began for me in 1965, in Falkensee, a small town in East Germany nestled on the western border of the island-city of West Berlin, the most controversial national boundary of modern times.

Finding my town was simple. Measured in a straight line, Falkensee was 15 kilometers from downtown West Berlin, but for us, actually getting into the city of East Berlin meant a tiresome journey of 90 kilometers. It was necessary to circle all the way around the forbidden perimeter of West Berlin. A bird flying south through Spandau would journey only 10 kilometers from that prewar suburb where the prison housed Rudolf Hess until his death. Continuing southwest, the woods and parks of Spandau thinned, giving way to a level countryside dotted with villages, clustered houses and collective farms. Here and there, the land held water in small lakes. The smell of animals and soil was in the air and Hungarian-made tractors dragged slow loads of sweet, ripe hay balanced high on the backs of rubber-tired wagons. The earth was fertile and dark, holding promise of plenty for those who were willing to work. In the spring, visitors were immediately struck by the profusion of living colors. Houses, stores, factories, and even the mechanically arranged rows of deathly gray apartment buildings were dotted with the color of flowers growing in their seasons. Falkensee lived up to its nickname, 'The Garden City of Europe.'

The town boundaries were roughly rectangular, about three by six kilometers, with a two-acre lake set into its center like a muddy jewel. In the summer, the lake was a favorite place for parents to bring small children to swim or sail model boats.

Babies sometimes got away with naked bathing, but adults who wanted to sun their more sensitive parts had to visit designated beaches on the Baltic. It was a place where conservative values persisted despite the razor-sharp edges of the twentieth century. The intersection of Strasse der Jugend and Spandauer Strasse marked the center of town, the location of the Rathaus, city hall, and the city museum, which mainly housed a chronicle of communist triumphs since the last war. Significant local businesses included the Gebaude Wirtschaft, the state-operated building and construction operation where my father, Fred Kaaz, was in charge of remodeling operations; Radio & Fernsehtechnik, where electronic devices and appliances were repaired, and local manufacturing concerns like Polymath and Plastik Werk. Residents shopped at the same grocery store, went to the same Poliklinik for medical problems, and stopped at the same Apotheke to have prescriptions filled.

To go to a movie, it was necessary only to drive three kilometers and cross the east-west rail line on the south end of town. Management was allowed to show preselected Western movies twice a week, the other days being mandated to run material of East Bloc origin. Other local landmarks included the ubiquitous monument against fascism and the inevitable concrete bust of Vladimir Iliych Lenin. Winter snows softened the contours of the great hero's nose and piled impossibly high on the black aluminum letters that made up the monument's message. There was one Eisdiele, carrying ice cream in season; one Intershop, where high quality foreign goods could be purchased if the buyer had Western currency; and one fire department, that depended on volunteers to operate the single water-pumper engine if the alarm bell began to ring. My mother, Barbara Kaaz, worked for Haus der Dame, the specialty women's clothing store on the Strasse der Jugend. Eastward toward the Wall, sat the Huehnerfarm where eggs and poultry were produced mainly for export, the best goods going to West German customers. The Schweinemast was an odd two-story structure of reinforced concrete, and probably the only former panzer factory in the world converted to serve as an upstairs-downstairs pig sty. Half a mile from Schweinemast, the

Grenztruppen, East German border guards, parked vehicles, stock-piled supplies and maintained small barracks in their own depot on the cobblestoned Spandauer Strasse. Old people said Spandauer Strasse was an important street before 1961, but for as long as I could remember it simply ran eastward, terminating at the Wall with an unpainted concrete guard tower as a kind of odd exclamation point. Falkensee had a jail, a cemetery, a restaurant that was recommended more for its convenience than its food, and a centrally located paved community parking lot where young people congregated to socialize in the evenings. It was a place where a young person could grow up enjoying the best of two worlds; close enough to the cities of East Berlin and Potsdam, near enough to open country eyes to the possibilities of twentieth-century life, but far enough removed so that in the night, the honk and hiss of auto traffic was nothing more than a distant muttering often smothered by the sound of crickets. Old and slow, it was a place where a young person could mature, getting to know about the world but still having enough quiet to learn of his own heart.

Divorce is very common in Eastern Europe, and in 1969 my natural father left Mother and me, taking his alcoholism and abusive nature along. We remained alone until 1971, when Mom married Fred Kaaz. Although never legally adopted, from the time I started school, I used the name Kaaz.

The dozen or so homes in our neighborhood were built in the early Thirties. Most escaped destruction in the war because the town was on the side of Berlin opposite the main thrust of invading Soviet armies, and there was little of military value in the area. They were wood-framed, sturdy structures that for the most part stayed in very good condition due to constant repairing and care. We did not own our house, nor did our neighbors. Possessing land or real property was impossible in our society.

Frau Kosa, the widow across the street, was determined to remain in her home despite advancing age and periodic illness. She came closest to owning her own home because she had lived in the same place since her husband built it before the war. Since they stayed through the siege and bombardment of Berlin at the bloody end of the Third Reich, she felt it was her home no matter what any government said. Her husband, Willie Kosa, had been a mechanic in the nearby tank assembly plant and had somehow escaped internment by the Soviets when the machinery was dismantled and its engineers and technical people shipped away following Germany's surrender. They continued life together until later in the 1970's when Willie died.

We children could always get an extra piece of candy in exchange for good manners and a few minutes of conversation. She had an inexhaustible supply of grandmotherly hugs and unsolicited comments on the state of the present world compared to the times of her childhood. She would paint word-pictures of magical, blooming Berlin, wistfully recalling how even in the depths of an event called the Great Depression it had been alive with new ideas and world-moving personalities. We munched the candy and acted as though we had some comprehension of what she was saying.

"Just wait until you get older and you go to Berlin," she said. "You will never forget that." To us, Berlin meant East Berlin and we knew only that to get there it was necessary to travel around the other Berlin, a place so full of evil that our government had built barriers to protect us.

Surveying precious blooms, her tired feet shuffled and her bent body stooped as she teetered, steadied by a cane in her small yard.

"Don't step in the flowers, you little sweethearts," she told us.

"Yes, Frau Kosa." We took great care to avoid the flower pots crowding the front steps, and with lips still smacking resumed our games elsewhere on the dusty street.

The back of Kosa's house was 20 meters from the inner barrier, our side of the Berlin Wall.

Fifty meters down Zwingli, north of Frau Kosa, was Jerke's place. Herr Jerke was a production worker at the state-owned Plastikwerk Company, where one of the main products was fiberglass food containers for the army. He was a quiet, nondescript man of medium build, and like many of our other neighbors, kept well-groomed gardens and a small barnyard.

He was particularly successful in producing eggs with the dozen or so chickens he kept inside a wire enclosure. His son, Ronald, a peripheral member of our group, was slow-witted and too heavy to keep pace with our hyperactive ramblings. Frau Jerke, a woman who always seemed to know everyone's business, was a clerk at the Konsum, the local convenience store near the bus turnaround on Calvin Strasse. They were silent fixtures in the neighborhood, keeping mostly to themselves.

Helmut Schirmer lived in the last residence on the northeast side of Zwingli Strasse, in a house even older than ours. He was a tall and lanky, swaggering, loud-talking man whose Leipzig accent stood out noticeably among the older residents who still used Berliner idioms and verbal inflection. Schirmer was a border guard, a Grenztruppen, whose duty station was several kilometers away, in keeping with the custom of not assigning guards duty near anyone they knew. All border guards faced well-known social hazards since they were not accepted into the rest of society. As a group, they were purposely excluded from informal neighborhood social functions such as cook-outs and parties. This left them to congregate mainly with others of the same vocation. As with many specialized occupations, they tended to see themselves as apart and above the rest of the locals and fostered this image by communicating in their own jargon, particularly addressing each other as 'Genosse,' comrade, when offering a greeting. As in the case of Frau Kosa and Herr Jerke, Schirmer's backyard was bordered by the four-meter high inner-wire barrier of the Berlin Wall.

Our side of the street also was not crowded. The Krippner and Haan residences were separated from my home by vacant lots. Henrik Krippner and Jens Haan were boys about my age, and like weeds, we grew up together exploring the local lots, the pine thicket, and our favorite playground, the swamp. It was the flattest place in our area, and water would stand for many days after a hard rain. To us it was the place where on demand we could find any combination of imaginary alligators, lurking Indians, and anthropomorphic monsters. In the spring, the swamp was the first place we would hear the toads croaking and the fragile peeps of newly hatched birds. It was a place that a

11

Author's parents, Fred and Barbara Kaaz, in front of their home at
Number Four, Zwinglistrasse, in Falkensee, East Germany — 1990

Carsten Kaaz with his homemade toy, a Winchester rifle —1974

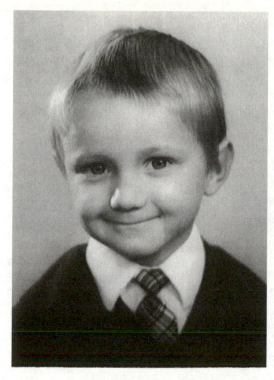

The
author
in
1970

child could appreciate for its marvelous potential.

In the beginning, the wider world and its troubles held few cares for us, for life was new and bold in our veins and the days were for playing. We could buy molded plastic Kalashnikovs in the department store — replicas of the Russian automatic rifles carried by our own army and border guards — but I preferred something different. Western films were often shown on West German TV stations, and I was able to watch all of the West Berlin programming because we lived so near the border. One evening I watched 'Winchester Seventy-Three' starring Jimmy Stewart. From that time on, "The Wild West" with cowboys and Indians was my favorite play scenario. To preserve the spirit of the game, I took a piece of wood from Dad's tool shed and shaped it with saw and knife into an approximation of a lever action rifle. After some ardent persuasion, my friends and I

13

would choose teams, drawing twigs for the privilege of being the cowboys. Usually the neighborhood girls also wanted to play, so we would make the role of Indians the price of their admission. When I was about six, we made a treehouse from scrap lumber and fashioned an old black shirt into the neighborhood's first skull and crossbones. We knew that some kids liked to play army, but from the beginning, our group was possessed by a frontier spirit. Even then, we loved the rain in our faces and the whisper of the breeze in the pines that spoke in a secret tongue of the incomprehensible vastness of the world. We acted out our unconscious exploratory longing in innocent games. For me, the seeds of a singular vision were quietly opened in the sunlight of those simple days.

One day when I was about six, Mom and Dad came in from the backyard. They seldom argued, but Dad was waving his arms in uncharacteristic hostility. They were very angry.

"Jerke's grass is dying, and his garden is gone, too. I saw his wife at the Konsum, and she says some of their animals are even sick," Mom said. "They said it was some kind of poison."

Dad stood by the window, looking out into the backyard at our strawberry garden.

"You can see the same thing here," he said. "It has to be herbicide. The rabbits are just lying there not eating, and the shrubs by the fence are wilting. It must be something the guards sprayed on the Wall and let drift over this way on the wind. Schirmer probably knows, but he wouldn't tell on his dear comrades, so I'm not going to give him the satisfaction of my asking."

"That's it then. We'll never know for sure," Mom said. "There's no point in asking, because no matter what happens, they don't have to tell us anything unless they feel like it."

The conversation trailed off into silence, and Mother shuffled slowly back to the kitchen. Pots and dishes made familiar clinking sounds, and Dad continued to stare at the strawberry bed. After a long moment he turned away, lips set in hard lines, eyes glistening with involuntary silent tears. He was a steady man of quiet strength, but the depth of his frustration was clear. I cataloged the incident, feeling more puzzlement than anything else. They were angry, but at whom? Was there someone to fight against?

More neighborhood gardens were lost over the years. When the wind was right, the herbicide that was sprayed in the forbidden area drifted with the breeze and killed whatever vegetation it touched. I saw the same anger later, and the same cold silence that always followed. It was all part of life's heavy rhythm.

From time to time, some local event would provide excitement, and the dinner table was where we always found out.

"Did you hear about Stutzer?" Dad said.

Stutzer was one of our most interesting neighbors. He and his family lived one street behind us on Pestalozzi Strasse. His home was situated on a large lot, and like most residents he kept animals. But where others had only a few rabbit hutches or a chicken coop, he had those and a stable and two horses.

"Carsten, please eat the Brussels sprouts," Mom said. "What about him?"

"You remember that he lost his driver's license for driving drunk?"

Mom nodded. His genial nature and love for alcohol were legendary.

"He wanted to take a drive yesterday afternoon, so he hitched up the four-wheeled wagon to both horses and took off down Pestalozzi."

Mom shrugged. That didn't sound so unusual. Everyone knew that he had a wagon and that he sometimes drove it.

"He was drunk this time too. The horses were running for all they were worth, and he was hanging onto the reins, yelling at the top of his lungs."

Mom coughed and forced her food down. They both laughed, and as I smiled, Dad caught my eye. "You would have enjoyed that ride, cowboy," he said.

Mom's eyes got big and she coughed again. "Never ride in that wagon unless you ask me first!" Then to Dad she asked, "So, did anyone call the Vopos?"

Dad shook his head. "He calmed down before anyone

thought about that, and I don't think he went by Koch's house anyway. Weber was home, but you know that he wouldn't cause trouble unless someone was in danger. He'd be a really good neighbor, if he wasn't a Vopo."

Herr Koch and Herr Weber were in law enforcement, but they were very different from each other. Weber reminded me of Spencer Tracy on West Berlin TV; a tough but kind man who would never hurt anyone unless there was no other choice. Although not very tall, Weber was powerfully built with thick biceps and broad shoulders. His police duty was as a bicycle patrol in another part of town with the constant companionship of his trained shepherd police dog. Instead of looking for reasons to report people, rumor was that he remembered his own failings and left citizens alone unless some real crime was being committed. He didn't fit the usual mold of the Volkspolizei because he didn't enjoy their perpetual game of intimidating as many people as possible, most often using nothing more than an unblinking stare and putrid, feigned politeness.

Koch was an inspector for customs in Staaken, about three kilometers away. He spent a lot of time outside in the yard, pulling weeds or working on his car, but I never saw him stopping to comment on the weather or pass the time with neighbors. About forty years old, he was a quiet man, but his was the kind of quiet that happens when the crickets stop chirping in the night because there is something wrong. His presence was silent and ominous, like something unwelcome and threatening had come close and other living things wanted to get away. His torso was thick like a flour sack from overeating and inactivity, but the sharp, dark eyes never relaxed their darting, probing gaze.

As the early years passed, I grew among these people, getting to know them by reputation or association and filtering my understanding of life through interactions with them. But like most children, I was most interested in how to have fun.

Zwingli Strasse was not paved, but was surfaced with dirt and crushed rock, packed hard by decades of vehicle and foot traffic. Mom and Dad bought me a bicycle with training wheels, but it was awkward and unstable on the lumpy road.

To my five-year-old mind, the solution seemed simple — find pavement. Looking around, I could see the undulating grey ribbon of the first Berlin Wall in the distance. The second, inner wall had not yet been constructed, but a barbed-wire fence blocked anyone from approaching closer than fifteen meters. The wire barrier did not seem to be a threat to me and my friends, but fell into the same category as a rock, tree or guard tower. It was simply part of the neighborhood. I noted the paved surface that paralleled the fence on the inside and decided to give it a try. Every day, I saw the Grenztruppen motorcycles putter by on its hard black surface, and none were present at that moment, so why not? The next nearest smooth roads were a kilometer away, so this one was ideal.

The chain made a buzz-click, buzz-click against the chain-guard as I wobbled the new two-wheeler southward down my street. Ahead was a whole new dimension in riding pleasure. How perfect, I thought. The closer I came, the more I appreciated its smoothness. I pumped the pedals harder and steered onto the black granular surface.

Click-buzz, click-buzz. I stood hard on the pedals and accelerated, weaving and tipping, caught by the auxiliary wheels, the delicious breeze washing my face.

From somewhere far behind came an odd thump and the creak of reluctant hinges.

"Hey," the voice called. "Hey you, kid!" In an iron-cold, commanding tone. "Hey, I'm talking to you!"

I quit pedaling and coasted to a stop. Turning in the seat, I could see the man's face and shoulders as he leaned out of the guard tower window. The bike tipped and I lurched, trying to regain balance.

"You can't ride out here. Go someplace else." Even from ten meters away, his snarling face was visible. A very mean-looking face! He was going to stand there and watch until I did what he said. Adults did that sort of thing sometimes, but this one watched with unusual intensity.

I turned the bike as quickly as possible without getting off the seat by pushing on my toes, involuntarily teetering from one side to the other. Not daring to look at him again, I pedaled back to Zwingli and turned onto the dirt. Far behind, I heard the sudden squeak-slam of the tower window as the guard returned to his endless vigil.

When I reached home, Mom listened to the story, then sat me carefully on the couch. Her expression was a curious mixture of the love that was always there when she looked at me and a profound tiredness, which I had really noticed only a few times before.

"Don't be afraid, but don't go back out there, either. Times are different now, and you have to be careful to follow all of the rules." She hugged me tightly. "Just try to understand. There are things we can't change, so we have to live with them."

I didn't understand the fence, and I didn't understand the wall beyond it. The only thing I was beginning to comprehend was the guards in the tower. They had been around ever since my earliest recollection, but had never mixed at all with people in the neighborhood, acting even more distant than the police. If they were our protectors, their faces showed little enthusiasm for the work. A few months after that, trucks turned onto our street from Calvin Strasse and down climbed men with power saws.

I whined at Mom, "They're cutting all of the trees down. Why?" The smell of two-cycle oil and wood chips mingled in the gentle breeze, and curious eyes peered from neighborhood windows. Bushes and trees disappeared piecemeal into the back of trucks, punctuated by the grunts of sweating men. No more treehouse. No more pirate flag. Nothing but a few scraggly bushes surviving where our swamp used to be. I began to cry, and Mom tried distraction by turning me away from the window as she explained, "They want to protect us, I think. When the trees are gone, there won't be anywhere for anyone to sneak in and hide near our houses or in the vacant lots."

I nodded, but it was incomprehensible. In a primitive way I knew that more was being lost than just a few trees. Now there was no familiar lair in which to hide and play. The trees had meant a lot to me and my friends, in the summer shading our games, and in the winter bowing gracefully low under the weight of large, wet snowflakes. Beneath their branches, we had dreamed our seagoing adventures, fought as cowboys and

Indians, and played hide and seek. The trees had no names, but each one was as personal as any of us boys. They fell one by one beneath the chewing steel and screaming motors; inside I was also wounded. The workmen dismembered their limbs and trunks into handy pieces and took them away without ceremony.

The advice was simple, and my parents had said it so many times that even then I knew it by heart. 'There is nothing you can do about it, so just don't let it get to you. Focus on something else. Don't let your mouth get you into trouble. There are things so big that you can't change them.'

The next morning I went for a closer look. Severed stumps oozed pitifully in the morning sun. Abruptly, there was no more joy in the barren land, and a profound sorrow impaled my heart.

August 13, 1961
East German guards seal off the East/West Berlin border

An early picture of the Wall before it gained height

# CHAPTER TWO

In the proper season I entered preschool, which comes after kindergarten. We studied math, German, art, geography, and had programmed physical exercises. At 2:00 p.m., daily classes were over, and those of us with working parents were supervised at school until 4:30 p.m., then I walked home with the other boys and girls of the neighborhood. Dad and Mom came home, and the evening pattern began.

"Let's see your daily workbook," Mom said. "You got another 'A' in math! You can't do better than the best! What's this, another note that you're talking too much? You have to behave, because if you don't, the next thing will be a conference with the teacher. You don't want to embarrass us, do you?"

Dad told what happened at work. We discussed the rain, the weather getting hotter or colder, and other events of daily life.

"No cabbage again today," Mom said.

Dad shrugged.

"And the potatoes are so small it's ridiculous. You can't tell me they can't grow bigger potatoes. All the women are saying how small they are."

"Of course, they grow bigger ones," Dad said. "Everyone knows the government sells the best from the state farms to West Germany so they can get their currency." The shrug again. "Nothing we can do about that."

"What about the coal, Fred? Our coal-ration card says we can only get half the usual amount. If this winter is long, we're going to be cold." As she spoke, she was looking at me, and fear was leaking through her brave mask.

"Neues Deutschland says it is so cold that the miners can't

dig enough," Dad said, and clicked his tongue. "Some of the men at work say they've seen trainloads rolling West across the border every day. Two kilometers of our coal headed for West German furnaces. I hope they enjoy being warm."

I looked from one to the other.

Dad tapped his fork roughly in the plate.

"I know what you're thinking, Carsten, but there's nothing we can do about it. The government is in charge, and they do whatever they think is best." He shook his head and pushed the food about aimlessly. "We'll get through it all right." Another sigh. "Everything goes its socialist way."

One of my routine duties was tending the rabbit hutches and fertilizing our garden. Rabbit dung was good nutrition for strawberries, but spreading it was not an intellectually stimulating activity, so after moving a few shovels full my attention would wander.

"Carsten," Dad said, "I can see that you don't like this, but you should look at this job and think about life." He studied my face, hoping that I was actually paying attention. "If you want strawberries, you have to carry fertilizer. For everything that you enjoy here, there will be something connected with it that you won't like. You have to learn to be happy with things as they really are. There will be many times in your life when you'll see something that should be different, but to change it is impossible because that's the way things are. It's impossible because there are men who have great power who will do anything to keep it. It doesn't do any good to go around mad about it either, because causing trouble will get you on someone's list, and if that happens more than a few times, they'll never leave you alone."

His hands had tightened nearly into fists, and I could see anger there, calloused and concealed, overburdened by a massive, accreted strata of silent frustration. For just a moment it was like looking into an open furnace door, with the flames and heat reaching out to consume anything near, and then the door closed again, and Dad was talking to me.

"Are you paying attention? If you do it like I am telling you, life will be a lot less trouble."

On blustery spring days I rode a Diamant bicycle through

the neighborhood with friends. We went like a dusty cluster of buzzing, squealing gnats blown about on a friendly breeze. Pedaling furiously north on Zwingli Strasse we stopped, tires skidding, in front of the guard tower where the street went beneath the inner-wire fence. There was a family, a mother and daughter, who lived in the last house on the north end of the street. The girl was about my age, but never played in our group. One day I saw them packing cardboard boxes into their old car; they were moving.

"I suppose it's because of Frau Schroder's daughter," my mother explained. Her face betrayed genuine empathy. "The neighbors say that she has been too friendly with the guards stationed in the tower near the house. After school she would stop and talk to them from the front yard before going inside."

Grenztruppen Officers had found out that the guards were sending the girl to the Konsum, a local convenience store, for cigarettes, and they reported the child to civil authorities. The Schroders were forcibly relocated to an apartment building in town, and a few days later a border-guard officer named Hildebrandt moved in with his family. They already knew that it was no use to try and mix with the normal people of the neighborhood, so they followed the pattern of Schirmer and Koch, not even attempting to make friends.

"I wave at the men in the towers sometimes Mother, but they hardly ever wave back," I said. "Why do they stay up there?"

"They're here to protect us," she said. It was as though she was reading words from a poorly written book. "Don't worry about it, but don't hang around there."

I nodded. "Protect us?"

She glanced away, then patted my head.

"The government just doesn't want anyone to distract the guards from their work." She was looking at me in an odd way, searching my eyes, perhaps assessing the depth of my concerns, worrying about the future of an inquisitive mind.

Not just anyone could visit my family, because to get there you had to pass the large red and white signs that stood on every street-corner approach, and at intervals down every block at the frontier boundary. There was no mistaking their meaning.

23

YOU ARE APPROACHING THE FRONTIER AREA
UNAUTHORIZED ENTRY IS FORBIDDEN

Directly adjacent and parallel to the Wall was a security zone two blocks deep called the frontier. In order to enter this area legally, persons over age 14 had to possess a special stamp on their ausweis, or identity card. Living there was not a problem until a person wanted to expand friendships and social activity, and for practical purposes children under fourteen were free to come and go at will. On the other hand, entry for those adults not living there was virtually impossible except in very rare circumstances. Social isolation was an unavoidable side effect of living in the area.

The greatest compensation for frontier residents was being able to live in single-family dwellings while most other citizens could never dream of the possibility. In town, it was common for adult children to still be living with their parents even as they began to raise their own families.

The everyday rhythm of our life was predictable and quiet for the most part, but occasionally we were awakened in the night by Ringo, our German shepherd. Standing awkwardly in his undershorts, looking out through the parted drapes, my father could see the shadowy forms of the police or border guards on random street patrol. Another of the frontier regulations required keeping our one and only ladder secured in the shed with a lock and heavy chain whenever it was not actually in use. As for fear, I was never afraid to go outside day or night, because I knew that the security of our neighborhood simply was not an issue at all. No outsiders would dare venture past the red and white warning signs to commit a crime. If there was any mischief to be made, it was by the neighbors or their children. Mom and Dad told me to always be careful, but it was also clear that they did not fear harm coming to me as I played in the nearby lots and yards.

To our young minds, the fears and restrictions of adults had little meaning, except to raise initial curiosity; so the frontier area rules and the striped warning signs went ignored simply because they did not have any direct effect on us. They were too high off the ground to hide behind and too tall to climb.

24

They were of no consequence until later in life.

When I was about nine, an inner wall was built where the fence had been. It happened like a surprise summer shower. One minute the sky is clear, and in just a little while something covers the sun and the drops begin to fall.

One day we went to school, and in the afternoon when we arrived home, the wire fence had been replaced. A whole section of wall 80 meters long between the guard towers had been constructed in one day. All the local children were amazed and got together for a discussion, sitting in a small circle eating cookies and chattering like squirrels.

"What's going on?" Henrik asked.

"Another wall," I said. "They put it up in a hurry!"

For a country where almost anything takes forever, we knew that it was really fast work.

"It's really close, right behind my house," Ronald Jerke declared. He adjusted his glasses and pointed. "You can come out back and see."

We ran together in a shoe-scuffling gaggle past his chicken coop and around the back of the gray wood-frame house.

In the distance, we could see the construction proceeding with undiminished haste. Mostly there were soldiers wearing the Grenztruppen greenish-brown uniforms, the trademark of the border guards that we had seen all our lives. Working in groups of four and five, stripped to the waist, they carried materials, sweating and swearing as the line of upright steel supports was extended one at a time. Modifications were also being made on the inter-wall area, but these were saved until after the barrier was in position. That way no one could see between the walls, and the newly installed alarms and obstacles were shielded from view.

We sat in a line, like little birds on a fence, watching and pointing at things of interest. A large truck had some kind of post-driving machine mounted on the bed, and it pounded the steel beams deep into the earth one at a time. Farther down the line were other trucks and a small crane that lifted the concrete slabs high so the soldiers could guide them down into the grooves between the beams. Men in regular clothing measured and marked, pulled string and marked again, indicating the path the wall must follow. They were not sweating.

"They're getting ready to start another post," Ronald said. He adjusted his glasses and squinted his defective eyes. "My dad says that they'll scare our chickens so bad that they won't lay any eggs for a long time." We could hear repetitive thuds and metallic pounding as another beam was forced into the earth.

First the wire, then another wall. What did it all mean? When we discussed it, we found that our parents had all given the same basic story. My mother explained it later that evening, but something was still out of order. She reluctantly explained that there was an army across the wall with tanks and guns, and that there might be some fighting if the governments couldn't work things out. She had never spoken fearfully of the West before, but even then it seemed less fear than resignation to the obvious fact that the governments that were created by men had so little success in governing them. In the end, we children simply repeated the reasons for the wall to each other, not really understanding, and went back to play. I lingered for a moment, just staring, wondering at the sheer, gray mass. Whose idea was that thing anyway?

That night, my family sat at the dinner table and Dad passed the Brussels sprouts toward me. I made a face as usual. His hand never wavered, so I took a little one, never intending to let it touch my lips.

"Maybe the new wall will really turn out to be a good thing," he said. "There's talk at work that the government is thinking about opening the frontier area, normalizing it for visitors now that we are better protected."

"That would really be wonderful," Mom said. Her face flashed momentarily with a bright smile, then slipped into a wistful, sad look. "It has been a long time since we had visitors."

"Maybe it's not good to get your hopes up too much. You know how it is now, with all the politics and trouble. I wish things would just settle down."

"It's hard to understand it all," Mom said. "You'd think they all had enough of war. Maybe it's different when you don't have the destruction in your own country. You don't have to get up every morning and see it."

"They ought to live here for a while. We still have bombed-out buildings on our block, and the streets aren't even paved." Dad picked at his food. "I wonder what the people in the West really think about us?"

"They're just like us, I think. It's probably just their leaders who have a bad outlook. This restriction is very hard to live with, but then we're really lucky to have a house. So many have to live in those dismal apartments. It's depressing to even think about it." She sighed and brushed back her blonde hair. "It's better to be stuck in the frontier than stuffed into those concrete apartments like herring."

Even through inexperienced eyes I could see that all around were people like Mom and Dad, the essential underpinning of my country — hard-working, contributing to the economy, honorable, and willing to bear hardships in order to support the social order. Their lives were examples of willing obedience to society's rules. I watched their struggles and, like every generation of children, gradually developed a silent determination that I would not suffer as they had, that my life would somehow be different and better.

Although it seemed that our everyday existence was much better than most, I could detect the muted stirrings of repressed anger pervading my parents' life. On one hand, they were grateful for having a home, food, and safety, but on the other, everyday life was a constant struggle against something unseen, something very heavy that slowed and dulled the normal cadence of life. It had no name, no face, but I could feel it wrapped around our lives like an old, damp coat. The undercurrent of dissatisfaction that I saw in them was subterranean, a desperate day-by-day grinding existence scarred by superficial coping and unrelenting frustration.

Life began in earnest with the passing of preschool and kindergarten. The grade-school years signaled embarkation into a plan designed to prepare our minds for assimilation into an intense educational process. We were expected to study hard and really learn, not just receive grades, and it was clear to everyone from the beginning that academic performance was an essential key to options in later life. We were too young to really comprehend the implications of those ideas, but understand or not, we were pressed by teachers and parents to achieve. As part of the overall plan, our political education began with the commencement of history classes and our induction into the Jung Pioneer, the ubiquitous youth organization.

Although sponsored by the educational system, the youth groups were really organizations of preparation and selection for the Communist Party. They were designed to function in an extra-curricular mode, and held regular, weekly activities after school hours. Attendance was mandatory, and appropriate participation was demonstrated by students preparing reports, learning to repeat political doctrine, and becoming thoroughly familiar with our country's official version of world history. With the exception that the programs imbued us with a socio-political intensity found elsewhere in later youth, we were like children everywhere. Staying after school to sing patriotic songs and listen to speeches grew tiresome, and when that special night of the week rolled around, our stomachs tightened with negative anticipation. What would it be this time?

Wednesday meant Pioniernachmittag, and all day we waited with uncomfortable anticipation for the evening's subject to be announced. We were packing books into our schulmappen backpacks before going home and whispering that perhaps the teacher had forgotten what day it was when his voice came, cutting through the polite buzz of our own conversation.

"There'll be a movie tonight in Falkensee, and you all need to be there. Don't forget to wear your white shirts."

Barely audible groans were silenced by his sharp glance.

The announcement could only mean another war movie. I had seen them all, mostly Russian produced, of the marching socialist legions. Classical music brought dramatic feeling to images of battlefields filmed in black and white, with their fountains of earth erupting to the resonating, over-dubbed explosions. Men fell so cleanly, without a cry, dropping like discarded dolls in a crescendo of violins, crashing cymbals, and thunder rolling drums. Over and over the enemy was vanquished and forced to admit its bloody works, and then came the parades, the adulation of the victors. The Fascists were the bad guys, and the Communists were the good guys. Did we have to attend? Of course. Attendance was expected, and we were being trained always to do what was expected. Liking the presentations was never an issue, but being there was as much a requirement of the education program as learning arithmetic.

The teacher nodded affirmation to the group and resumed his work, so we packed our books and papers and left school in small groups, heading for the city bus stop or our own bicycles.

The films and the instruction sessions were supposed to ingrain a sense of loyalty to the country, an understanding of our ideological foundations, a desire to conform to the needs of the state, and, finally, a hatred of the West as the author of World War and all misery. As children, we were not good at nurturing hatred. It was an adult curiosity that didn't yet fit our basic natures.

Constant reminders of the last world conflagration and assertions that the Fascists were now all in the West overshadowed our minds. The government wanted us to fear the West and harbor fear of warfare, which they said the capitalists would someday start. To prepare for all of this, they said, we maintained an army and were supported by our benevolent Soviet neighbors.

After a little familiarization, we were in slack-jawed awe of the modern battlefield tools. What child didn't shiver at the prospect of driving a house-sized tank? What child didn't stare with jaws agape at the shiny steel bayonet and automatic rifle, symbols of power wielded by heroes? What malleable mind could dispassionately view the marching ranks of stern, resolute faces whose courage was proven on bloody fields where cannons breathed death? When we fought, our reason was defense, they said, and we were the ones who stood for freedom.

Then they told us of greed, a Western lust for material things so ravenous that it knew no bounds. We heard of places like Hiroshima and Nagasaki, ghettos and homeless paupers, and saw pictures of shining automobiles costing millions of marks driving through neighborhoods where children cried from hunger and garbage littered the streets. From the beginning, the

29

West was painted as a place of pain where only the hardest and most avaricious prospered.

In this setting we were molded to comply, taught to obey, counseled to conform to the instructions that descended from above. Our leaders were our salvation, they told us, and they had sacrificed, bearing unimaginable hardship so we could live in a safe, orderly society. Most of us were not really afraid of the West, but the very mention of that word caused the automatic recall of compound horrible images. For the majority, afraid or not, we knew what was expected if shooting started. If our names were called, we would step forward.

I arrived home as usual, had a snack and flopped on the couch to watch the clock. Mom and Dad were still at work, so I munched my cookie and considered options. Going to the movies might not have been so bad, except that it was required. That imperative immediately removed any possible entertainment value. We were expected to go home from class at three-thirty and report to the theater by five. Roll would be taken before the film, so staying away was no good without a written excuse, and anyway these films were as much a part of our official political education as classroom lectures. At that point in life, we knew only that political doctrine was repetitive, boring, and very distant from the concerns of daily life. It was also in-escapable, and although most of the teachers were not enthusiastic in their political presentations, we understood that our knowledge in that area was to be tested. As a follow-up to the audio-visual experience, we would discuss the film's contents the next day in class and be graded on our understanding of the plot and moral points. After the test, we could forget everything if we wanted, and no one would ever ask again.

There was no escape from this recrudescent drill, so like the other 30 kids in class, I grumbled to myself and waited. Finally, the clock's hands crept into position, and it was time to go.

Heading out on my bicycle, I cleared the bus turnaround on Berliner Strasse and saw Ulf Kubicki about 25 meters ahead. He noticed and slowed so I could catch up. After greetings, we exchanged 10-year-old perspectives on the upcoming activity.

"Did you bring anything to eat?" he asked.

"No." I stood harder on my pedals. The afternoon breeze was picking up and it was getting harder to keep any speed. "Is Zickert's mother going to keep her sick little boy home again?"

Ulf laughed and matched my pace. Did he want to race again? Not today, please! Zickert was a gawking, ignorant bully who had been held back for failing grades. He had to repeat that whole year of school and unfortunately landed in our class. His presence was a constant problem. He was able to avoid attending at least one of the Pioniernachmittag after-school meetings every month because his mother would send a note saying he wasn't feeling well and had to go to the Poliklinik for an aching stomach. We were always glad if he didn't show, because having Zickert around meant having to stay out of his way so he didn't punch or trip you. All the kids looked forward to his sixteenth birthday, which would mean he was old enough to be taken out of regular school and put into training for a factory job.

Ulf and I rode side by side, talking when the ground was level, puffing a little when we hurried across Strasse der Jugend, watching out for the cars, and then the railroad tracks were before us.

Almost there. I could see other kids straggling in ahead, but it didn't help to know that in this particular aggravation we had a lot of co-sufferers. We parked our bikes and I drifted away from Ulf and into the building, dropping greetings here and there in the tittering crowd and settling on a place in one of the back rows. Picking the right seat was essential because it determined what you were going to have to put up with. Sitting too close to the teacher meant you would have to act like you were paying attention, he could actually see you in the flickering light. If you sat with the goof-offs, you might get into trouble, because when the lights went off, they always started talking or shooting paper wads. I was learning that the best thing to be was invisible. Small pockets of kids formed like clouds on a summer afternoon, each with their own particular endurance strategy, but for that hour I preferred to sit on an end row, aloof from any of the particular groups. Maybe I could take a nap after watching enough film to see where the simplistic plot was

31

headed.

The air in the theater was stale, laden with essences of a thousand spilled drinks, dropped candies, and pervasive decay. Parts of the screen had lost the silver reflective surface, the dull patches lending a moth-eaten ambiance to the structure. We all went to movies for recreation, but West German television was the main source of true entertainment. We understood that this theater was merely an extension of school, another instrument of the state's incessant prodding of our minds with Communist ideals. There was no relief from the pressure to believe and conform to officially sanctioned doctrinal thought, and even those who considered Marx's ideals valid admitted that they sometimes needed a rest from mental bombardment. The over-told tales changed fewer minds than the same ones might have, told once and told well. It was simply another class session where we would witness the same stereotypes. Neither plot nor actors mattered, because we could surely predict what was about to be stamped into our doctrine-weary minds.

There would be a brutal Nazi and a humane Russian, probably a farmer or a history teacher, who rose to defend the Rodina even though he didn't really like to fight, and some Soviet peasants who would be slaughtered by bombs, shells, or shot against a bullet-pocked wall by glowering gray-clad soldiers. The Nazis would have the upper hand until this reluctant citizen-soldier Russian saw an opportunity to stop the invaders by an act of self-sacrifice, which usually resulted in his death. After the bad guys were visited by some appropriate vengeance, the movie would abruptly end in a crescendo of gallant, thunderous music.

It was all very predictable, and our boredom had deepened past the point of taking the trouble to be critical of style or plot. It simply didn't matter. If they were trying to teach us something about war, what we got was that in the long run it must have been brutal and that there wasn't much hope either for the victors or the vanquished. Wounds of the body and spirit were suffered by both, and as long as men hated each other for any reason, there would at best be only cessation of open conflict, never true peace. They reminded us that all the Nazis had either gone over to the Western powers or been killed. We thought that the latter, at least, was true, because Erich Honecker was jailed by the Nazis for his Communist connections, and it wasn't likely that he forgot his former tormentors.

The teacher called for quiet and looked around taking roll. It was good to have a seat away from the major troublemakers, even better that I didn't have to sit next to anyone who was going to feign interest and start some kind of a conversation about the film. Those people were rare, but they did exist. I was also seated not far from some of the better-looking girls. Among them was Vivien Taschner, a girl my age whom I had just begun to notice. The dim light softened her features, lending a suddenly curious intimacy to the moment. I was three meters away, but it seemed as though she was very near. Her head turned slightly. Was she looking at me?

Vivien's home was three blocks from mine. Growing up in such close proximity, I had learned something of her circumstances. The first of two children, she was from a family of educated, well-connected parents. Her father was an independent electrician, which meant that he operated the business under charter from the state but did not own it. That arrangement was different in that he was not obliged to report to the state system but was still required to meet the yearly plan output quotas and charge for his services as prescribed by current state regulations. He had considerable responsibility and, at work at least, was respected.

Vivien's mother was totally devoted to being sure that her daughter had the opportunity and the motivation to succeed. From an early age, Vivien showed outstanding talent in art and was constantly being pushed by her mother to expand her capabilities. She tended toward the serious side, but that was better since I found intelligent girls the most interesting. Vivien glanced my way again, but it was hard to say whether she was smiling at me or someone else nearby.

The lights dimmed, and I imagined her sitting in the adjacent seat, her head resting on my shoulder.

Classical music began, convoluted weaving sounds of busy violins signaling the gathering of the battle-storm, then Cyrillic characters flashed across the screen. I could read the words because since the fifth grade we had studied Russian. Proficiency in that language was not optional, and we were told over and over how the Russians were our friends and had saved our land from the Nazis.

I settled further down, slouching in the wood-backed seat as the shooting started. German dive bombers swooped from the flak-puffed sky, sirens howling their death song, and civilians stood frozen in horror as their world crumbled beneath thundering bombs. These were Russians dying beneath the German onslaught. What did I really know about Russians anyway? I recalled the times when they had sent army personnel to Pioniernachmittag to instruct us. They'd been different from the Russian troops we saw occasionally in town, their pale white faces peering from a tarp-shrouded camouflaged troop truck. Traveling only in groups, carefully controlled, they were herded like cattle by their officers.

During one visit, I saw my first Soviet officer up close. He seemed very tall, more than a normal man, and was decorated with uniform medals and carrying a gun. He told a few stories of the Great Patriotic War and assured us that he was our friend — that he and others like him had saved our country from the criminals. He said that they fought our country, but they didn't look at it as fighting Germans; they were just fighting all the Fascists. It was an important and often-repeated distinction.

His pressed uniform, shiny buttons, polished shoes, and proud posture were impressive, and the Kalashnikov rifle was impossibly heavy.

"Handle it," he said. "This is what we use to defend you from those who want to make war with your country. And watch out for your fingers. The bolt will smash them if you are careless." The weapon moved slowly from hand to hand, the boys taking aim and imitating gunfire.

The girls gave the sleek metal a polite, but hesitant, examination, then passed it along.

We understood when he spoke of those wanting war. From the preschool and kindergarten days, we knew that America was the enemy. We knew that they had made war before and wanted

34

to possess our land and use it to grow richer. They were the only nation ever to use the atom bomb against their fellow man. They locked black children out of their white schools; they were filled with lust, greed, and evil. We heard that story a thousand ways, directly and indirectly, until it stained our understanding to the core, becoming as much a part of our knowledge as the alphabet. The kids stirred in their chairs as the officer finished his presentation, and after he left, the teacher initiated the inevitable commentary.

"That was interesting, wasn't it? Now, what do you think about our friends the Soviets?" The canned speech proceeded. "They suffered 30 million dead in the war, and now they want to make sure that there is never a war again. That's why they are here among us. They are protectors and trusted friends."

There was no mistake about the viewpoint we were supposed to take, but even then it didn't seem quite so simple. From what we heard outside of school, Russia was a miserable place, with shortages of everything that people needed to carry on daily life. We had our own phrase for that: 'It's not available'; but they had another: 'I've never heard of that.' Even knowing this, their society was constantly held up as a model for ours to follow. The lessons were different at inception, but identical in closing. Over and over came the themes of self-sacrifice, enduring hardship, and subordinating our will to that of the state, but try as they would, those seeds hardly ever sprouted. We simply were not fertile ground for the abstract ideas that prophesied conquest of the world by the Communist masses. Few of us really learned to fear or to hate from the words of our teachers.

The projector flickered on, clicking its background harmony, and memories paraded randomly as my mind tried to compensate for the overwhelming dullness. Eyelids sagged involuntarily and the nap overtook me. I nodded off, slouching awkwardly deeper down in the hard-backed seat, and dozed until the lights came up and one of the other kids nudged me.

On the way out of the theater, I motioned to Ulf. "What was it all about?"

He laughed and adjusted his glasses, "Give me 30 seconds

Ulf
Kubicki,
friend
of author
— 1982

Carsten
with his
brother
Roberto
— 1978

Author's
best friend,
Uwe George
at age 14

Annelies Kubicki in her garden

and I'll tell you everything."

Our grandparents harbored dark, blood-stained memories of Berlin's conquest by the Red Army. The school books were pro-Soviet, but from hearing casual conversation, unguarded comment, and outright condemning witness, we knew the hearts of our elders held no love for the protectors. Like many of my peers, I memorized our history lessons, but non-official sources were also available to help round out my perspective.

Within my own family, I had a sort-of lesson every time I was with my grandfather, Kurt Grossert. His worn, aging body held a robust mind filled with intricately woven stories of his youthful days as a soldier in the Wehrmacht, when he had traveled all over occupied Europe.

France, Spain, Italy, and Crete were only names on a map until his deep, growling voice told of their sights, sounds, and smells.

"Greece was beautiful," he said. "Like some kind of postcard. I never thought that ruins were much until I stopped to touch them. Did you ever run your hands over the side of a building? They have a life of their own, a personality. Imagine how they must have looked when they were first created. It's kind of like the Brandenburg Gate. You can't comprehend how magnificent that was before the bullets and bombs came to Berlin."

"Tell me about the trees again."

He laughed, convex belly vibrating like waves in a viscous pond.

"There was peace in those Greek olive groves, a feeling that was almost sacred. The trees were very old, nobody knew just how old. Maybe a hundred years. Maybe a thousand. I often thought about it, almost feeling the presence of a living thing that was centuries old, twisted and bent like an old man who refused to die. I imagined them with names, and I wondered what they would say if they should one day be able to talk."

I could imagine it, too. All of it.

He sat quietly in his living room, hands resting on his stomach, the favorite chair holding him like a friend, kindly in its overstuffed embrace. Thus comfortable, his eyes would search the corners of the room, focus into the infinity of time and space, gaze shifting rapidly back and forth, blinking and squinting to see the past, as unbidden memories flooded back from their deeply hidden nesting places. He had also served on the Eastern Front.

"Russia," he said, "went on forever. There was no end to the land, no end to the sky. It was as though we were at sea a thousand kilometers from anywhere with no hope of finding home." His thick fingers gripped the chair more tightly, holding on so he would not slide irretrievably into a fearful, bleeding past. "It was incredible, like looking into eternity. The emptiness was terrifying, like being slowly eaten alive. Nothing made by man could ever subdue that land, and it devoured everything, everyone." He shook his head. "I remember our Panzers going through the fields making tracks in the grass. Mostly no roads, only muddy paths. Then when the last battles were lost, the Russians were all around, pounding or nibbling, but never leaving us for a moment. While our own generals went to dinner parties at the chancellery in Berlin, we ate dead dogs and dragged our dying comrades across the frozen earth trying to escape the trap. All around nothing but an eternity of space and the knowledge that we would never come back. Most of us didn't. There was fear and death in everyone's eyes, and we couldn't even bury our dead. Sometimes I think I died there, and this life is some sort of dream." Opa's face tightened, and with visible effort he shook the agony from his mind.

Then his face brightened. "Crete. Now there was a place to just live and forget everything." The strong hands stretched, flexing calloused, retired fingers, now masters only of the rake and hoe. "Crete was the kingdom of the sun, like a jewel in the Mittelmeer, a real place to retire." Another bitter laugh. "But no one got the chance to retire from the Wehrmacht. They either died or ran away when the end came." A genuine, deep sadness moved like a cloud across his rough features.

"We were led by idiots. Idiots! It was nothing but a miracle that we got as far as we did. Some things never change. Germany is a great land, and her people are strong, but we have had very bad luck with leaders."

I asked why he was so fat.

He laughed like it was really funny. "I lived through two world wars, Bummelschen. All around me people were being killed, or just giving up and dying. I was hungry a lot, so I said to myself, 'Kurt, if you ever get food you should eat. You should not be hungry anymore.'" He laughed again and patted his belly. "So now we have food and I appreciate it," a short pause, "maybe a little too much, but I really appreciate it."

I listened to his stories for hours, absorbing details like a sponge, but at the same time a certain sadness crept into my heart. Although my mind's eye could see the sun-bleached columns of the Acropolis, I knew that I could never go there. Most of the places he had wandered would be forever forbidden to my footsteps. The world seemed such a fascinating place, full of mystery and possibility. Why were we forbidden to leave our tiny corner of Europe?

Sixth and seventh grade civics class became a recurring problem, and I saw that my feelings were gradually separating me from most of my peers. We all talked of life and our hopes, but there were few of them who seemed to share the intensity of my fundamental discomfort. Friedrich, the civics teacher, taught us to draw the slanting line depicting the evolution of civilization. First came nomadic, non-civilized man, followed by feudalism, capitalism (with imperialism being its highest form), socialism, and finally communism. The line sloped from the bottom left to the top right of page, signifying continued advancement toward the ultimate good — a workers' utopia where everything was harmoniously shared and people governed their lives without the superstructure of a state.

Somehow that didn't feel quite right. Perhaps more study would help me understand, so I resolved to really try, to really do my best to understand all of the things that my country wanted me to know.

"This is the history and the destiny of mankind," Friedrich would say. "Right now our system still has a few problems because it is not yet purely Communist, but we are the only thing between the capitalists and their dream of world domination. Always remember the motto you repeated every morning before class when you were in grade school:

'For peace and socialism be ready.' Then you answered, 'Always ready!' The capitalists' main goal is to possess land, commodities, and to oppress our people. Their people want to be free of the exploitation, and you are their hope for the future."

"Are most of their people in that situation?" I asked.

His wary eyes scanned my face, looking for intent, weighing the question while framing the answer.

"Yes, but the small upper class keeps them under control. It is a capitalist oligarchy, a ruling class like the old feudal kings and nobility."

"Why don't their people escape to our country?"

No hesitation this time. "They have been seduced by the decadence of the materialistic society," he said. "They don't realize how badly they are exploited."

"Maybe I wouldn't mind if I could live that way. Most of them seem to have it pretty good," I said. From the corner of my eye, I could see a few of the kids shifting uncomfortably in their chairs.

Zickert muttered, "That's right."

It was embarrassing that the class thug would agree while the rest only sat in silence.

"That's exactly what they want you to think!" Friedrich said, glaring first at Zickert, then me. Then he changed the subject to Che Guevara, and his voice took on a fervent, missionary tone, his arms gesticulated, drawing in the air how Che and his brothers in arms were liquidated by mercenary imperialist killers. Death in such a cause was glorious, was it not?

"Just believe what I tell you," Friedrich said. "There is no reason to consider any other viewpoint. Trust that I'm telling you the way things really are."

They taught us honesty in the classroom, but everyone, inside and outside school lived in a maze of contradictions. We professed to be democratic, but any open disagreement with official doctrine brought hard stares and hastily scribbled poor-conduct notes from the teachers. How could we ever grow intellectually or emotionally if no other viewpoint was even allowed?

Lights burned late in my room every night, and through

study, piece by piece, the puzzle of knowledge began to interlock, forming order from the chaos of unsatisfied wondering. In the beginning I breathed easier, but then I began to worry again when the more I understood about what I was supposed to believe and defend only grew a new crop of irritating inconsistencies. In class the tests came, and although I wrote the right answers, I couldn't reconcile observations of daily reality with what was taught. It soon became apparent that there could be no peace in simply regurgitating appropriate information to obtain a good grade.

School progressed at its normal six-day-per-week pace, and I did well. Then a totally unexpected event occurred.

"It's time to appoint another political discussion leader," Friedrich said. "Who shall we elect this time?"

An unidentified voice rose from the back of the room. "Everybody vote for Kaaz!"

I shrunk down in the seat wondering who had spoken, then like a pack of dogs, they all took up the same howl.

"It's Carsten's turn."

Friedrich tapped his pencil on the desk and conversation ceased.

"All right. Does anyone else wish to volunteer? Fine, let's see your hands if you want it to be Carsten this year." Through a patronizing half-smile, he surveyed the grinning faces and wagging hands, then smiled at me in an almost kindly manner. "I'm sure that you'll do a good job."

Knowing my growing propensity for debate and unorthodox views, he could have simply refused to accept the nomination, but to my great surprise, Friedrich immediately appointed me Mitglied des Freundschaftsrates.

Becoming discussion leader was an honor to some, but to me it only represented a lot of extra work. The leader's task was to clip articles from official newspapers and guide periodic discussions by introducing a specific political topic during civics class. Having seen others in this role, I understood that the purpose of presentation was not designed to debate our country's viewpoint, but to understand and extol its ideological correctness. Discussions were in reality more expostulation than an exchange of ideas leading to understanding. There was no blessing, no benefit, no promise of enlightenment in the assignment. Still, I couldn't refuse without jeopardizing my grades.

As class dismissed, Friedrich motioned for me to wait.

"You have a real opportunity here, Carsten," he said. "I can see that you have all the talent necessary to be successful, and I want you to use it wisely. These principles are the foundations of the future, of your future. This is the pattern for the new order that will someday rule the world. You can be part of it. You can be one of those rulers if you will embrace it with all your heart. You have a quick mind. Seize this opportunity and bend your life to the path of future glory!"

I looked into his face and saw an unusual expression, like the distant, glazed eyes of a man with a fever. He really believed in what he was teaching, and he wanted me to believe, too. He wanted to save me from heretical ways before it was too late. I listened without comment and nodded in acknowledgement when he was finished.

For the first assignment one week later, I came to civics class with a folder full of newspaper and magazine writings on a timely subject.

"Neues Deutschland says that the dictator of Chile, Pinochet, runs one of the most repressive regimes in the Western hemisphere. They say that many people are secretly executed without trial by death squads that roam the streets at night looking for victims. The situation is the same there as in El Salvador, where it is impossible to say how many have been put to death for no crime at all." I took a deep breath and continued, "It seems that this type of problem is common in dictatorships all over the world . ...."

"Let me interrupt for a moment," Friedrich said. "There are many Western countries that say they are democratic, but in reality are very dangerous places. This is an example of how the military and secret police can be used to repress a population through outright force."

I spoke quickly as he paused for a breath. "I believe that a similar sort of thing happened in Russia under Stalin, some say under Khrushchev and Brezhnev, too."

"That has not been proven, and besides governments often make mistakes. Where did you read that, in some Western paper?"

"Didn't Khrushchev denounce Stalin? Even Pravda wrote about Sakarov being exiled and confined in a psychiatric hospital for behavior damaging to their national security."

"What's your point? The Soviets are our allies, and they have done a lot for us."

The answer filled my mind, and left my mouth with a will of its own. I could not hold back speaking what every other person in the room knew to be the truth.

"We've done a lot for them, too. Didn't they take our rocket scientists to Russia after the war? Didn't they dismantle and ship whole factories back beyond the Urals and take German technicians and engineers with them?" None of that was in our history book, but Western television had shown numerous documentaries giving what seemed to be a fairly complete view of that period. I had heard some of the older people talking about relatives who disappeared during the early months of the occupation. After 35 years they should have been able to get events pretty much figured out, and besides, if one part of the Western media told something the others didn't believe, the rest would attack the assertions without hesitation. I believed what I was saying and looked Friedrich straight in the eye.

He sputtered for a moment, then recovered and waved his pencil at the class.

"There was a lot of mutual trading of resources after the war," he said, "but we are the beneficiaries of peace and order under their protection." His eyes narrowed to hard slits, and between stares at me he scanned the class, assessing their acceptance of my comments.

"Still, isn't it true that …"

He interrupted with an anecdote about Socialist heroes and their virtue in the face of constant opposition. As his voice rolled on, I settled in the chair. There was no point in arguing with him anymore, and anyone in the room who was going to get the message had probably already gotten it.

Class was dismissed and I noticed Friedrich staring at me. On the way out of the door, one of the tough guys tapped my arm playfully with his fist.

"Bock zum Gartner," he said. Then he laughed and slouched away, shuffling down the hall. He was right. Having me assigned to be the Mitglied des Freundschaftsrates was exactly like appointing a goat to be the gardener. There were fundamental contradictions I couldn't leave alone, and the teacher would neither back down nor engage in a fair debate. Whatever path was true, school wasn't going to lead me there.

From then on, I did only what was necessary to fulfill the assignment, and at every presentation he was ready for me. The pattern of classroom conflict held constant, and at the end of the year, Friedrich wrote an extra note under 'Betragen' on my report card. "Argumentative. Always wants the last word."

Pythagoras, Newton, and German grammar displaced political concerns, but outside the classroom some of the other kids spoke their real opinions. They weren't so sure about the value of death in a glorious cause, when making something out of this life seemed to be struggle enough. We were intensely counseled to prepare for the time we would have to make career choices, and living a good life would be a lot better than going around thinking about glorious death. How could all of the contradictions possibly fit together? Where in the world did the teacher get those ideas? The thoughts bounced around my mind, and I repeated them to my parents at dinner.

"It doesn't make sense. The teacher is always telling us how bad they are in the West, and how any day their people are going to rise up and throw off their chains. But we can see on TV that they live in better houses, drive better cars, it just doesn't make sense." I looked straight into Mother's eyes. "What is the truth? Are we right or are they right?"

My parents exchanged glances, and Dad cleared his throat.

"The truth of things is often hard to find. Sometimes it takes a long time to figure out. You have to remember that our country is our country, and we owe it loyalty. We don't always agree with the government, but they have taken good care of us. We never go hungry, and we are safe from harm. We have a nice home, and in a few years I'll be able to get a car. Maybe that is all we need for now. Maybe we shouldn't ask for anything more."

The conversation faded, but their worried expressions remained, amplified as they reflected back and forth. Maybe I was like the crocodile in the Peter Pan story, maybe a little taste of the West was only the appetizer. Maybe these questions about truth and freedom really were only the beginning. It was certain that none of the answers I got at home or at school put my mind at rest. I did not yet comprehend the depth of my questioning, but in order to sort things out, I began to seriously evaluate the West and its way of life.

The authorities taught civic responsibility in a special way to grade-school children. The sixth grade brought the opportunity to do "volunteer" work in local industries for the purpose of learning how to work while also producing commodities or products. Two days per month were set aside for this mandatory activity. One of the days was class time where the principles of work were discussed; production lines, quotas, and State goals expounded. The other day was an actual visit to a factory where we were given work. In the beginning we had simple tasks, such as making small fish nets for aquariums, while the older children in the class were given more complex tasks and moved on to other factories. Our work was supposed to help industry make its yearly quotas, but our effectiveness was questionable since we had to be more carefully watched for safety purposes. At least one of the main reasons for the monthly excursion was fulfilled. The government was determined to have us learn first-hand at a young age the necessity for productive work and contributing to the society, and we got the message very clearly. The experience also helped many of us understand our career options more clearly. We would soon have to make decisions that would bind us to certain career paths, and I decided early on that the fish net factory was not for me.

Toward the end of sixth grade, while watching 'Kung Fu' on a West German TV channel, I had an idea. The hero was a great example of peaceful intent coupled with the ability to defend himself. Maybe I could learn martial arts. There was some kind of school right on the bus route within a few kilometers. It didn't have a phone so the only thing to do was go the next evening and ask some questions.

The practice room was large, like the dance studios I had seen, but instead of a highly polished floor, it was covered with thick padding, and the students wore pajama-like clothing. The air smelled of sweat and unwashed underwear, and the instructor looked me over like I was a horse for sale. I weighed about 30 kilos soaking wet and was not exactly formidable.

Then Herr Naujock gave me the speech.

"We meet three times a week, Monday, Wednesday, and Friday, 6:30 p.m. to 8:00 p.m. The charge is five marks for a kid your age. Do you know anything about martial arts?"

"No sir. Actually, I would like to learn karate."

He shook his head immediately. "I'm afraid you're out of luck. It's illegal for me to teach that. Judo is the only thing allowed."

"Why?"

"Look at it this way. With judo you can defend yourself against any single opponent, but using karate you can defeat a number of people. In addition to your hands, you learn to use knives, sticks, anything and everything as a weapon. Knowing karate is actually like owning a weapon, you know, a gun, and that's against the law. It's considered a threat to society."

On one hand this was an exciting opportunity, but it didn't make sense. The rules weren't Naujock's fault, and there was no point in arguing since they never changed the rules for anyone, so I just wrote my name on the line. Somewhere deep inside, I felt an irritating sliver. It was a thorny jabbing, and otherwise normal flesh was beginning to swell, reddening with corruption. Why would I want to use karate against a group of people? What people? Who made those rules anyway? At ten years old, what kind of threat was I? Six months later, my interest flagged. It was a large class with little personalized instruction, and I gave it up. At least I had learned how to fall without being injured.

The years passed with surprising speed, and my interest in extracurricular activities continued. At age twelve, I volunteered to teach elementary electronics to fourth graders after school every Thursday evening. Before making a final decision, I reviewed it at home.

We had our usual conversation at the dinner table, where Mom and Dad encouraged me to follow through with the decision.

"That's very good, son," Dad said. "How many will there be in your class?"

"About six I think. Did you ever teach?"

"Only at work, but that's not exactly the same thing. What made you decide to do it? My men pretty much have to do what I ask them, but your students are there because they want to know. That is a great opportunity to help someone else."

Dad was right. I was amazed that the young children would sit so still and behave. Why did I do it? It just felt good to see their faces light up as they crossed new thresholds of knowledge. Was it my teaching or did they just love to learn? After about six months, I couldn't get sufficient new materials or parts, and we ran out of projects to do. At that point, my only other choice was to go out and buy things for the class myself, since the school couldn't provide them, so I stopped the sessions. We just couldn't do anything without additional support. I was as upset as the children when we had to quit, so like a limpet, I began looking for something solid to which I could attach.

On August 17, 1977, my family and I were packing a suitcase for a vacation at the Baltic Sea. I came downstairs carrying clothes for the trip and found mother sitting on the veranda sniffling.

"Mom, what's wrong?"

"I just heard that Elvis died." She wiped her eyes and looked at me as though I ought to feel something, too.

"Who's Elvis?"

"I'm talking about Elvis Presley, the American singer. I grew up hearing his music. The news said that he was only 42 years old. We used to dance to his records all the time when we were kids." More sniffles, and she rehearsed a brief biography for my benefit. She had never mentioned him before, and I wondered how any singer could be important enough to bring tears to

Mom's eyes, since I knew her to be very strong and composed.

We packed our bags and caught the train later that day. Upon arriving at the resort six hours later, I began to feel nauseated, so while Mom and Dad went to the beach, I stayed in bed and listened to the radio. The tuner was stuck and the only station the old device could receive was West German. The program featured Elvis music interspersed with stories and comments about his life and exploits. My English was fair by that time and most of his songs were understandable, so it was only a short time before my spirit began to feel an affinity for this man. There was some kind of resonance with my own life. Some of the songs were strong finger-snappers, and others were soft and mellow, filled with subtlety of feeling and deep emotions. I propped myself up in bed with the pillow and forgot about my stomach. Embedded in those lyrics and melodies were messages, and I wanted to hear them all. Behind that music there seemed to be a depth of personality. I knew what a ghetto was. The words to 'Separate Ways' were touching, reviving memories of the bitter aftershocks of divorce I saw in many of my friends' lives as well as my own. Perhaps I could more nearly understand my own changing emotions by hearing about his. I resolved to learn more about him.

After vacation, life settled back to its usual routine, until one Saturday night when Dad came upstairs to find me half asleep with the radio playing as usual.

"Son, there is something on TV I think you might like if you're not too tired."

I mumbled something and stirred.

"You don't have to get up, but it's an Elvis movie on one of the Western stations. It's called 'Viva Las Vegas.' Give it a few minutes and see."

That got my attention enough to drag downstairs and plop myself on the couch. As Mom and Dad sat holding hands, the West German commercials babbled, pleading that we should rush out and purchase things that we could never afford, things we could never even find in our stores. Watching Western advertising was strange because after a while we ignored it in the same way we would have ignored invitations to ride a rocket

49

to Mars. Then the screen changed and the adventure began.

It was amazing. Even though I knew that Elvis was dead, I found myself admiring the qualities of his character in the film. He was a down-to-earth man who was fighting to succeed in an unfriendly world. The voice track was well dubbed, and I became immersed in the experience. Honesty, strength of character, and belief in the eventual triumph of right were foundation themes. Were these the values that all Americans held dear? If the United States were anything like what I saw in the film, it would be a place where anything was possible, but it would be frightening to live in such an unpredictable place. The teachers told us how lawless America was, but maybe that wasn't the whole story. In the films, there were powerful bad guys, but the honest good guys won in the end. Would real life be like that? Could compassion and hard work provide a better life than getting your way by simply using power? Then the movie was over, and I was left with much to reflect on. The next morning while getting ready for school, I studied my hair in the mirror. If I combed it back a little more, it might look pretty cool, maybe I would even look a little like Elvis.

A few weeks later, Dad greeted me first thing in the morning. "I woke up late last night with a stomachache." His eyes sparkled with the yet-untold secret.

"Does it hurt now?" I mumbled, munching my toast.

"No, it's fine, but I have a surprise for you." He pointed toward the living room. "RIAS had a special program on Elvis, and they're going to be playing his music for the next few months until they've gone through every record he ever made." He pointed toward the living room again, waving his finger in a small circle. "I taped the show for you."

I immediately got up from the table, crumbs falling from my half-opened mouth, and headed for the recorder. When I was finally able to listen to the whole thing, I found that he had taped a whole hour of Elvis music that began with his first records and came forward chronologically. Toward the end, the disc jockey noted the time and date of the next broadcast. This was a real stroke of luck. Taped music was just as good as the radio, better if the music was special. Many of my school friends liked

50

AC/DC and some of the other Western groups, but I felt that this was something quite special, something that might endure a lot longer than contemporary screamers.

The next day I made a point of talking to Henrik Krippner about it.

"Dad taped a whole hour of Elvis music for me," I told him.

"That will be worth something for trading. Do you remember when we talked about my writing a letter to my uncle in West Germany to see if he could find me a book on Elvis? Well he did, and I just got it in the mail! Come on over and let's look at it."

Henrik was my first connection with anyone outside my own family who had an interest in Elvis. Over the next few weeks, I spent a lot of time with him, finding that, though he liked Elvis, it was a casual interest more connected to monetary value than anything else. Still, he was someone I could talk to, and together we entered the local trading channels.

At the same time, I became aware that other friends were feeling the influence of Western music. Ulf Kubicki and I knew each other from childhood, and one day after English class the subject of music came up.

"I'm getting tired of the hard rock," he said. "What do you think about country?"

"Some of it is good, but my favorite is Elvis. I'm getting a good collection of his music and a few articles, too. Do you have anything to trade?"

"No, but I have some really good country music. How about Hank Williams Jr. or Alabama?"

I shook my head, those were only names to me.

"Come on over this weekend and I'll introduce you," he said.

The next Saturday we sat in his living room listening to pirated and smuggled tapes. Lester Flatt and Earl Scruggs, David Allen Coe. New names, new sounds filtering into my mind and new passages opening. Theirs were ancient rhythms of the earth, sounds of sweat, pain, wasted lives, raw regrets, and drunken anger flailing against an uncaring cosmos. Toes and fingers tapped out the new beats, and the hair on the back of my neck tingled when the steel guitar cried out. This was pretty

51

good. I was just resolving to add another dimension to my interests when I noticed a large, beautifully framed picture of Hank Williams Jr. standing next to his father.

"Where did you get that?"

"My mother. She's an industrial photographer for a factory in Henningsdorf. The picture was in a book, and she shot it, then developed and printed the film in the back room."

"You mean here in the house?"

"Sure. Come on and I'll show you."

Frau Kubicki had a fully equipped darkroom with an enlarger. That suggested some interesting possibilities.

"Do you think she might be able to take a few pictures of my Elvis stuff?"

"Let's go ask."

That afternoon marked the beginning of an important friendship with Ulf and his mother, Annelies. Over the following weeks and months, I brought books and clippings, which she photographed and printed. Even after paying for the chemicals and paper, the resale value of the prints and blowups was tremendous. I began a lively barter and sales operation that steadily increased. One evening I came to visit carrying the usual sack of materials.

"Tonight you are going to learn how to do this yourself, Carsten," Frau Kubicki said.

At first I was afraid that I had made a nuisance of myself, but then I realized that she really wanted me to learn something that would be fun.

The greatest benefit of that new enterprise was realized the day Vivien Taschner approached me at school.

"How are you doing?" she asked.

A strange feeling fluttered in my chest, and I managed a smile. She was even more attractive up close. I had only kissed one girl, Heike Puttnins, when I was six, but Vivien's lips were looking very inviting. Her eyes scanned my face, and my insides warmed. She was saying something.

"I heard that you like Elvis."

"Yes, how about you?"

"Me too. I heard that you have some taped music."

"Some of his best. I have almost every song he ever did."

She hesitated, but not for long. Vivien was assertive. "Would you mind if I taped some of the songs you have? I have my own recorder, and I really like his music."

What a stroke of luck. Silently, I thanked Dad for having that upset stomach and caring enough about me to start the recorder that night.

"Would you like to come over to my house?"

She nodded and returned my smile. We agreed to meet a few days later, and she excused herself to go home.

On the appointed afternoon, I stood at the front window wondering if she would really come. At 3:30 p.m., I saw her bicycle round the corner off Calvin Strasse, heading my way. In the midst of my excitement, there was an important question. Why was she really coming? Was it to see me, or was it only for the music? Why did it even matter? These confused, exhilarating feelings were new, and something very important I did not completely understand was stirring in my heart.

For two hours we sat in my room listening to the tapes, talking mainly about Elvis and her, and exchanging shy smiles. She was seriously interested in art, concentrating on painting with the eventual goal of becoming a graphic artist. Then it was time for her to go, and she reached out to take my hand. Her fingers were warm and soft, supple yet firm, and I could hardly speak for the beating of my heart.

"Thanks a lot for letting me come over. Perhaps we could get together again sometime," she said.

"Sure, anytime."

I stood, a politely smiling tongue-tied statue, on the front steps as she pedaled away down the street, blonde hair flowing like a lovely fountain in the afternoon sun. I watched her receding form until she was completely out of sight. It had been a wonderful day.

In the fall of 1979, the pursuit of Elvis collectibles took me into an entirely new realm. One by one, I traded with the kids in my class, then other classes and grades, until I knew almost everyone in school with an interest. Continued inquiries brought me into contact with the architect of a new adventure.

Bernd Riebisch was two years older and had the reputation of being the most well-stocked Elvis trader in Falkensee. One of my friends introduced us, and I asked if it would be possible to stop by his house on the way home from school. He agreed and we met as planned.

"You collect Elvis stuff?" I said.

"Oh, a little," he replied. "Come on in and let's talk."

Inquiries revealed that he was not only well-stocked, but a sharp trader, so I assumed the role of student come to learn at the feet of a master.

"Actually, I'm just getting started," I told him. "You have quite a lot from what I heard." In two years, I had managed to accumulate about 300 different items including photographs, articles, and a few records smuggled from the West by various grandmothers and acquired at exorbitant cost. Original pictures stayed in my inventory because Frau Kubicki had taught me how to photograph and print them for resale. After some general discussion, I showed him a few of the pictures.

"Not bad," he said.

Then I saw the poster on his wall. It was one meter square. That was something of great value, and I was openly impressed.

"Where did that come from?"

"I got lucky. There was a record jacket that had his picture with only the name Elvis on it. No record company label to ruin it! Then I went to a studio and had it blown up." He smiled and winked. "Eighty marks."

I whistled.

He smiled again. "It's good to see that you appreciate things like this. I think we can do business."

Over the next three weeks, we concluded some mutually profitable trades, and a lively friendship began to develop. Bernd, like too many of my other friends, suffered deeply from a troubled home life. His father and mother were constantly fighting, and it was both embarrassing and painful for him. He seldom spoke about it, but when I realized that his father would get drunk and mean, a part of my own childhood came flooding involuntarily back.

It was a tiny fragment, a faded piece of rotting canvas dimly illustrated in a confusion of dark colors and swirling impression. I must have been only two or three years old. There was a room, softly illuminated by the wavering glow of a single candle. The muted sound of a woman crying came from my mother. Her husband, my natural father, was a man thwarted by life, a problem drinker, and with the drinking came the yelling, and her choked cries from the violence of his staggering rage. At three years old, my mind could not comprehend the depth of her suffering, and there was nothing to do but cling to her neck speaking a child's hopeful benediction that things would be all right. I could still see the wavering flame, a tiny undulating sliver of orange light against the palpable darkness. I could almost recall the confusion and the pain I felt just seeing her hurt. Like most remembered agonies, it was mercifully impossible to relive. My father moved out of our home when I was three, leaving Mom and me to work life out alone. Since that time, I saw him only two or three times. Our meetings left a numb, hollow place where I reasoned that some love for him ought to have been. The scene closed to my view, folding into itself, retreating behind the scar tissue in my memory.

Bernd was standing by the door to his room, when his face changed to a deeply thoughtful pose, then brightened with the apparent resolution of some question.

"Since we are friends, I have something special to show you, but you have to promise that you won't tell anyone else. This is privileged information."

I waited, not sure what to expect.

He opened his dresser drawer and removed magazines. Bravo, the popular West German teen magazine! They were special issues full of Elvis pictures. I was stunned. What a treasure! His hands dug deeper, then retrieved a hard-bound book by Becky Yancey, Elvis's private secretary, about her experiences in his employ. These were unbelievably valuable!

"Where did you get these?"

Bernd smiled.

"I wanted to tell you last time we talked, but you have to know that you can trust someone before you tell them any secrets. Have you ever heard of Ketzin?"

55

"Sure, that's where the West Berlin garbage is dumped after they truck it in. They say the whole place is fenced and guarded."

Everyone knew about Ketzin. It was another of our country's wonders. Motorists could see the West German trucks swaying under their putrefying burdens, whining on large, wide tires along the F-5 highway. The West paid our government a lot of money to dispose of refuse there. Although eager for the hard currency, the government was at the same time fearful that even through the medium of garbage, malignant capitalist ideas might spread to our people. The landfill itself was encircled by a high chain-link fence topped with several strands of barbed wire. Inside there were many armed guards, accompanied by dogs.

"Well," he said, "I know my way around there pretty well, and I've been inside a few times." He grinned. "Never been caught! If you get there an hour or two after a new drop, you can usually find something, but if you wait much longer, the bulldozer is likely to come and turn it all under. I have a good idea of their dump schedules, too."

I took everything in, listening with genuine fascination as he explained how to penetrate the fortress.

"You got these Bravos there?"

He smiled and nodded.

"I was thinking about making another run this Sunday morning." He paused and was staring at me.

I stared back.

"Well, are you interested?"

"Me, to go? Sure, I'm with you." I could see it all, the magazines, maybe a poster or a discarded record. West German garbage was better than our own stores on the best day.

While the rest of our town slept soundly, I got up at 7:00 a.m., ate a light breakfast and set out on my bicycle to cover the easy mile to Bernd's house. When I arrived, he was waiting, and together we pedaled down Strasse Der Jugend to F-5, and turned north. An occasional car passed, and we rode easily, enjoying the quiet of that sunny morning. Drawing nearer to Ketzin, I could see the perpetual cloud of circling birds that marked the dump itself. Though the wind was at our backs, the

56

smell filtered through anyway, and the musty, heavy odor penetrated everything, clinging even to the trees and rocks. There was no such thing as fresh air at Ketzin.

Soon we left the main road, taking a side street, and concealed our bicycles in the trees to make the final approach through the bushes on foot.

Bernd's face changed; hard lines of concentration marked his eyes and the corners of his mouth.

"Now you have to stay cool and remember what I am telling you. Wherever you see hills, that's where the bulldozers have already been, and things there are smashed beneath their treads and the blade or buried so you can't get to them. Don't bother with that. Look for the valleys and loose papers. Where there is loose paper, nothing has packed it in, and it hasn't been there long because the rains would have made it soggy and flat. We have to go under the fence, so be sure you don't get your clothes tangled in it. Are you getting this?"

"Yes." I swallowed involuntarily.

"The fence bottom has sharp wire ends, and if your shirt gets caught don't panic or struggle. If you're stupid, it will make a lot of noise and the dogs will be sure to hear. So you have to stay in control and untangle yourself quietly." He studied my face for a moment, assessing the effect of the instructions.

I stared back, trying not to show the rising apprehension. This was quite different from sitting on his porch in Falkensee.

"All right. Now one last thing. Stay low. Never stand upright, and go from mound to mound very quickly, like the army men in the movies when someone is shooting at them. If one of us gets caught, the other one ditches his bag and tries to get away without being seen. They are sure to arrest you, and then they'll call your parents. They'll make all kinds of threats, too, but you have to really stick to the story that you came alone just to see what was going on and maybe get a few souvenirs. They call it a conspiracy when two people work together, and that's really bad to have on your record. We'll meet next to that big mound over there at noon. Any questions?"

High on the fence I could see the sign.

## BETRETEN UND BEFAHREN VERBOTEN

No trespassing! Maybe the guards were so busy scavenging for themselves that they wouldn't be looking too hard for intruders. I shook my head in the negative and focused on what he had said. This was one of those times in life where there could be no mistakes. Suddenly, I felt a curious detachment of mind, as though it was not I but someone else about to go under the wire. It was almost amusing, sneaking into a garbage dump like some kind of commando just to get a few used magazines.

We loosened the bottom of the fence, slipped under and split up. In a few moments, he disappeared behind the rotting landscape. Then it hit me. I was actually inside! Initial excitement evaporated, leaving crawling fear, a paralytic feeling of nakedness beneath the uncaring sky dotted by wheeling flocks of birds. For a moment, I imagined guards laughing as the beaks tore at my dying flesh. Then I regained control. In the distance, I could make out a few brown-uniformed figures, with smaller shapes at their sides. Those would be the sentinels and their shepherds. Maybe the rotting stench would mask my scent from their inquiring noses. I scrambled quickly between the mounds, plunging to the knee in the putrid earth, searching ragged ravines for trophies, stuffing my sack with an electronics catalog, some newspapers, and a few magazines. When the time was up, I scuttled like a rat to our rendezvous point, and in a few minutes Bernd appeared dragging his sack of plunder.

"I hit it big today," he said. "Let's get out of here."

As we slipped beneath the fence and into the woods, we heard barking. Even near the fence we were subject to arrest, so we ran panting to the bicycles and pedaled breathlessly down the highway.

"That's too close even for me," he said, "but if they come now, we can drop the bags and say that we were just looking around."

"Too bad we couldn't get some of the larger stuff. I saw a neat toaster. Maybe I could have fixed it," I said. Western appliances were valuable in trade.

The ride home was carefree, spotted with laughter and survivors' banter, but in the back of my mind, I weighed the whole experience. The risks were substantial, and the reward was not that great. That was my last trip to Ketzin.

One day after school as I was headed for my bicycle, another kid called me by name. It was Uwe George, who lived a block from my house, down on the south end of Pestalozzi Strasse.

"I hear that you like to collect Elvis things," he said. He was two years younger and spent time with a different group of kids. Although I had seen him around the neighborhood for years, we had never struck up a friendship. Uwe was stocky and of medium height. One of his eyes turned outward at times due to a muscle imbalance, and I wondered if other kids picked on him. Probably not too much, because he was solid, and looked like he could take care of himself if necessary.

"Bring your stuff over to my house tonight. Number Four Zwingli Strasse," I said.

Over the next few weeks our friendship grew steadily, and I found that although he was not a serious student, he was an honest and thoughtful person. Before long, we had developed a strong bond of mutual respect. Often we would take walks at night around the neighborhood talking of life and values. Our trust finally evolved to the point where I could speak of some things that weighed on my mind.

"How can we possibly believe all of the stuff they tell us in school?" I asked.

"I don't know many who do," he said. "They just don't talk about it."

"But we have these discussions in civics where I am the only one objecting. I don't see anyone else with my viewpoint except the kids who are always getting into trouble. You know, the ones who start fights and wear stupid clothes."

"I never say anything myself."

"That's not the same. I know that you have a mind of your own."

"Carsten, I think that Duckmauser comes earlier to some people than to others. Maybe that's what you are seeing."

Perhaps he was right. Duckmauser was our slang term for the people who went along with everything the party and the government said. Order, obedience to rules, and productivity

59

were the foundations of our society, and as long as these were evident in a person's social behavior, the requirements were fulfilled. The Duckmauser person went along because it was the only thing they knew how to do. They went along because no one had ever taught them how to decide for themselves, how to be their own person. They were the fabric, the backing of the society. There can be no absolute rulers without compliant followers.

We decided that there were three classifications of people.

The first were the non-achievers, the troublemakers, the smart-mouth kids who never knew the answers when the teacher called on them in class. They were the ones who sneaked cigarettes into school and got funny haircuts. They protested out of a generalized rebellion against authority, and they would have done the same no matter what society raised them. Their school records showed a lack of intelligence or desire. They inhabited the fringes of education, learning just what was necessary and waiting eagerly for the day when they could go off to work in a factory and disappear forever into mediocre oblivion.

Second was the greater mass of students who could see that the political stuff we were being taught was shot through with lies. They knew it, but they also knew by now that it was necessary to start planning their career path, and that if they had any brains, they must try for a good job. To get the best employment, they needed good grades, but even more importantly, they had to have a clean political record that showed that they had the right kind of attitudes. If a kid made a major behavioral mistake, it would be written down somewhere and follow him for the rest of his life. They were beginning to see how this controlled their future, and they had decided to some degree to go along with the game on the surface.

The best that East Germany had to offer was promised to the obedient achievers. We called them "Red Socks." These were the ones who always flew the East German flag on May Day and participated at the Jugend Pionier meetings. They were the ones who frowned at jokes about the government, and stood up in class or at assembly to quote what they read in Neues Deutschland. They were the ones who looked through narrowed eyes when something negative was said about the party or public officials, and settled comfortably in their chairs as they saw the teachers taking note of their correct behavior.

The third group was smallest, those who had to question things for reasons of conscience. They saw both sides, the good and bad of the system, but they were unwilling to submerge their reasoning simply because a school official said that things were a certain way. Some of them studied, understood and could discuss Communist doctrine backwards and forwards, but didn't believe any of it. Others were less academically inclined, but all of them worried what to do with their lives as they realized their nonconformist behavior might soon seal all doors to the future. They had talent and could achieve in society if they chose to play the game like group two, but their own hearts would not tolerate it. Most felt the first stings of official disapproval at an early age but resolved that possessing their own heart was worth the cost.

In most of us, these behaviors were only just being understood on a conscious level, but no matter which group a child belonged to, there was no escaping the constant discomfort of living with so many contradictions. I felt the itch myself and began to realize that somehow there must be a resolution or my personality would be hopelessly fragmented.

For all of our talking and walking, Uwe and I were not quite able to solve any of the world's problems. Our friendship was strong, but my intro-spection had exposed an awful void. How could it ever be filled?

Uwe went home that night, and again my lights burned late. How did my chaotic feelings fit into the order that seemed to be all around? Most of the people I knew seemed to go about daily life without any outward sign of distress. What was wrong with me?

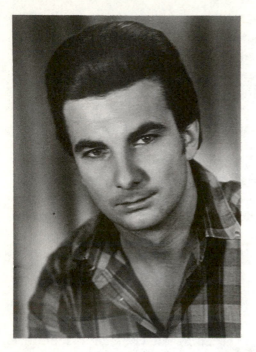

Lutz Bobzien,
one of
author's
best friends

Vivien
Taschner,
author's
first love

# CHAPTER THREE

From my earliest recollection, Mom and Dad had shown that it was necessary to fit in. Their lives were unspoken testaments of compliance. I began to notice at home that they were often critical of the government, but not in a conscious, calculating manner. Their behavior seemed to say that they would appear to go along with the system to have a place in the society. Without that anchor, what would life be like?

At the beginning of the eighth grade, I realized that it was time to make the best showing possible if I were to have opportunities for the future; so I decided to make all A's for the rest of Oberschule until I graduated. Serious study became a rigid evening routine, but as the year began to develop, another complicating problem arose.

Uwe came over one evening and sat heavily in a chair.

"I ought to be happy, but I feel awful," he said. "Thursday's my birthday."

"I thought it was going to be soon. What's wrong with that? You'll be getting some stuff won't you?"

He frowned. "None of that is going to make much difference if I can't come to visit."

Of course! He would be 14. Celebrating that day meant he would have to present himself for a photograph and fingerprinting at the local police station. A week or so later, he would receive the Ausweis, a mandatory ID that every citizen was required to carry. In addition to name, address, and occupation, it also had spaces for recording other life events, like travel permits and arrest records. Any time a police officer wanted, and without need of justification, he could require a citizen to produce this document. I had one already, but mine had a special additional stamp that allowed me to enter the frontier area because I lived there.

The problem wasn't imaginary. Uwe lived a block outside the frontier and was fully aware that his official entry into adult society also signaled that he couldn't legally come to my house unless his Ausweis too had a frontier stamp. That, we both knew, was utterly impossible. The police would never give him one just to visit a friend.

Although I had known the law all my life, this was the first time it had a direct impact. No matter how we looked at things, the choices remained only two. If we obeyed the rule, our friendship would be awkward. Since Uwe's parents had already made it clear that I wasn't welcome at their home, we would have nowhere to get together but some street corner at the frontier boundary. If we ignored the rule, there was a good chance in the long run that he'd be caught, and since there were criminal penalties for unauthorized frontier entry, it would go on our record forever. I looked at him, and he looked back.

"Well you're my friend, and I don't see why you can't slip into the backyard by coming through Detlef's fence." Our back-yard neighbor, Detlef Jasmund, had a gap in his fence that was hidden by bushes. He was not well and often went to bed early, so the danger of him seeing Uwe sneaking around was minimal.

"If they catch me here, they'll at least fine you. Maybe arrest you, too." He looked at his palms, rubbing them in the nervous habit he sometimes displayed.

"Some things are worth the risk. Like I said, you're my friend, and that's more important than what the police say. If you're careful, they won't catch you anyway."

His strong face softened, moisture showing at the corners of his eyes, mouth working silently, trying to speak, trying to swallow. After a long moment he spoke.

"You're better than a brother."

The next night he slipped quietly through the hidden gate and arrived looking a little flushed and excited, like he had just done something supremely dangerous. Over ensuing months, his surreptitious transits became routine, and our biggest worry was avoiding becoming complacent and inattentive. Just breaking the law was no big deal, because by that time in life, everyone was getting around a lot of rules some way or other. For starters, most of the kids trafficked in smuggled goods, like recordings and clothes, so life was already taking on dimensions of risk. Some results were worth getting arrested for, and some were not. We were learning first-hand that the main point was to avoid being caught. There were times when that attitude felt extremely uncomfortable, as though I was exchanging honesty for the chance of having an everyday life.

While Uwe and I covertly challenged legal limits, other pivotal events were brewing. My relationship with Vivien was intensifying, and I realized that my lack of appetite, and preoccupation with everything about her, signaled that I had fallen in love for the first time. From the time we realized that our attraction was serious, we could talk of everything except a future together. Even when we became sexually intimate, tomorrow was defined strictly in terms of mine and yours.

Vivien expected me to be successful in school so opportunities would be available for my own advancement, but a problem soon emerged that became a major test of our relationship. She developed a strong dislike of Uwe.

"You shouldn't spend so much time with him," she said.

"What are you talking about? We've been friends for years."

"You're different people, Carsten. Uwe's not going to amount to anything. You need to be with people who can teach you, people who can help you out. You have to start developing the necessary connections."

"Sure we're different, but he's one of the few people in the world that I completely trust. My life would be safe in his hands, and that's worth a lot! Besides I won't be friends with someone just for what they can do for me. I'm not like that."

She shook her head and changed the subject.

As our relationship continued, I noticed her mother's continuing coolness toward me. I made a few attempts to build a rapport, but was unsuccessful. Frau Taschner and I never spoke of substantive matters unless they were connected to my schoolwork.

"I've decided to make all A's for the rest of Oberschule."

"That is commendable," she said. "And what then?"

"I'm considering law school, but as of right now, I have a contract to receive advanced electronics training."

"There is obligatory service in the army, I believe? And after that, you will become a technician?" She lingered over the last word, watching me closely, taking in my mannerisms, dispassionately inspecting. She knew very well about the military obligation for everyone receiving specialized training, and by the faintly sour look on her face, I had the feeling that she thought her daughter could have chosen a more promising consort.

"Hmmm," she said.

Her expressionless eyes never wavered, and I imagined that this was how the frog must feel just before it was dissected to prove some point in biology.

And so I came to understand that Frau Taschner did not approve of me and that Vivien would be fighting an uphill battle if she wished to stay attached to me over the long term.

Considering the whole equation, the only way to keep my ties to Vivien and not discard a longstanding friendship with Uwe was to simply allocate time to spend with each. I didn't discuss Uwe with Vivien anymore, because I grew tired of constantly having to counter her deprecating remarks. She'd often come to my house to study math, and our conversations fell into a pattern.

"How's your geometry coming?" she would ask.

"Great! I got a good grade on the last test."

"How good?"

"B+."

"That's all right, I suppose, but you know that you can do better. I thought you wanted to graduate first in your class. Have you changed your mind? Nothing will ever come of your effort if you don't stay serious about goals."

We sometimes talked of life and aspirations, but she could never comprehend my persistent unrest where personal freedom was concerned.

"I can't see why you're so worked up over these things.

You'll never change them, and all you'll get for your trouble is problems with the police." She took my hand and looked deeply into my eyes. "You can really become something, Carsten, but you have to get serious. There's a lot of competition for the real opportunities."

I saw iron determination in her eyes, not kindness, not encouragement, just a smoldering, consuming drive to achieve. Was it for me that she desired success, or was she simply trying to be in charge, to direct my life the same way I had noticed her mother directing the lives of their family?

Days melted into months, and we, the youthful hope of our country, grew in stature and experience, repeating the endless cycle of discovery and conflict that has driven the adolescent heart since the dawn of time. Even in my quiet neighborhood, human drama was abundant.

It was a soft summer afternoon when Jens Haan met Silvia, his girlfriend, at the bus turnaround and walked up Calvin Strasse toward his house, about a block down the street from mine. He was 16, and she 15. They exchanged glances. Jens was shy, tentative as his hand reached for hers. At last, holding hands and talking quietly, they moved slowly up the street to the intersection of Zwingli Strasse and Calvin Strasse, savoring the mystery of adolescent romance, prolonging its unfulfilled magic.

If they had been paying attention as they passed Pestalozzi Strasse, the red and white frontier-area sign might have provided an effective reminder. Since they were both over the age of legal responsibility, each was required by law to possess the special frontier stamp on their Ausweis. If they were discovered without one, the penalties were very clear. Jens' Ausweis had the stamp, but Silvia's did not.

Their stroll did not go unobserved, however, because our neighbor Herr Koch was in his yard digging at something as they passed by, wrapped in the ambiance of fluttering hearts and teenage fantasies. Koch's probing eyes noted that the girl was not from the neighborhood, and presently he went inside. Jens and his guest reached their destination, but they had hardly been inside the Haan house for 15 minutes when a green Wartburg containing two Polizei came creeping very slowly up Calvin

Strasse, then stopped in front of the house where Koch had resumed watering his already-soggy flowers. The two uniformed patrolmen sat in the car talking with Koch for several minutes, like tourists asking directions. Then the Wartburg backed up and proceeded south down Zwingli at the speed of a slow walk, finally pulling off the road just past Schirmer's house to park on the grass with the motor off.

The kids' visit at the Haan house lasted about 40 minutes, and they had no idea that the Polizei were waiting. Jens and Silvia came out of the house, turned to walk north up Zwingli, and froze in mid-step as they saw the car. They both knew what was about to happen. After a moment's pause, they resumed walking on the only course possible, one that would carry them past the car. As they approached within three meters, both Polizei opened the doors and got out, speaking their standard polite, but cold, greeting. Shuddering fear must have seized Jens's insides as he sought some way out, but it only took a moment to realize that there were no options; he could see that the police were expecting them. He must have pulled himself together, muttering something encouraging to her. After a few predictable questions including demanding the Ausweis, both kids were put into the back seat and the car drove away. Silvia buried her head in her hands, long brown hair catching the last slanting rays of the afternoon sun, and Jens's expressionless white face peered forlornly through the back glass as his home disappeared in the distance. A few reddish swirls of drifting dust marked their passages, and then they were gone.

As the Wartburg turned the corner, Koch shut the water off, carefully coiled the hose and went inside.

Word of the arrest circulated through the neighborhood quickly, and it was obvious that Koch was the Spitzel who had summoned the authorities.

Neighborhood reaction was a mixture of understanding and condemnation. It was not unusual for the Polizei to question people, but in the court of local gossip, it was judged unjust to treat youth so harshly unless there was some major violation. There was no question that Jens had illegally brought Sylvia into the frontier area, but it was Koch's obvious action in calling the Polizei that ran like an electrical current through the neighborhood. Many eyes had seen the whole thing through drawn curtains.

Jens did not return home until he was released 12 hours later. His angular face was etched with a haunted, fearful look, like a dog who gets kicked every day. For weeks, the slightest noise or sudden movement sent him twitching. The budding romance was extinct, smothered in the fear that two children could not overcome. Strangled and buried under the daily reality of the Polizei and their informers, it disappeared into the dust of our frontier streets.

Koch probably didn't anticipate the full cost of his act; from that day on, it was as if he no longer existed. His verbal greetings and waves to neighbors on the street were now totally ignored, and in a short while he realized that there was no use trying to be friendly. When the smell of barbecue sauce and grilling chicken drifted on the Sunday afternoon breeze, he went inside and shut the door. There were no common pleasantries from the other citizens in the neighborhood, and he was forever sentenced to cook Sunday chicken with only his own kind.

Jens was never again the same, becoming more furtive and restless over the next year or so, and as various neighbors experienced thefts of personal property, he was strongly suspected by many in the neighborhood.

Since my friend Henrik Krippner had noticed some of his own possessions missing from the family storage shed, he and I decided to set a trap and capture the thief ourselves, using money as bait. I had to pass his front yard three times before I saw Jens on the porch.

"Wie geht's, Jens," I said, "Henrik and I have been having a great day. How are you?"

"All right, I suppose," he replied.

After some small talk, I pretended to have other business. "Well, I have to go now. We made thirty marks today so we stashed it in his room and we'll spend it tomorrow." I tried to appear casual. "See you later." It sounded so phony to my ears. Would he possibly believe?

Both of Henrik's parents had gone shopping, so he and I

waited outside in the bushes next to his house. In about half-an hour our patience was justified as Jens came around the corner. I carried my illegal pneumatic pellet rifle, and even though it had no stock and was scarred from age, it was powerful and accurate. At that moment, I could not really say whether or not I would shoot. If I did, that would bring a whole new set of problems that might have put me in more trouble than the thief.

We saw Jens enter the house by using a knife to slip the lock. Henrik waited a full three minutes before going quietly inside and locking the basement door from above so Jens could not retrace his steps and escape. The only other way out of the basement was through a window. Presently, Jens had found no money and tried to leave. Finding the door locked from the other side, he came to the basement window and began to push it open.

The gun was loaded, cocked, and I was waiting.

His eyes met mine and he flinched. I was so close I could see his pupils struggling to adjust to the sunlight.

"You'd better stop," I said, gesturing with the gun.

His face went white.

"I was waiting for Henrik. I wanted to borrow something."

"He already called the Polizei. You can tell it to them." That was the conversation. With no other way out of the basement and not wanting to be shot, Jens resigned himself to capture. He sat heavily on a nearby chair, and through the window I thought I could hear him crying. Henrik called a warning to me when the patrol car turned into Zwingli Strasse, and I ran home to hide the rifle.

Peeking back around the corner of my house, I remembered how Jens and I had played together in past years. There had been many summer days when we rode bicycles and chased our dreams through childhood's rosy fog. Now he was just a small-time thief, and I a small-time vigilante. Adrenalin subsided, leaving a hollow gnawing in my mid-section, and I began to feel somehow guilty for exposing him.

The Polizei asked Henrik a few questions, had a very short conversation with Jens, then handcuffed him and took him away. He spent two days in jail, was tried and convicted within a week, and was fined 450 marks. He never again stole anything else in our neighborhood, but ended up being arrested years later and serving 24 months in Rudersdorf for other offenses.

The school year ended and summer break came. Vivien went on vacation, and in a way it was a relief from the constant tension I felt at having to avoid being with both Uwe and her at the same time. Juggling a close friendship and a demanding girlfriend was uncomfortable work.

During Vivien's vacation, she stayed a week with a friend near Rangsdorf. Upon returning, her account of the visit was filled with unusual enthusiasm.

"You aren't going to believe this," she said. "While we were in Rangsdorf, we decided to go to a movie. We went into the theater, and when I went to pay, I saw three huge Elvis posters behind the old woman taking money." Her face was animated. "I asked if I could buy one. I never saw one that big, and I know I could have traded it for something really good or sold it for a lot of money! Well, she said they weren't for sale, but that if I wanted to talk to her son, the manager, he would be available after the show. We watched the movie and then went upstairs afterwards to talk to him." She took a breath and continued, even moving her arms around. Very unusual for her. "You wouldn't believe it. He looked exactly like Elvis!"

"What are you talking about?"

"His hair, his eyes. I couldn't believe it. You should have seen Jane flirting with him."

"Only Jane?"

Her eyes narrowed. "Don't be ridiculous, and don't interrupt. He's about 23 and his hair was combed back and shiny. You know, like this." She brushed her hands across my hair to demonstrate. "Well, after we recovered our surprise, I asked him about buying the posters, and he told me that he got them from the West side but they weren't for sale. When he asked if we were fans, we told him yes, and then he said that he had a few records if we'd like to come over to his place to look at them."

Jealousy flashed through my veins.

"What do you mean, his place?"

"His house. He only lived a kilometer away."

"And you went?" It was too much. What else was she going to end up telling me?

"If you don't shut up, I'm not going to say any more."

I shook my head and stared at her, trying to hide my jealousy. Thinking of my first and only girlfriend with some older stranger who looked like Elvis and ran a theater wasn't good at all.

"Anyway we drove to his house …"

"You drove? What did you drive in?"

"He has a red Moskwich."

"Red?"

Vivien put both hands on her hips, the same way I had seen her mother do when she was telling off Herr Taschner.

"This is the last thing I'm saying if you don't shut up and let me finish." She stared me down. "His name is Lutz. We went to his house, the three of us, and I saw more records and posters than I ever believed could be in our whole country!"

I had one of the best collections of posters, photographs, and books in Falkensee. How much more could anyone possess?

"How many?"

"At least 70 albums."

My jaw relaxed involuntarily.

"And I counted at least 20 posters on the walls, maybe more. I couldn't believe it!"

In that instant everything changed. Vivien had unwittingly discovered a kindred spirit. This Lutz was a real find.

"Does he have any books?" I had books, three different biographies of Elvis, all in good shape, all ready to be traded in the right deal. If he didn't have books, maybe I still had something that would interest him. A collection the size Vivien was describing was unheard of, and had to contain some rare finds. My mind raced as she continued.

"He said that he liked to trade sometimes, but he didn't seem too excited when I told him about your collection." She paused, studying my reaction. "I have his address if you want it."

Her voice continued in the background, recounting the rest of their adventure, but my attention was focused on this new collector and how to meet him.

I wrote a letter, being sure to mention books, and about a month later a reply arrived with a polite acknowledgement and the suggestion that we meet. I invited him to visit my home and a time was set.

I struggled to contain my excitement as the Moskwich turned the corner and drove slowly up Berliner Strasse. Lutz was the first person over fourteen other than Uwe that I had dared to bring home for a visit.

Vivien had been precise in every detail. The car was spotless, and obviously well-maintained. He parked on the grass next to Siedlereck, and since the bar was closed during the day, there was no danger of anyone bothering it.

"Lutz Bobzien," he said, extending his hand.

"Carsten Kaaz." Vivien was right about his appearance, too. Definitely an Elvis look-alike, and I tried to avoid staring.

"I brought a few things along for you to look at," he said. "Which is your house?"

We were eight meters from the frontier, and the red and white signs loomed before us. This was going to be tricky. Lutz lived nowhere near the border and was probably not aware of the severe restrictions. I indicated a general direction and we began to walk up the street, talking informally. As we approached the first warning sign, he paused for a moment studying the red and white message.

"What's this? Am I going to get arrested or something?"

I swallowed and chose my words carefully.

"You're supposed to have a pass to come in here, but I know my way around pretty well. Just stick with me and there won't be any problem. We have to leave your car here or the neighbors will be sure to notice."

If a border guard or a policeman happened by, our meeting would be cut short in a hurry, and I'd have to try to persuade some officious VOPO not to haul him away. But if I didn't bring him to my home, there could be no acquaintance at all. I reasoned that, like most people, he probably understood that in order to live anything like a normal life, it was necessary to break some laws with regularity. I was counting on my new

Carsten Kaaz and Vivien Taschner — 1982

Carsten Kaaz — 1984

Author's high school graduation class
Falkensee, East Germany — 1982
(Carsten in front row, kneeling, third from right)

friend to have at least an average level of East German cynicism.

That day we were lucky. We avoided Koch's eyes by cutting down Pestalozzi Strasse and slipped without incident into my yard through the hidden gate in Detlef's fence.

We were both excited to find another person who had a comparable level of interest, and our eagerness to exchange ideas and information made me oblivious to the time. We talked a whole two hours and did not even bother to have coffee. During that brief time, I began to feel as though I had known him my whole life, almost like a member of the family. Lutz lived with his aging mother and retired father and had decided to devote as much of his own life as necessary to helping them finish out their lives in comfort. It also became obvious that he was not the same as many collectors, only interested in how to gain advantage in a sharp trade, and that friendship was important in his life. As the weeks passed, he visited several times, and on one visit carried a bag.

"I brought a little something along for you," Lutz said.

It appeared to be a record. I took it hesitantly.

"I have another one of these at home. It's not like I'm giving my last one away," he said.

It was a brand-new Elvis record, unopened, worth at least one hundred marks. I examined the jacket and stuttered appreciation.

"My dad is retired," he said, "and every time he travels to the West side, I get him to bring back a record or something special. Once he bought this one without knowing I had a copy already, so now I'm giving it to you. It's important for friends to share."

That gift held much more than monetary value, because I realized that he liked me as a friend, not simply for the purpose of trading. Relationships with other collectors were always business, but from that day on, Lutz and I were like brothers who saw the world through the same set of eyes, and wanted to help each other make our way through it. Being six years older, he seemed to comprehend the full range of my feelings, and offered advice from his maturity and experience. Over the next few months, our trust developed to the point where I could freely speak my mind on any subject. In a land where neighbors would turn you in, it was a rare thing.

Over the months, my Elvis inventory grew, and a fascinating picture began to form of this controversial entertainer.

Our official press noted bad habits that were said to include drug and alcohol abuse. The few news clippings I had added that he gave some of his friends automobiles at Christmas. Reading this, I scratched my head. Being successful, did that mean he was one of the cruel capitalists I had heard about all my life? How did this fit with Elvis? I was amazed to learn that he came from a poor family and had very little formal education. In my country, anyone who wanted to become a professional musician had to attend special schools or they would never even be considered, no matter what the talent. Perhaps America was a place where a person could have the opportunity to try things just because he wanted to. Perhaps if a person changed his mind, or failed, he could try something else. But America was supposedly our enemy.

It was a Saturday, and my parents had taken my brother Roberto and gone for an afternoon drive. Uwe and I got together and discussed life. Then the inevitable subject of the West came up.

"What do you think?" Uwe said. "Is America as crazy as it looks on TV?"

"I don't think anything is like it looks on TV," I said. "Some of it may be true, but the Western programs about our country aren't completely true either."

"I wonder why that is?"

"Maybe it's just because people are so different in some ways and similar in others. Maybe we expect everyone to be like us and then call them stupid when they do things differently. Sometimes I catch myself thinking like that."

We lay on our backs in the grass in the backyard and fell silent, looking up into the cloudless deep blue sky.

"Here comes another one," Uwe said quietly.

Then I could hear it, too, building, steadily building to a whistling whine, rushing of air, roaring, venting of compressed gasses.

"They all come in the same way," he said, "just like there are tracks."

Then it was upon us, and our very bones shook as the big jet shrieked overhead, so low we could see the oil streaks on the engine nacelles in the moment when it blotted out the sky. The lingering kerosene fragrance of burned jet fuel would soon reach us.

Uwe raised his voice as it roared away in a northerly direction.

"Another one for Tegel. What do you really think? Is the rest of the world as bad as they say?"

I thought about it, remembering things we had been told by the teacher only last week. Herr Friedrich had said, "The capitalists oppress their people. They keep them in poverty and exploit their energy and lives just to make money. Then just the rich people have the wealth and the rest of their people go without."

"Herr Friedrich," I had countered, raising my hand, "that may be true, but they seem to have a lot of possibilities. You know, they can change jobs whenever they want, they can ..."

His raised hand cut me off.

"Sure they can. But have you ever thought about what happens when they are unemployed? They can be thrown out of their house, they can't get medical care. They'll go hungry and be sleeping in a car somewhere."

"But ..."

"You can't understand until you get older," he continued. "Security is everything. How would you feel knowing that someone could just throw you out of your house? You have seen their own news programs with the slums and the millions of homeless. What kind of a society allows that to happen? Where is this thing called freedom that they boast of?" His last sentence carried the usual zealous inflection.

For the moment, I was without a reply. Clearly there were problems in the West, and all of the injustices he cited were true. Still, they appeared to be basically happy. It didn't make any sense.

Returning from my reflection, I said, "I don't know, Uwe, but Americans seem different from anyone I know about. They talk like they can do anything. Some of them are arrogant and think the rest of the world is backward. Others seem to love everyone. It must be a place where there are many contradictions."

"I wonder how it would be to travel wherever you wanted?" he said.

"Where would you go?"

"I always wanted to see Australia, maybe catch a kangaroo. Walk across their great desert, I think it's called the outback." We laughed and I hoped Uwe would always have the spirit of adventure. His was a quiet hope supported by inner strength that enabled him to be more patient, to bear more hardship than anyone I knew.

Jet noise rose again in the distance, and we stopped speaking to take in every part of the sound. I had read Mark Twain's "Life on the Mississippi" and thought how it must have been to sit on the bank and watch steamboats pass, puffing and thrashing up and down the river. It would be absorbing to learn about the passengers' destinations, their names, why they traveled on the back of that huffing, churning vessel, and what thoughts ran through their minds as they noted the observers on the riverbank. Faces were too far away to be recognizable, but from the distance, it would be possible to distinguish a top hat, beard, or the subtle curve of a feminine shape beneath an unfurled parasol. The thought became too convoluted to continue because I found myself on the boat looking at myself on the bank. It was the same feeling we now had as Uwe and I watched the giant screaming shiny thing flash overhead. Blue and white letters. Pan Am. If the angle was a little better we might have been able to see a face pressed against a double-layered window. Why couldn't those faces have been ours?

We read everything we could find, good and bad, on America. We watched every program on television. Western views and that of the East Bloc were sampled and integrated. The picture began to form, then solidify. The cities of the Northeast, in fact all of the really big cities, seemed to be dangerous. Crime, unemployment, and overcrowding were serious problems. American public education was declining in effectiveness, moving towards a collective comfort zone that would eventually leave it in the low ranges of mediocrity. A person could make a life there, and by working hard and trying to succeed, the basic necessities of life would be available. What were the basic necessities? If a person didn't get too greedy, food, shelter, and a respectable job would be adequate. I already had these, but family and personal relationships were my deepest core, my inner life, and without them daily existence would be unbearably cold. Big cities probably snuffed out personal relationships, replacing them with economic interdependence or some other artificial attachment, but that would be true in any country. I didn't want that. Life was good when it was filled with productive activity and a circle of close friends and loved ones.

"I dreamed," Uwe said, "that if I went to America, I could start a business in woodworking. I bet there are some people who really appreciate good furniture."

I agreed. "I think I could make it too. Maybe my own company repairing electronic equipment, or translating languages. My Russian is pretty good."

"Where would we travel if we had the chance?"

"I want to see it all," I said. "But for sure I'd go to visit Graceland, and South Fork in Dallas."

Uwe chuckled. He and I, like most of the people in East Germany, were fascinated to distraction by the TV show, "Dallas." Everybody knew J.R., and was amazed by his continual capacity for evil doing.

"Then I'd like to see some of the cities: Chicago; Washington, D.C.; Los Angeles. But I never want to live in a big city. Near one maybe, but never in one."

Uwe fell silent, withdrawing.

"What's the matter?" I said.

"I was just wondering if you and I would still be friends, if we would still be able to take a walk now and then to figure out life and all the things we have to face?"

I shook his shoulder.

"Come on. You and I have been like brothers since we were twelve. We'll go to America together and help each other. Our friendship will never change, because there is no material thing either of us has that is more important than that."

He nodded. From the distance came the rushing of air on polished metal.

"Here comes another one from Tegel."

Near the end of my eighth grade school year, my Berufsberater(guidance counselor) made an appointment for me to interview the school director. Herr Kuke was a friend to me and many others because of his sincerity. During my interview with the director, he reviewed my good grades and recommended Erweiterte Oberschule (extended high school). If I chose not to attend that next academic level, I would have to go into vocational training immediately and enter factory work. This was a critical turning point, and a mistake here could irrevocably ruin the rest of my life. At 14, the decision was heavy, and what to do filled my waking hours. Finally, the time came to have my official interview to review all of the options.

Kuke's office was small, even by our school's standards, and sparsely furnished with a worn wooden desk piled high with a multitude of papers, like most of the desks in our country. I perched uncertainly on the chair to his right and waited as he finished signing something. Papers rustled and I studied the wood. How smooth it was, polished to a milky perfection in odd places by an infinity of rubbing. How many elbows had rested there, and how many fingers had touched the top above the drawer as their owners pushed away to stand. Every important person I knew found something to sign at the moment you came into their office. He acknowledged my presence with a nod, and steepled his fingers in a gesture of thoughtfulness.

"Let's talk about your ideas for the future," he said. "I have been looking your records over, and with the exception of conduct, you have a lot of potential. What do you think you'd like to do about a career?"

"Maybe I'd like to be an attorney," I told him.

"That's entirely possible," he said. "Pre-university training will prepare you for higher studies after your military service."

I knew that military service wasn't optional. "How long would I have to serve?"

"For the professions, three to four years before university entrance."

"Before?" I knew that in my mind, but now it came home to my heart. "Before?" I stared at his sallow face, thin and angular in the starkly-lighted room.

"Carsten, listen to me," he said firmly. "It's a trade you're making, one which most young people never have the chance to even think about." His fingers brushed my file on his desk blotter. "If you do something for the government, the government will do something for you. One never goes without the other. It is that simple."

Reluctance rolled through me, and my eyes averted reflexively.

"What's bothering you anyway? It works the same way for all of us. That's how I got to be a teacher. That's how you'll get the opportunity for a career. Even if you instead choose

81

technical training, you'll have to go to school for two years under contract to a business, then go to work there after graduation until you're called to go into the army."

"I'll think about it. I like electronics too."

"Don't sell yourself short by taking the easy way. Do you understand the doors this could open in your life?" His dark eyes fixed upon me with unwavering concentration while the overhead incandescent bulb cast stark oval spots of light upon his cheeks. "Everyone has an obligation to the State, but the best students like you have the chance to rise up. It's your life we're talking about. Think it over carefully. This is the most serious decision you will make for a long time, and the rest of your life will follow the path you choose in the next few years."

The explanation continued, and I weighed not only his words, but what I knew of reality. Succeeding in school for the love of knowledge was something I had already begun. As the world and life unfolded from pages in a book, I drank it in, savoring the variety and enlightenment, but even by eighth grade we had been advised that our future was to be ordered according to a formalized set of rules. Grades determined access to higher education, and failure in the early years irrevocably closed certain occupational doors, so those of us having any ambition wanted to keep the doors open, and we worked hard. But business success, becoming the director of some state-owned company, or receiving professional training as a doctor or engineer wouldn't bring large financial rewards because the higher-ups made only twenty percent more than the workers. But there were other rewards to be had. The managers and professionals gained access to networks of connections, the chance to develop personal relationships with other people who controlled state resources and materials. Those who controlled the acquisition and redistribution of those assets had something much better than East German currency. With a phone call, they could cause a load of lumber to be dropped off at a certain place, part of a shipment of appliances to be held in the warehouse for special pickup, or a plant purchasing agent to obtain foreign automobile parts under a state priority purchasing order.

Where money is no good, connections are everything.

Doctors took care of lawyers' bad feet, technicians took care of the plant manager's stereo, and carpenters took care of the clothing store manager's new porch with wood from a state apartment building project. Judges, engineers, and anyone having specialized training traded favors and such commodities as they controlled. A vast informal network of connections allowed those with some of the right things to bypass the shortages and non-availability of so many other things in the society. That was real power, and real wealth.

Kuke stared. "Are you paying attention? You'll have to make a choice or we'll make one for you. Think it over and remember that you're the only one who can say what is going to make you happy."

The door closed behind me and I added up the time. Finishing Oberschule, then going to the army, I would be twenty-three before even beginning university studies. Another four years to a degree was an eternity of waiting.

At supper that night, I went over the options with Mom and Dad.

"I'm thinking about training in electronics," I said.

"You're smart, and you know how to work hard, Carsten," Mom said. "I know you can become anything you want."

Dad nodded his approval and swallowed his food.

"There are many opportunities now that didn't even exist when I was your age. You're really lucky."

The words flooded out of my mouth.

"But what if I am successful?" I said. "It won't make much difference in pay, and I'll be trapped like everyone else in this country. There's no reason to excel unless there can be fulfillment in life, and I don't see much of that when I look around. I'm not going to be jammed into a mold!"

Their speechless looks of alarm shot back and forth. "There are many things to understand before you make a final decision, son," Dad said.

He was always the pragmatist, but I was in no mood to compromise. The anger had surprised me, erupting from some inner chambers.

Mom joined in.

"You have a lot of potential and we don't want to see you hurt. Please think things over carefully, and talk with us before you sign anything at school."

I thanked Mom for another good supper, and excused myself.

Feeling aloof and immersed in silent pondering, I went to my room that night and lay in the dark, going over the paths that lay ahead. In my heart I had already decided. Though I had the grades and knew I could master law studies, I didn't want to live with the trade that I would have to make. Irretrievable youth would be consumed and no one could enter the desirable jobs without first serving in the armed forces of this eastern kingdom. I didn't fit that category, and suddenly I was glad. The feelings reminded me of when I stood on the front porch looking westward into the frigid winter wind that howled in from across the Wall. Even though it slashed pitilessly with its moaning cold daggers, I felt strong because I could withstand its worst and still not shrink away. I was facing a different wind now, but I wasn't about to flinch. The faceless ones were not going to win! It was now a point of honor.

If I changed my mind about studying law while in the army, it would make no difference, because once I joined there would be no backing out of the three-year obligation. Waiting around was another possibility. If I were simply drafted to fill the mandatory obligation, I would only have to suffer through 18 months in that unhappy organization. What about just joining? A local example was Schirmer, my neighbor Grenztruppen Captain. I couldn't see myself following that model. Bernd, the garbage commando, was drifting in adolescent despair as his home life deteriorated. He talked about the army as a means to buy some time, a way to avoid making a serious decision about choosing a direction. Another example of the military product was evident in Danilo Krys, a schoolmate. Danilo seemed to lack all motivation, having failed a year. He was older than the rest of us, but his lack of success in school never appeared to cause him worry.

"It doesn't matter that much about school," he said on one occasion. "My dad is a major in the Nationale Volks Armee, and

I can always join up anytime I want. You can join, too, if you want. They are always looking for men. They'll take almost anyone."

He was right, and that fact bothered me even more. The army would take almost anyone who had both arms and legs, so it was said that the only men who stayed for life were ones who could rise in the ranks. Therefore, if I joined the army, someone like Danilo would be giving the orders. Our army took its orders from the Soviets anyway, and they made no efforts to humanize the recruit's time in service. Their custom was to station troops inside East Germany, but as far away from home as possible so they wouldn't be distracted during their term. We had some troops in Angola, but that was a volunteer assignment and only the most hard-core commando personnel qualified. Most troops were due eighteen days of leave in eighteen months, but none of that was available until six months had elapsed. None of the military training was designed to give soldiers skills transferable to everyday life, and men who served voluntarily for long enlistments were regarded with suspicion when they reentered the civilian world. They were branded as party men, staunch Communists not to be trusted by the commoners. No one with ambition wanted anything to do with the army, and in my understanding, enlisting was an admission of failure in life.

Whatever happened, I had no intention of failing, but how could I fit in?

Others were raised in the system, were used to its well-worn paths and appeared normal. Among them were my parents, uncles and grandfather. Truly among the best people I knew, they were sober, kind, full of love and caring for family, and good friends to many, but what of their day-to-day lives? Were they happy? If so, I couldn't see it. They would have a vacation every year in some neighboring country where Communists still ruled, and they would eventually own a car. Beyond that they would never dream of having their own independent business or really doing anything unusual in life unless their aspirations fell within the special restrictions of state law. They would love their family and raise children to be obedient to them and those who directed their lives. Was there some tomorrow for them beyond retirement to a soft chair and overeating? They were in the same cage as everyone else, and they ran round and round, pushing the wheel on and on until the day they would no longer be obligated to run. Then they would simply get off and settle in a corner to await the end.

How could my own life be any different? Who would I become? What did I want from life? Following the standard path, I could hope for a car by the time I was 30, maybe an apartment in town and getting married, having a few children. If no political shocks occurred, I could expect to vacation on the Baltic or in the mountains twice a year. Beyond that, I'd have to work away my life in one of the state-owned enterprises until retirement.

Whatever I was going to do, it would have to be soon, because the time for decision-making was upon me. If I did not choose, a decision would be made for me, and then I would be forced into a career path whether my perspectives on the future were accurate or not. No matter which road I took, the number of future possibilities would be further reduced. Somehow, there had to be a way to go forward with life without having to choose so very early. My head hurt from going over everything so many times. The system was squeezing me and all of my classmates, steering, channeling, herding us toward choices that would bind us for the rest of our lives. There was no way I could see ahead to preserve options, no way to escape the imperative to choose now, to make commitments that would forever exclude other possibilities. Surely this was how an animal must feel when it finds itself in a trap. No matter whether it understands how the trap works or not, it is still caught and the jaws still hold fast with their merciless grip. After a while, the animal tires and ceases to struggle. There are some, though, who would chew off their own leg to escape.

There were many possibilities, but which ones would lead me to a happy life? Was the substance of life only found in career status? How important was the family? Where did a wife and children fit in?

Lying on my bed in the quiet of the evening was almost painful. In the silence nothing stirred but my fears. A faint white light filtered in through the attic panes, casting a trapezoidal pattern high on the bedroom wall. It was as though the small window was the only means I had to look upon the world. It was a small opening facing north, with a narrow angle of view looking out over the gray rooftops. There was nothing else to see but the distant white lights of the Wall.

It was impossible to count on anything being a certain way tomorrow, but I could guess at what it would be like. Salvation from the fate of living oblivion would only come if there were powerful goals to direct my little life. Forming those goals would mean more choices, all of them as irrevocable as the one now forced upon me. I wanted to remain an intact person, a whole functioning entity, and to keep the power to direct which way I turned as the years passed. To have less was to disappear, in a way to die. Every time that thought occurred to me, my heart was awash in fear.

Somehow I had to survive without giving myself to the system. Somehow I had to find my own way in the face of the inexorable current dragging me toward a gray uniformity. My goal would be to make something good of myself, to become someone of whom my parents and loved ones could be proud, someone who was at peace within.

With a mind full of worries, I tossed in bed for hours wishing for sleep. Finally, it stole in quietly to the bedside and led me gently away into a painless, fuzzy nothingness.

The Unter Den Linden, the main street of East Berlin

The East/West Berlin border in 1963 at Potsdamer Platz

# CHAPTER FOUR

Weeks melted into months and I burrowed into my books, spending hours each day in pursuit of intellectual understanding. The quantitative studies fell into place, and I arranged time to help Ulf Kubicki with his English. Vivien and I discovered the depths and the limits of our attraction, and despite the obvious missing pieces, we continued to see each other regularly. Uwe and I took regular walks through the pine thicket, noting the seedlings that seemed to grow even as we did from year to year. We lived each day, laughed and cried, together and alone. Our lives were in motion, and the horizon drew nearer.

Ninth grade history was an enhanced version of what we had been hearing since the beginning. No matter what the course title, it wasn't really world history, but rather it concentrated on developments following World War II, the organization of the Communist party, the formation of the Eastern Bloc, the Warsaw Pact, and COMECON, the East Bloc trading organization.

In that same year, we began compulsory Pre-military training one full day per month, and it was always longer than a regular school day. The first half-day was spent in coeducational class, studying ideology and military history and tactics. That was followed by specific classes on military education including detailed discussions of the deployment of NATO forces in Europe, and the probable path their invading army would take when they started World War III. My old civics teacher, Friedrich, was the instructor. He was still of undiminished Communist missionary fervor and untiring enthusiasm for the calling. His wiry body was leathery and lean, like an underfed horse; his light gray eyes were never still. Constantly probing, watching, cataloging every event, each subtlety of speech and inflection, he would report students for both what was said as well as what was not said. We were wary of him the same way a dog sees a snake coiled in the path and, while not fully comprehending the threat, all the while knows that an evil presence has come nigh. A few kids in the class were friendly toward him, but their choice carried the cost of close friendship with the rest of us. Those who joined the government club at an early age soon came to know that isolation was the price of their proclivity towards authority.

"Let's talk about their latest weapons system," Friedrich said. "They call it an enhanced radiation weapon, the neutron bomb. It's the capitalist's dream, designed to produce massive amounts of hard radiation that will penetrate shelters and kill all of the people."

Many in class shifted uncomfortably in their wooden chairs. We had read a lot about the effects of radiation following nuclear detonations, and had been shown pictures of people and buildings at Hiroshima.

Friedrich continued, his slight body upright, sitting at attention.

"In three or four weeks they'll come in, dispose of all the dead bodies, start up our factories, and move into our homes. They'll pile the corpses in vast heaps and set them afire with diesel fuel the same way the Fascists did in the death camps during the war. Your mothers and fathers will all be dead, your brothers and sisters will be dead. There won't be a dog or a cat to chase the rats, but the capitalists will have the land and all that we now possess."

He paused, adding putrefying details to that vision of desolation until satisfied by our reaction; then he was in control. Out came the recognition charts; he tapped the poster with the wooden pointer. Name them all, left to right, silhouettes of NATO armor and aircraft. We named everything without hesitation, so he continued.

"This is the American M-60A1 tank. Notice that it has a machine gun in the commander's cupola. It has the 105mm cannon, and night driving gear that does not need the infrared searchlight. You can see the difference between its silhouette and the British Centurion and Chiefton. More rounded. This is the AMX, latest series, but we do not believe that the French would be serious opponents. They don't have a history of reliability as anyone's allies. Then there is the latest armored destroyer to come from the fascists. They call it the Leopard, their newest battle tank."

One of the boys spoke up, noting the caliber and type of thermal sight of the Bundeswehr tank. Friedrich smiled and complimented him. What a good example he was. I could see other boys shaking their heads in contempt. "Red socks," we called them, those who sniffed the political crap, bought it, chewed it, and swallowed it all the way down.

"You should all be proud that your country has no warlike intentions; that we stand for peace."

My mouth moved before I could think.

"The Czechs are proud of their country, and the Poles are proud to be Polish, but I don't know any who are proud to be East German." My eyes swept the room. No supporting nods, but no disagreement either. Mostly they resembled statues.

Friedrich's face went blank for an instant.

"I am proud," he said, but his shifting eyes betrayed hesitation and doubt. Then the lecture ground on, settling on Western armor, but we already knew about enemy tanks. The previous week we had a class on how to successfully attack them with the shoulder-fired Panzerfaust anti-tank rocket. If you could get close, a direct hit on the turret or the rear quarters could be lethal, but a broken track would take the machine out of action, too. He continued, diagraming the way a high-explosive-shaped charge burns through armor.

I took out my graph paper and tapped on the desk. Ulf caught the movement and raised his eyebrows. It was time for a diversion to pass the rest of the lecture — Schiffe versenken, our version of the Western game known as 'Battleship.' There was little inherent risk since we didn't receive a grade for the training, and the teacher's only threat was a nasty note at the end of the year. After taking a minute to draw the location of my four ships on the paper, I tapped the desk again. He nodded and mouthed the words, 'F-6.' I shook my head and fired my salvo, 'H-8.' He grinned and shook his head. Back and forth we went until he got lucky.

"Boom," I said softly. "A hit."

The other boys snickered, and Friedrich looked sharply in our direction. We bent over our papers pretending to be taking notes and fired our "guns" more discreetly.

In the afternoon, the girls went to other classes to learn first aid and CPR, then the boys all went outside to dig individual fox holes, the schutzengraben, and later gathered to construct an observation bunker. The sun was full in the cloudless sky, and we each tried to avoid the hardest work of filling sandbags or hauling the excavated dirt. Our mentor stood by, urging us onward.

"Learn how to do it right," he said. "You'll be protected from the radiation if you dig the hole deep."

"What a bunch of garbage," one of the boys said after Friedrich strutted away. "Who wants to live if the world is covered by radiation and everyone you love is a rotting corpse? What kind of world is he talking about?"

Another boy spoke.

"If there is ever a war, they'll come drag us out of the classrooms, shove a rifle in our hands and tell us to go kill fascists. Then we'll march out to be gutted by a machine gun, or smashed by a tank."

"You're forgetting something." The random sound of shovels scraping earth punctuated the sentence. "If we're a little too slow, our own officers will put a bullet in our heads. They have to be sure and kill someone."

Were we eager for war? No. Would we fight if we were told? Yes. For my part, I enjoyed the private joke among some of us that nuclear combat would be a unique thing, so that would be the time to jump out in the open and look directly at the burst. After all, you'd get to see it just once, and that would be your best chance for a really good show.

I shoved my spade deeper into the dirt and thought how sticky the soil was, not at all soft and rich like in my mother's garden. This drill-field earth was dead, trodden upon and dug to death, stuffed into and emptied from gray sand bags over and over. Used as a rehearsal for the end of civilization, it was employed to legitimize a futile academic exercise on how to survive and prosper after some group of fools had murdered the human race. All around I heard the grunts and curses of my classmates, and I cursed, too. What kind of childhood was it where so many days were spent immersed in learning the business of death?

A boy's voice rose above the scrape of shovels.

"Do you think there'll be another war?"

Another replied, "There will if you don't keep digging. I'm not doing this all by myself."

"I'm serious," said the first one.

"The West has a lot more to lose than we do. Why should they start it?"

I threw my shovel down and stepped away from the bunker entrance as my mind was seized by an involuntary vision of the squat mound of dirt collapsing beneath the squeaking treads of a camouflaged tank. We built it exactly according to the book, and it would make an efficient grave. Friedrich would be pleased at that.

"What's the matter?" Ulf asked.

"I have to go to the bathroom."

He wiped his brow, pushed the glasses up on his nose and began to fill another bag.

As I walked away, stumbling on the deep brown dirt clods, I felt guilty leaving them behind. Something was terribly wrong. Was the problem with me or the society? Sweat ran down my back, cooling my body in the gentle breeze, and for a moment soothing my mind as well. I would have to decide who was wrong, me or them, and I would have to decide soon. Life was running out, and if I didn't figure it out, there would be no more choices and someone else would end up saying who and what I was going to become.

It was nearly three in the afternoon when we finished the bunker, but instead of sitting down for a rest, Friedrich gathered us on the edge of the large field next to the school.

"We're going to run now," he said. "As soon as we get done, you can get your things together and go home. One kilometer run. Get moving!"

Groans. When Friedrich said 'we,' he meant that the running was for us kids, and the watching was for him.

"Save the complaining for your mothers. Get moving, and you have to carry your accessory bag."

My curses mingled with the others as we began to trot. As we neared completion, Friedrich ran out on the field toward us waving his arms.

"Gas! Gas! Put on your masks! Gas! Gas!"

Between panting breaths and more curses, we dragged the black round-snouted rubber things from the bags, fitting them over our sweating faces. The sticky perspiration made a good seal.

"Run," he yelled. "Run another lap! Come on, you babies, your mothers can't help you now!"

Although Soviet-designed chemical equipment was supposed to be superior to Western gear, we could barely get enough air at a brisk walk, and immediately the heat became unbearable. Some partially unscrewed the filters to allow a little more airflow, but I preferred the method of pushing the thing up on my face until the seal was compromised, causing a nice breeze along the lower edges. Then it was over. Friedrich, standing on the edge of the field hands on his hips, our would-be Kaiser, waved an end to the torture. We passed him without speaking. The only sounds were scuffing steps and the harsh rasping of boys' respiration in the relentless afternoon heat.

A few weeks later, I arranged to meet with a potential sponsor — the director of a Falkensee electronics repair facility. I had to pass his Wartburg sedan parked in the reserved space, the presence of which was sure testimony of Herr Doktor's connections. The office was nicely furnished with a dark hardwood desk, brass lamp, West German electronic calculator, and a fashionably framed photograph of Erich Honecker on his light green wall. The director was writing something on a pad, but stopped as I knocked at the open door.

The interview began with his polite questions about my

family, but quickly progressed to the important part.

"There are really no openings now, Herr Kaaz." Doktor peered with heavy-lidded eyes over his bifocals at my shiny ninth-grade face. "Tell me about your performance in school."

"Straight A's, Herr Doktor," I said proudly.

"Ah, yes." His gaze shifted back and forth. "And you will be choosing electronics for certain?"

"Yes, I'm really interested. I have taught elementary electricity to young students."

"Ah, yes." Of course he knew that because he already had read my file. "There is the matter of your military obligation as well. Assuming something could be worked out, there are conditions. After you have finished school and our on-the-job training program, you will owe the army three years. In that way, you can feel as though you are returning something to the state in gratitude for all it has invested in you."

"Three years." My face betrayed the lack of enthusiasm. It seemed like such a very long time. "Yes sir, I understand. When will I know if we can have an agreement?"

"Well, there are some things that I must check with Nauen, and who knows. ..." His voice trailed off and the sentence ended in a slight smile, superscribed by the careful, precise eyes. "You must also remember that you can only get training by keeping good grades. Otherwise, you'll be out of the program and assigned to a non-technical career path."

That meant anything from a truck-driving job to checking train cars in and out of a freight yard all day.

"I'll keep my grades up," I promised.

That was the answer he wanted to hear, because three days later Doktor notified the school that I had been accepted by his company as a contracted trainee. I had chosen because it was choosing time, whether I liked it or not. I also knew that I was not picked just because of good grades, nor because I happened to talk to someone having some political pull. The army was so much in need of personnel, that future employment in the technical or professional specialties was directly linked to military service. Industry and educational leaders were instructed by the government to be sure that young people were regularly funneled into this path.

The contract I made with Radio und Fernsehtechnik secured a valuable education, provided for actual job training during technical school, guaranteed the company a trained employee following the military obligation, and paved the way for another body in the Volks Armee. But in reality, it was most important to Herr Doktor and my school guidance counselor because they could stay in good standing with the ever-watchful state as military recruiters.

I imagined that working for Doktor would make life predictable. I'd have a place to live, food to eat, clothing, and, if I simply showed up and made some visible effort, employment would be mine as long as I wanted it. I imagined the adventure of a real career with an aching heart, because I believed I could succeed. Contemplating years in the army evoked nausea. I could feel part of my life draining out, but what other course was possible? I put the pen to the paper.

Somewhere in the innermost corners of my adolescent mind I heard the slamming of distant doors. I stood on the edge of the chasm. Just another of the multitude, I wandered between the tufts of grass in a mediocre pasture. I had eaten from the trough because there was no other food to be had. The rough, cold bars pressed against my face as I probed for some other avenues. But the keepers were well practiced in their art, and I began to see my life as just another in the endless stream of faceless beasts filing through the chute into the final corral. I wasn't a citizen, I was a calf to be fattened until a steak was needed.

Uwe and I found time again for an evening walk, and I couldn't help pouring out my ambivalent feelings.

After recounting the experience there was nothing but silence. I had known Uwe for years, and by now it was certain that he could be trusted with the most carefully hidden feelings of my heart. Otherwise, I would not have dared to utter the next sentences.

"There must be something wrong with me," I said. "Everywhere I look there's another rule, another official like a traffic cop telling me I have to do this or believe that. I don't hate the West, and I don't want to waste three years of life in the army learning how to dig holes and repair tank radios. The army is worse than school. They watch you every minute to be sure you don't defect or steal some secret, and it's full of Spitzels who'll turn you in for a politically incorrect belch. I've heard all the stories. I wouldn't be allowed to see my family for nearly a year. How can I ever become a whole person if I'm not even free to say how I really feel without fear of being reported?"

Uwe said nothing, but kicked a rock, sending it skipping away into the pine trees.

"It looks to me like nearly everyone around us is just going through the motions of life. The only people who seem to be really happy are the Friday-night drunks at Siedlereck," I said.

"My parents live each day as best they can," he said softly, "but they live without hope." He kicked at another rock, but it didn't budge and his sneaker bounced off.

"What about you, Carsten? Do you have hope?"

"I don't know exactly what to hope for. I have you for a good friend, my parents love me, and Vivien means a lot, but otherwise there isn't much worthwhile. The things you can buy here with money are hardly worth having, especially when we can watch TV any night and see how much better off the rest of the industrial world is." I added, "But none of that is really important anyway. Anything we can build or buy will wear out and decay, but I believe friendship can last a lifetime."

"What can we do to be happy?" he asked.

I stopped walking and turned to face him, although I knew he could not actually see my features in the dark.

"I almost believe that living here in East Germany isn't for me. Maybe I ought to try and find some other place."

"Leaving here isn't like moving to a new job in Potsdam. It's more like ordering a new Trabant and settling in for a ten-year wait. The only ones I know who make it out are the old people and the few who live to tell about going over the Wall. Where would you go? How would you get out without getting into trouble?" he said.

"Maybe there are laws or emigration regulations that we don't know about," I muttered.

We resumed walking and a heavy silence descended.

There we were at Pestalozzi Strasse again. A full circle through the neighborhood brought us back to where we started, and nothing was any different. The houses looked the same, all buttoned up for the night, quiet as though abandoned.

"I know one thing," I said. "Living here is like going to a funeral every day. Everybody says how natural the corpse looks, but they all know he's dead. Who are they kidding?"

Uwe shuffled his foot in the dirt and said, "I don't want to end up like everyone else, but I don't know how to stop it from happening." In the dim light I could see his head tilted backward, gazing up into the dark sky. "I guess I'll go to bed." Then he said good night and disappeared into the shadows. I heard the sound of his shuffling gait all the way down the street. At that moment, it seemed as though there was nothing else alive on the whole earth.

Even though my awareness of the surrounding fear and frustration was growing, there was still the business of living to be handled, and I sidestepped the growing unrest to focus on my studies. School was a serious place, where serious efforts were made every day.

The weeks passed into months, and time was consumed by studying for school. I had made the decision to make all A's, to be the best student in the school, and was beginning to realize that goal. The only hope for the future was to be the best, and that ambition began to consume my heart and mind. I even dreamed about math problems occasionally.

About the middle of ninth grade, the whole school was shocked by tragedy. Henrik caught me by the sleeve before class.

"Did you hear about Torsten?"

"What about him?"

"He's dead. Kerstin was riding home on her bicycle and found him hanging by his neck, you know, from a rope." He held one hand to his throat in a choking gesture.

I shook my head. "Dead?"

"He left a note."

"He killed himself?"

"Right, hanging from a tree where he used to play.

98

I heard that he wrote about the way Friedrich had been picking on him all the time. The other kids said Friedrich used to make him stand up in front of class all the time if he didn't know the answer to math problems. Then he'd call him stupid and laugh."

"He's done that to a lot of kids."

"I also heard that Torsten broke up with his girlfriend a few days ago. Maybe it just got to him." Henrik tugged at his belt, idly flipping the loose end. "We weren't friends, but it's not right that something like this should happen. He wasn't smart, but a teacher shouldn't tear a kid apart like that."

"What do you expect?" I said. "It shows just what Friedrich really cares about. I wonder if the school director is going to do anything about it?"

"One other thing," Henrik said, "Some of the kids are saying that Friedrich is a murderer. They actually whisper the word so he can hear it as he passes."

"I wonder what he's going to do about that? He can't intimidate everyone in the whole school, can he?"

The students shunned Friedrich and continued their whispering campaign until a few days later, when the administration chose to act. An assembly was called, and the director explained that Torsten was a troubled young man who had a bad home life and difficulty with personal relationships. That, he said, was the reason why young Torsten put a note in the mail, a noose around his neck and stepped off a lower limb of the oak tree. It wasn't anyone's fault, he said, but we were forbidden to discuss the subject anymore. He asked if there were any questions, but of course there were not. During the assembly, Friedrich sat on the benches with the other teachers, impassive and distant. It was clear that public accountability for the tragedy was not going to fall on him. The director ended by saying that Torsten was probably crazy, and that his parents failed to bring him up correctly. No one in authority was willing to admit that a teacher had helped torture this confused young man until he chose a kicking, gagging death on the end of a rope over another day of life.

The rest of high school passed in a blur, an ever-accelerating montage of tests, reports, and intellectual challenges.

We bent our energy to assimilating ever-increasing quantities of technical and language information. Even for the slow-learning students, there was no question that they were expected to learn something in school. It was clear that there was no place in our society for the ignorant and uneducated. Even the worst students could read, write and perform basic math computations. Our membership in the state-sponsored youth organization evolved, and we passed the last three years inside the final enforced political participation framework that the state had constructed for the young. FDJ stood for Free German Youth. Membership meant that our uniform changed to a blue shirt and red scarf, and the level of our required participation rose to new heights.

Individual ideological feelings were firm by that time, and everyone with high aspirations planned to seek early Communist Party membership. Connections and career advancement would be very limited unless they joined as soon as possible and were active at least until their professional reputations were established. In later life, being a member on paper was good enough most of the time. If the next stop for a student was pre-university training, erweiterte oberschule, they would be expected to look, sound and behave like the good Communists they would soon become. We were already beginning to understand that it really didn't matter what we felt in our hearts, but only how we behaved around those in authority. To be positioned for future advancement, it was necessary to repeat the right slogans, fly the flag on May Day, read the official newspaper, and show up at the right meetings pretending to be interested in the program. It was clear that within this group, there were those who really believed and those who didn't, but the point was that they all had to act the same. These students recognized that the quality of their connections would determine their business futures, and they had made a conscious decision to follow a path designed to make the best of things as they really were.

Since I had chosen the technical education path, I, too, was conscious of these needs, but I also knew that in my arena ideological ratings were far less critical. I reasoned that the government was most concerned about the attitudes of those entering the professions, because it was from this pool that future political leaders would emerge. They weren't so concerned about what the electronics repair personnel thought as much as how the future Minister of Transportation behaved in party meetings.

In another way, it must have been the same for school children in every land. We saw the end of Oberschule approach and possessed a measure of satisfaction. We were all ready to get on with our lives. We saw it as the end of being treated like a child, herded and force-fed with political dogma. We felt that now, somehow, we would be able to really live, to be our own person at last.

Since Ulf and I were classmates from the beginning, we finished Oberschule at the same time. Toward the end of our senior year, the graduating students were assigned by school administration to participate in summer community work projects. Most of these had to do with agriculture, and ours was to pick strawberries. I had stayed over at Ulf's house Friday night, and we arose at 4:30 a.m. A breakfast of scrambled eggs and toast was prepared, and we sat in appreciative silence in the soft gray of dawn on his patio. It was only a couple of blocks from his house to the bus stop at the intersection of Calvin and Pestalozzi strasses, so we rode our bicycles down the silent streets. There was nothing but the rhythmic sound of the bicycles and the hollow buffeting of the wind on our ears. Lights went on here and there in the houses, and I imagined the people sleeping, eating, or taking an early-morning shower. The oily buzz of the chain and the scrape of pedals against the chain guard made a kind of primitive music in the silent morning air. The front wheel wiggled on the cobblestones as I considered our present situation. Working on the nearby collective would pay us next to nothing; it was just another of those civic duties that we all had to perform. It wasn't that I hated helping with work projects, but I did hate being forced to do it, and inside I could feel the hatred growing.

We locked up the bikes and waited with the crowd at the bus stop until the Hungarian-made monster, trailing a dark cloud of fumes, arrived to scoop us all up. The bus wallowed near on its wornout springs, headlights shining the dim yellow beam that comes from poorly grounded, corroded electrical circuits. Like tired cattle, we stepped up into the belly of the machine. The driver's indifferent face shown pale in the green instrument lights. He didn't react as we boarded, but leaned heavily on the steering wheel staring blankly ahead into the darkness. Even though I was nauseated by the exhaust fumes and the ponderous rocking of the bus, it was restful to see buildings give way to fertile fields as the sun rose. After a brief pep talk from the collective farm manager, we were pointed in the direction of the fields. It didn't take long for our minds to be seduced from the labor of picking to the pleasure of eating. Ulf and I ate strawberries. A lot of strawberries.

"Carsten," Ulf said, "What do you suppose they'll do if they see us eating this much?" He laughed as the juice ran down his chin.

"Fire us perhaps?" I said, and we both cackled. It was good to see him loosen up a little. His ever-present rational attitude was superfluous here among the strawberries.

We ate some more and I lay down between the rows gazing up into the deep blue morning. Now and then a solitary bird would pass, and I noticed for the first time how different they appeared, even though they all flew in the same sky. Sparrows were fitful, nervous little things, painted in the colors of the earth itself. Although they performed amazing acrobatic maneuvers, they seemed more creatures of the dust. Dirt, not the heavens, were what they were all about. Hopping appeared to be just as interesting as flight to them, and I couldn't comprehend why anything that could ride upon the air would choose to scrape its feet in the soil. Crows moved their wings in a peculiar rhythm, and then only when absolutely necessary in order to remain aloft. They constantly looked around as though trying to find some lost treasure. I wondered how it would feel to have no barriers but the strength of your own wings. Thinking of the unfettered birds brought on a certain sadness, so I forced my attention elsewhere.

We dozed, picked some strawberries, ate some strawberries

and just talked of life. The other workers' zeal carried them in the opposite direction, and we were more or less alone in that forgotten corner of the tract. Ulf squinted at the newly yellowing morning sun.

"This is the most boring thing I've ever done," he said, munching. "And I swear I'll never eat another one of these for the rest of my life."

"Not me," I said. "Listening to Friedrich was even worse because we had to stay awake."

I relaxed between the reaching shoots, laden with their red fruit, and touched both ends of life. Like the strawberries, I was rooted to the soil of my homeland and painted like the sparrow with the colors of the earth. But until I could somehow shrug off the invisible weight pressing upon my life, I might as well save my energy and remain grounded. To make only short excursions would eventually transform me into a sparrow, and I would live out my life in flashes of hope, followed by deadly tempests of despair. An unseen, heavy embrace was ever tightening around my life. To simply fend it off was not enough. There had to be a way to rise above it all.

The next day we got up at 4:30 a.m., ate scrambled eggs, and appeared again as scheduled at the bus stop on Calvin Strasse. Five-thirty came and went. Small groups formed like graded eggs, the young with the young, the old with the old. Men and women shuffled, stretched and mumbled. Cigarette smoke mingled with the drifting mist. Six o'clock and no bus.

"What do you think, Ulf?" I asked.

"This is stupid," he said. "Do we have the wrong day?"

Six-thirty. No rattle. No diesel fumes. No bus.

"Come on," I said "Let's get out of here."

"Do you think we should?"

"They'll never even miss us," I said. "Besides, it was the people at school who said we'd do this, and they can't do anything to us now. We're going to graduate no matter what because we finished the work."

For show, we made a lot of loud, indignant comments and disappeared down the dusty Calvin Strasse.

That summer I really saw into the depths of the abyss, into

View of the Wall and West Germany from the Kaaz home in East Germany

The landmark Brandenburg Gate by night, a long-time punctuation point between the two countries and worlds

the yawning, gaping pit where hopes were buried.

Trying to keep a perspective, I took inventory. By the definition of my peers, success should be coming because I had worked hard throughout Oberschule. I was the top student in our district of about 40 schools, spoke, read and wrote German, English and Russian. I had an appointment to a well-respected electronics training school in Burg, and was in possession of a contract to work in my own hometown after training and military service. There were many others who had insufficient grades or who waited too long to make a decision about the course of their lives and were simply absorbed into the meandering sargassum of East German society. Through luck, hard work, and what I began to understand was my native stubbornness, I had managed to dodge the most obvious pitfalls. But beyond the obvious lay the rest of a lifetime where I would have to continue to be an individual in an environment that didn't value individualism.

Looking around, other aspects of life began to come into focus.

All around me, others were infected by a creeping ennui. I began to recognize symptoms in peers that had been evident in older people for as long as I remembered. The ones who seemed not to care too much for life were those who didn't have a strong will. In that area, as well as many others, their wills had been leached away under the constant drain of a stupefying social inertia. Like Bernd Riebisch, they believed that they had no control over their future, so that became the operative truth. After a couple of decades, it didn't seem to bother them anymore, and existence settled into a predictable pattern. Issues of free will and basic human rights didn't crowd the stages of their minds very long, because fundamental problems of daily life occupied so much of their waking time. I began to wonder if most of the obvious inefficiencies of our society were the result of being constantly told what to do by authorities. And they were everywhere. From the Minister of Agriculture to the police on the corner and every major and minor official in-between, came an unceasing flow of directions and proscriptions on how to live, where to go, what to love, what to hate, and above all, what to fear. Quietly, softly they had stolen our wills and replaced them with blind obedience. Somehow, our generation had set up housekeeping inside a cage where creativity and human spirit vanished in habitual obedience.

Vivien had been accepted to an elite pre-university school specializing in the arts, and was on the verge of actually beginning her career. We dated regularly and spent a lot of time together, but all of my attempts to be friendly with her parents had failed. One evening while visiting Ulf, the conversation strayed to Vivien's family, and Ulf's mother, Frau Kubicki, gave me her opinion. She was an educated lady with a steady perspective on life, and it was enlightening to talk with her because she was well informed in so many areas. The Kubicki family fed me many meals, and I always left feeling that I could go there as easily as I could go home. I often thought of Annelies Kubicki as a second mother. She knew Frau Taschner personally and offered me some unsolicited advice.

"Don't say much around her unless you are sure of what you are saying. Her interest is narrowly focused in life, and she is a bottom-line person. You know, 'What kind of benefit can I get from this or that?'" Frau Kubicki's eyebrows arched. "She thinks that most people are pretty stupid, and that impression is made permanent if you aren't careful of what you say."

I thanked her politely, but was yet unconvinced.

"You are a very different sort of person than they are. Don't let yourself get hurt."

My head nodded politely, but my ears had only half heard the message. How could it make all that much difference, I wondered. After all, Vivien cared for me, loved me. But then she had never really spoken those words, and I began to evaluate. Can you be in love and never say it? If you never say it, how can you keep the feeling alive? I had said it many times to myself as though talking to Vivien, but had never gotten enough courage to express it to her face. What would she do if I did? What would happen to our relationship if I didn't? I was bulging with questions, but empty of answers.

Uwe began an important project. For as long as we had been friends, he had struggled to overcome a background of abuse and unrelenting domination by his stepfather. This heritage had left him with difficulty in making important decisions, but he was aware of the limitation and worked hard to overcome it. He wanted to be creative and original, and his latest idea was to begin another adventure.

Uwe's interest in the life and legend of Elvis was growing along with mine. We both had a few posters and newspaper and magazine clippings that had found their way through the restrictions of our country's press. We even had some records, but even with our enthusiasm, it was impossible to make much progress with just the two of us doing the looking.

"There are just a few people in the area who are really interested in collecting Elvis stuff, but we see so much of each other that we each know what everyone has to trade," he sighed. "It's getting boring because nothing new is turning up." He continued, enthusiasm rising in his light blue eyes, animated confidence spreading across his face. "We have to get a larger bunch of people together." He pointed, index finger snapping the paper as he poked it repeatedly. "I had this printed in Neues Leben magazine. Tell me what you think."

I read it once, then again.

"Elvis fan looking for connections with other Elvis fans via correspondence. Uwe George, Pestalozzi Strasse, 18, Falkensee."

"Well?"

"It's a great idea, and it'll be a big success. I'll bet a lot of people will write back."

He smiled, enjoying my approval.

There was no phone number in the ad because the George household had no phone. None of my neighbors had a phone except for the ones who worked for the government. In fact, there were probably not more than a few hundred telephones in all of Falkensee. It would have been so much easier if there were phones, but communications apparatus was mostly reserved for the government and those who served it.

"Do you think Elvis really used drugs as much as they say in the magazines?"

"It's hard to say. What do you believe?" I asked.

Uwe thought for a moment.

"Well, it's easy to think the worst of people isn't it? After all, he's dead and he can't very well defend himself."

"Whatever was wrong in his life, his music has brought a lot of happiness to me. I'm just glad he wasn't born here in East Germany."

We both had a laugh at that. If Elvis Presley had been a native East German, he would have remained a truck driver, because some official would have made him sign a training agreement when he was in ninth grade.

Uwe's project was an immediate success. Within a week of publication, about 50 kids replied by letter. The respondents were either from the northern or southern areas, so East Berlin was the logical central location for a first meeting.

Uwe was nearly bursting with joy.

"I scheduled it for August 16," he said, "9:30 a.m. - 10 a.m., right in front of the American Embassy." He was glowing with pride and expectation. A fan club for a Western musician would be a first for our town, maybe for the whole country. It hadn't occurred to Uwe that anyone would mind, especially since Elvis Presley was dead.

We had both arranged vacation time to be able to attend the meeting, and Uwe mailed the last of the notification letters. Everything was proceeding according to the plan.

On August 6, at 5:30 a.m., two men appeared at the George house on Pestalozzi Strasse and rang the buzzer on the gate. Uwe's mother went to the door.

"Is Uwe George home?"

"Yes, still asleep." She was not a particularly sensitive woman, but she surely knew that men in suits visiting at odd hours could only mean trouble. She went upstairs and woke him.

"There are two men to see you."

Stretching and rubbing his eyes, he stumbled downstairs wearing only the swimming trunks he slept in.

The unsmiling visitors stood in the small living room and appraised him like sharks deciding where to bite.

"You are Uwe George." It was a sort of statement, not a

question. Part of their power came from people believing that they knew everything, so they used the same approach over and over.

"You have to come with us. State Security." They made no move to show identification.

"What's going on?"

The Stasi looked at him in silence.

"Let me put some clothes on."

One of them shook his head in the negative.

"That doesn't matter. Let's go."

The brown Lada carried them to the Falkensee police station as Uwe shivered in the back seat. It was not cold that summer morning, but he was gripped by fear of the nameless, fear of the unseen and unexplained. The silence of his captors was a roaring terror in his heart.

He was put into an interrogation room with one of the agents who simply sat and watched. Uwe sat and tried to control his body tremors while the Stasi agent stared him down. Without warning the man spoke.

"What kind of music do you like?"

Uwe blinked in surprise.

"Different kinds. Some rock, some country, it just depends."

Silence and staring followed. Nothing else.

A great measure of Stasi effectiveness came from their ability to come and go without explanation, to enter any home, any business, to ask questions without having to justify the action. Although they never openly displayed weapons, they all carried pistols, the ultimate mark of power, since common citizens had no possibility of owning firearms. These silent watchers went about their business with unimpeachable purpose, offering no explanations unless doing so served their ends. Fear, the eternal lever, was used with practiced finesse upon a people unprotected by law or traditions of personal liberties. The Stasi usually didn't beat or torture their captives, but no one who had been in their embrace could deny that it was like being under a sentence of extinction with no hope of reprieve.

Imagine being nearly naked, seated in a windowless room in front of a grim-faced man who neither spoke nor acknowledged your existence except to watch your every move. Imagine the walls without relief, except for the shadows cast by the single shadeless overhead bulb. Remember the fear that was written across your mother's face and the silent icy stares of the Stasi when you asked them why. Imagine there was no way out, no one to call for help, no appeal. Then imagine being only 16 years old.

Four hours of waiting had tired the agent as well as Uwe, even though the agent had left the room occasionally for a break. Uwe sat in the straight-backed chair waiting for something to happen.

The door banged open; two men entered and nodded to the seated watcher, who rose and left without comment. The two new agents were large-framed, at least ninty kilograms, about two meters tall. They wore similar unremarkable gray suits that appeared to be almost a genteel uniform, closely matching that of the men who had brought Uwe to interrogation. Their features were plain, no warts or blemishes, no big noses or snaggle teeth. No one would remember them if passed on the street. The only remarkable thing was their eyes. Their polished attire became irrelevant in the context of their hard, piercing gaze. Appearance set them automatically apart as men who knew the uses of authority, men who commanded with a raised eyebrow or nod of the head and expected obedience.

One sat down in the empty chair directly facing Uwe, pausing to adjust his pants so the creases would be preserved. The other half leaned, half sat on the small table, one leg casually dangling, the other braced against the floor.

"We have come a long way to ask some questions," said the one on the table.

The other man interrupted.

"Do you write many letters?"

"Letters, well sometimes. Why?"

"Who do you write, Herr George?"

"Sometimes …"

"There's no use trying to fool us. Just answer the questions I ask."

The one in the chair leaned forward for emphasis, placing his hands hard on his knees as though bracing himself to spring. His eyes flashed with arrogance and obvious contempt.

"I will only ask you one more time. To whom do you write?"

Uwe shivered again, shrinking beneath the icy stare.

"Are you talking about the bunch of letters I wrote to Elvis fans?"

"What kind of music do you prefer?" said the standing agent.

"Mostly country and rock. It really depends on how I feel."

"Why do you want to start an organization?" the seated man demanded. "Did you get clearance?"

"Clearance? No, I …"

"You will give us all of their names. All of them! Do you understand that?" the seated man said. He shook an extended index finger in Uwe's face. "You will furnish a complete list of names and addresses!"

"But I just wanted to meet other Elvis fans, maybe to have a club or something." Uwe's panic was rising. What would they do to him?

The standing man spoke in soft tones.

"Did you apply for permission to start a club?" Then without waiting for the answer, he continued, "You picked an interesting place to meet, Herr George. Why in front of the American Embassy?"

"It is easy to find the street. It's in the center of the city near the U-bahn and bus lines."

"What were you going to do at the American Embassy?" The seated man's face was straining and red with rage.

"It was just a well-known street. Nothing to do with the Embassy."

"Addresses. I want all of the addresses right now."

"Addresses? I have a list, but I can't remember. I didn't try to memorize …"

The seated agent glanced back at his partner. "You can see that he isn't cooperating." Then he leaned suddenly back toward Uwe with cold hatred squeezing from every pore of his face. His voice rose an octave and he bellowed, "Do you think we are stupid? Do you think we have the time to play games with you? What kind of code was that in your advertisement? Who were you signaling?" The muscles stood out on his neck above the carefully knotted tie.

The room seemed to contract and Uwe felt as though he was being stuffed into a box, a very small box, by the pounding of the man's voice and the intensity of his stare.

Uwe spoke a name, then tried the address.

"Louder," the seated man said. His partner's pencil made a sound like a twig brushing against a screen as he took notes.

Another name. Tentative, not really sure.

"I'm not certain about the address. It was just for a fan club. It is impossible to remember."

The seated agent's face was hard as iron as he leaned even closer.

"If you are trying to delay telling, it won't do any good. We have all the time we need, but yours is running out. You're in big trouble."

"Where's the list?" the other agent asked.

"At home. In my room." Uwe's bowels felt loose.

"Then we'll go back to your home right now," the seated man said, relaxing slightly, as though an important victory had just been won.

As they rose to leave, Uwe could feel sweat running down the small of his back. His mouth was dry, lips sticking together, tongue pasty and thick. He now cared only for escape.

The ride home passed with his captors exchanging an occasional comment between them, but acting as though he didn't exist in the back seat. After what seemed like only a few moments, they were walking in the front door of Uwe's house past his silent, staring mother. No one spoke as they made their way to the bedroom.

"So this is how you spend the precious days of your youth," the angry agent said. He stepped close to the wall, examining an Elvis poster and the neat stack of Western records. "These must be your heroes." His lips made a spitting sound.

Uwe retrieved the stack of reply letters from the ad, and the address list he had used to return correspondence.

The silent agent scanned the information, while the angry one paced the room, picking up items, inspecting them, then dropping them as though they were contaminated. His face wrinkled and twitched in disgust, and snorts of displeasure punctuated his evaluations. The silent man read a few of the letters, then dropped them together on the foot of the bed.

Uwe stood in awkward silence fidgeting with his bathing suit tie cord.

"Records, posters. What other Western garbage do you have? Isn't there anything serious in your life?" the angry one said.

Uwe looked at his naked toes and shrugged.

"We have what we need," the other agent said.

The angry one left the room without further comment, and with heavy footfalls he clumped through the living room and out the front door. Uwe flinched at the distant bang as the door slammed.

The other agent remained for a moment.

"I think you have cooperated with our investigation." His manner was almost kind. "I need to meet with you one more time to finish this business. Come to the Zentral Restaurant tomorrow at 10:00 a.m." He paused and made eye contact for emphasis. "Look through your papers and bring anything that I have not yet seen. Don't leave anything out. Do you understand?"

"Yes, sir. 10:00 a.m. at Zentral Restaurant."

"Bring any other addresses you can find."

"I don't think …"

"Look carefully through your papers, Herr George. Do you understand?"

Uwe nodded and watched numbly as the quiet one's back disappeared through the front door.

Outside the car door thudded. The Lada's engine revved as they made a U-turn next to the frontier warning sign and the sound faded by degrees until it was completely gone.

"Udo is not going to like this at all," Uwe's mother said. "This is going to make him mad, and you know how he gets when he is mad." She turned away and began to fiddle with dishes on the table. "I have to get things cleaned up." Sounds of clinking plates filled the void as his mother's critical silence descended.

"I just wanted to have an Elvis fan club."

"If they come back when Udo is here, we're all going to have a bad time." Then she walked slowly back to the kitchen, wondering if her husband was going to beat her, again, tonight.

Uwe trudged slowly back upstairs and stood alone in the room. They were gone, but his little personal space was still awash with their presence. The records, magazines, after-shave, even his ballpoint pen seemed different now that the angry agent had handled them. The room still echoed with their questions and summary judgments. All of the things could be put back into physical order, but the place itself, the feeling that it was his own room, was forever changed. It had never been much of a sanctuary, especially when his step-father was drunk, but now something else, something permanent, was added. Like grease beneath fingernails, it wouldn't wash away. Maybe it would just have to wear off. The presence of the Stasi lingered like a stain.

Uwe told me the rest of the story in a few sentences.

"He met me at Zentral and asked if I had any more information. I told him 'no,' that he had all of it. Then he told me that if I went through with the meeting there would be serious consequences."

"What did you say?"

"What would anybody say? I told him I wouldn't do anything. You know, Carsten, yesterday I saw a girl from Rostock, one who sent me a letter wanting to join the club. She said that some Stasi visited her house, too. Her eyes accused me like I had turned her in or something. I guess they sent agents to everyone on the list." Uwe sighed heavily. "Look what happens when I get an idea. I never dreamed that something like this ..."

His upturned palms gestured impotent frustration, speaking what his trembling lips could not say, and I changed the subject, hoping to salvage something of the day for us both. It burned in my guts to think about my friend quivering in that shabby room while his slick-suited tormentors watched him squirm like an insect in the killing bottle.

June of 1982 was the formal graduation ceremony of my Oberschule class. We sat in the auditorium that afternoon in our best clothes looking around at each other, but with most of our true attention focused on that blind bend in the road we knew as the only future. Our paths were separating, many for the last time, but in our little circle we could reasonably expect to encounter each other off and on for years to come; on the same rutted streets and in the same stores our parents had patronized for so long. The school director, a principal in Western terms, had his say at the end of the half-hour meeting. His remarks were predictably dogmatic; we'd all have been surprised if they hadn't repeated the format we had become accustomed to over the years. There were no robes, and no stirring speeches about how we were supposed to prosper and save the world. Our futures were already mapped, and in most cases signed for, so we knew what career we would follow, and even what company would employ us. Graduation, then, was merely another meeting, and we simply returned to our homes that evening. No parties, no celebrations were in order. Now that we had learned our lessons, it was time to get to work and justify our existence to the state that had benevolently nurtured us for so long.

The transition into mainstream work life began in the summer of 1982, when I began scientific technical training. The electronics school in Burg was not far from a sleepy little agricultural town. Getting an education there meant we were quartered much the same way as the army, living in barracks, sleeping on bunks, eating in a cafeteria, and getting a daily dose of political instruction from someone who was either a very good actor or really believed that Communism was still going to conquer the world. The program was cyclical, consisting of school for four weeks, followed by four weeks in a specific industrial factory working for our future employer. This plan combined theory with actual work experience, and by the end of school we were supposed to have a good blend of practical knowledge and academic background. This made the transition to actual work life smoother, since the student would enter a company where he was known.

Since my future employer was in Falkensee, I was more fortunate than many of the young men who were forced by circumstances to spend nearly the entire two-year training period away from home. I was really missing my family, and contrived ways to get away more often. Andreas Henkel was one of my two roommates in the dormitory. At almost two meters tall, he was burly, strong and answered to the nickname, 'bear.' His hands were thickened by manual work, and I learned that he was a natural mechanic, having an innate ability to diagnose automobile troubles. Andreas and I got to be friends because, in addition to sharing room space, we held similar dislikes of the restrictions under which we lived. This commonality was reinforced by the presence of our other roommate. Bear would just snort and turn away shaking his head when Ralf began to spout politics.

Ralf Hasford was very red. Children have toys that play the same tune when you turn the crank, and we had Ralf for a roommate. No matter how his crank was turned, the same repetitive jargon came out. Ideas aren't necessarily foolish in and of themselves, but if they are continually regurgitated in the same manner without reflection, mindlessly as a rat running a maze, they soon seem ridiculous no matter what their intrinsic value. At first I argued some about politics with Ralf, but within a few days it became obvious to Andreas and me that our roommate was somehow captivated by Communist doctrine, and had no desire to test the merit of other ideas. We soon gave up trying to reason with the hawk-faced young man and resolved to endure the irritation. The only alternative was to privately punch Ralf around and threaten him with broken limbs unless he shut up. It was a hard decision, but we held our peace.

Like me, Andreas lived only to go home as much as possible, so together we concocted successful escape ruses based on the unwavering pattern of school's daily schedule. Sometimes on a Thursday night, we would walk the mile to the station and buy tickets for the next morning's train to Falkensee. Before retiring that night, our sports clothes bags would be packed and ready. Then Friday morning following roll call, when all students were accounted for, we simply slipped away. The morning class and roll check was held with daily mechanistic precision, completed at 8:25 a.m., that left exactly 11 minutes to make the train. For the first time in my life, I appreciated the value of hard workouts, and the physical conditioning paid off, since we had just enough time if we ran. Despite the two-kilometer distance and the fat clothes bags, we never missed a train.

Another successful Friday ploy was for my friend to exercise until he worked up a profuse sweat, then go directly to the infirmary. Just before entering, he would press the flesh of his face hard with the palms of his hands. This caused him to meet the doctor with a very pale look, followed by a flushed appearance as the blood returned.

"You look awful, Andreas," the doctor would say.

"I really feel faint."

"Perhaps you should go home for a couple of days."

"Maybe I can make it," said Bear.

"If Herr Kaaz has finished his obligations, I will allow him to accompany you. I don't think you should try it alone."

The doctor probably suspected our game, but I was never nearby when Bear visited the infirmary, and since my grades were all A's, I could go without risking academic setback.

The doctor sent a messenger to find me, and asked that I accompany Andreas, whose face was still mottled from his odd manipulations. Hiding my eagerness, I would consent, but not until after the train actually left the station could we relax and congratulate ourselves on succeeding in our studies while beating the system. Did we really fool them? We were young and thought that we were smart and they were dumb, but the truth was probably more like we were energetic and they were tired. We pretended to follow their rules, and they pretended to countenance something we were going to do anyway. We wanted no trouble from them, and they wanted no trouble from us.

"Getting away is great, but I still don't understand why the doctor hasn't figured this out," said Bear.

"Maybe he knows, but since it appears legitimate, he can have private sympathies," I said. "As long as there is a reasonable explanation for events like this, he isn't responsible. If you come to his office looking like death, who's going to tell a doctor that you aren't sick. Even the political teacher can't tell a doctor who is well and who is not."

"This is going to be a good few days. I have three cars to fix, and I know I'll make at least a hundred marks apiece. I'll be rich for a while."

We both laughed about that. Having money meant nothing, because there had to be something to buy. Otherwise it was only a substance of torment, fueling frustrations rather than dreams. Bear often talked of someday having a privately operated business so he could be a legitimate mechanic, but even as those words would leave his lips, he would shake his head as though it were only a dream.

Technical school did have some other positive features, however. We called Opa Theil 'Grandfather' because he was in charge of our dormitory and was so much older than the rest of the teachers. He was a veteran of World War II, and being responsible for us was probably the only job he could hold due to his age. Part of that duty meant that he had to read political lessons out loud to us once a week. We made no pretense of listening, but had to be present physically or be reported to administration. We felt sorry for Opa because we could all see that while his mouth was reading the words of instruction, his heart and mind were not convinced. He, like so many others, simply did what he had to do. Perhaps he had already given his best to the last government, maybe in a hedgerow near Cherborg or on the frozen steppes of Russia. He was overweight, but carried himself with a quiet dignity testifying to a greater man beneath. Opa Theil was still on the march, living out the end of his life as he had the beginning, by doing his duty.

The two-week military training camp was held during one of the four-week stays at Burg. We were invited to board a train and clattered away like refugees in the decaying passenger cars for our two weeks of basic training at a camp on the Baltic sea.

As in Oberschule training, we had compulsory daily civics classes, and the teacher was a retired army officer. As his eyes scanned the class, sizing everyone up, they flickered as they met mine. This was truly his territory now, and he had been briefed on who was who in our group before we arrived.

One day after a lesson, we had a few minutes left over, so he began an impromptu discussion.

"A recent article in Neues Deutschland says international terrorism is a serious threat to world peace," he began. "There are many examples of this problem in the world, and in recent months we have noted the shooting of innocent people in Lebanon by a fascist government that takes its directions from the Zionist state and the head of the imperialist conspiracy. The United States is a supporter of terrorism all over the world. Did they have some justification for bombing Tripoli?"

My mouth moved before I thought.

"It seems to me that they have some reasons for hitting back. Terrorists are against civilization itself. Most often terrorists kill civilians, and they disrupt a country's daily business so transportation and utilities are cut off. It's not very different from war as far as I can see."

He sat up in his chair, alert and defensive.

"It's foolishness to even discuss this aspect. The imperialist nation has made economic and military warfare on every continent; they dropped the atom bomb on Japan; they support the racist regime in South Africa. There isn't a part of the world that doesn't bear the bloody mark of their oppression!"

My face was burning red, and the other kids stared.

"What would we do if someone shot our citizens? Would East Germany defend its national honor?" Looking around the room, I could see puzzled looks on some faces, then two voices muttered agreement. They were poor allies since they were on the verge of failing the class. Not much to loose perhaps. Didn't anyone else think about things objectively?

"It looks to me like Neues Deutschland hasn't printed all of the facts. One thing is sure. The Libyans will think twice in the future before bragging openly about sponsoring attacks on American interests. I have to admire a country that will stand up for itself."

He bristled at that and began a canned speech about the evolution of history and the oppression of mankind. I settled in my chair. There was no point in further arguing.

All of the instructors were retired army or Stasi officers who seemed to take special pleasure in making young civilians sweat and wince. There was no hope of going home for a weekend with the family, so we made the best of the experience. The routine was simple and unchanging. Up at 5:30 a.m., running and various physical exercises for a half-hour, wash and shave, eat an army breakfast, class and lessons on various aspects of military activity, followed by more running and pushups until we were blind with fatigue. We ate what passed for lunch about noonday with a short rest break, then more instruction sessions or physical training until evening approached. At 6:00 p.m., we ate supper and were herded back to the barracks for final verbal harassment by an instructor before lights out. All but the most 'red' among us expressed obvious distaste for the experience.

Practice on the rifle range was the closest thing to enjoyment that most of us had. The 7.62mm cartridges were smooth, coated with lacquer to prevent deterioration of the powder and primer. Their dull casing and copper-jacketed projectiles were precise and symmetrical. I balanced and turned them in my fingers.

"Take your time and hold the weapon correctly." The instructor's voice was sharp and precise, like a closing bolt. I stood on the firing line and slipped the Kalashnikov sling around my arm, twisting it to gain a more steady position. "Hold your face back more, don't crowd the sights, and get a good grip on the trigger. The rifle is like a girlfriend. To get what you want, you have to treat it gently." He laughed and elaborated with a lewd short story about a woman he knew. "All right, now everybody will fire when I give the order and not a second before." He paused, waiting for someone to discharge early. No one jumped, so he swung his arm down in a vertical arc.

"Fire."

A splatter of six shots, and some excited murmuring from the young men on the line. The smell of burned powder was sweet in the soft breeze, and the rifle's bulk was comfortable in my hands. I liked shooting, but, otherwise, the army was a massive bore. I knew older boys that went off to the armed forces, but none of them had anything good to say about it. There was even less personal freedom there than in everyday life, and if you were in a sensitive job where anything was secret, your associates watched you like an enemy. Once the army got hold of you, they were no longer protecting you. You were their property, or even an enemy of sorts, and they were going to see to it that you did exactly as you were told. The older noncoms and officers picked on new soldiers, borrowed money without paying it back and made them take the dirty jobs. You could have two days off in the second year of service, unless they had some kind of emergency or you stepped out of line. Joining the army was more than getting a new job. They really did own you, and they were not benevolent masters.

"Shut up and pay attention or you'll be on your bellies doing pushups for the rest of the day. Now again, one shot only, check your selector to be sure you are on semi-automatic. Take aim, fire." He scanned the targets and nodded. "Not bad for a bunch of babies. Time's up. Remove the magazine and operate the bolt to clear your weapon. You'll be cleaning the garbage cans in Rudersdorf with your tongue if you ever turn in a weapon with a round in the chamber."

Of course he knew that each weapon had only been loaded with three rounds, and that we had all fired three shots. Maybe they were concerned with safety, but it seemed more likely they were just taking another opportunity to threaten and badger. Then we cleaned the rifles and returned them to their lockers. As we walked back toward the barracks area, I cursed and shook my head. Directly behind, I heard a voice.

"Don't let it get you down." It was Sven, a student from the northern part of the country. We met on the rifle range, but the acquaintance was only casual as far as I was concerned.

"This is so stupid," I said. "What are we supposed to protect anyway? What country would want to conquer us so they could have all this?" I swept my arm in a wide arc.

"I don't know much about that," he replied. "It doesn't get me too upset anymore."

I noticed that he looked relaxed and confident, yet I knew that the instructors had yelled as much at him as any of us.

"You're a little different," he said. "So I think that this might be of some help to you." His extended hand held a small black book.

My fingers closed around it and I knew immediately. It was a Bible. I was surprised and didn't know quite how to react.

"Go on, take it. Whenever things get to be too much, it's a special comfort. There is a lot more to life than just living it like these people tell you."

"You are a believer?"

He smiled.

"Yes, and I can tell you that it has brought many good things into my life. Knowing God makes me a better man. See you later."

Then he walked away, leaving me holding the little book. From my earliest years, I remembered the same thing from school. There was no God, only a universe that operates on natural laws. The chief and most obvious natural law was the inevitability of communism and the destruction of all things like religion that only serve to keep men in some kind of bondage. Sven didn't appear to be in distress because of his beliefs, in fact he seemed to somehow rise above the daily aggravations to a more ordered level of existence. I stuck the Bible in my pocket and made a mental note to look it over some day and see if he was right. If such a tiny thing could help a man keep his spirit intact in the midst of so many contradictions, maybe there was something to it after all.

19. September 1985

Herrn
Carsten Kaaz

1540    Falkensee
Zwinglistr. 4

Sehr geehrter Herr Kaaz!

Ich habe Ihren Brief vom 12. September 1985 erhalten, worin Sie sich nach der Möglichkeit der Übersiedlung nach den USA erkundigen.

Sie können jederzeit ein Einwanderungsvisum für die USA beantragen. Wie es scheint, sind Sie gut qualifiziert, um eine Anstellung in den USA zu finden. Sie haben in Ihrem Brief nicht erwähnt, ob Sie Angehörige in den USA haben.

Um Ihren Antrag voranzubringen, sollten Sie bei den DDR-Behörden Reisedokument (Pass) und Ausreiseerlaubnis beantragen. Informieren Sie mich bitte, wenn Sie diese erhalten haben.

Mit freundlichem Gruss

James S. Huffman
Consul General

Letter received by author from the Consul General at the U.S. Embassy in East Berlin concerning immigration to the United States — September 1985

# CHAPTER FIVE

I wasn't interested in being number one in technical school like I was in Oberschule, but even so, I got straight A's for my efforts; and in the summer of 1983, I was rewarded with a week vacation in Bulgaria.

Vivien and I had been dating steadily before I left for training, and I thought it would be romantic to take her. I brought it up when I visited her home, but her parents objected immediately.

"It's out of the question," her mother said. Then looking fiercely at Herr Taschner she commanded, "Explain it to him!"

He cleared his throat.

"Yes, well of course it's not a good idea. What would everyone think if we let our daughter go off for two weeks with a young man, and them not even married?" He glanced at his wife for approval, then continued. "Besides, there isn't that much to do in Bulgaria, and she probably wouldn't like it."

His argument was ridiculous, because it had to have been obvious to both of Vivien's parents that she and I had been having sexual relations for some time. That was a generally accepted behavior, carrying no moral stigma in our society. Where did they think she'd been sleeping when she spent the night at my house?

Frau Taschner nodded vigorously and interrupted.

"It's just not appropriate for a girl of her age to be leaving the country without an adult escort."

Inconsistent or not, they were adamant. After that failed conversation, I dragged over to Ulf's house, and as I complained, Frau Kubicki heard and offered her assessment.

"It's the same thing you've been facing all along; they have their own agenda for Vivien, and you aren't part of it. They can see how you have plans for the future, but they don't want her to be included."

She was right, of course, and I was beginning to realize how deeply fundamental the discontinuity was between us. Vivien was attractive, energetic, and had vast reservoirs of artistic talent, and the Taschners didn't want her tangled up in the life of a mere electronics technician. There were times when I caught Frau Taschner watching me through those cold gray eyes. When my gaze met hers, she wouldn't look away, choosing instead to lock eyes and try to stare me down. "There are many better than you," the eyes said with their pitiless, silent flickering. "There are better men than you for my daughter, and I will not let you hide her away for the rest of her life somewhere in a dirty little apartment with a bunch of crying children." Most of the time, Frau Taschner won the staring contest; she had the will to win in a game that I didn't even want to play.

She would have been attractive if not for those eyes.

Arriving home late that night, I told my parents Vivien couldn't go. In a couple of days, my mother found an opportunity to speak to Herr Taschner when his wife was elsewhere, and he reluctantly agreed to the trip. Vivien could go to Bulgaria, but it was knirschenden Zaehnen (with her parents' teeth grinding). I didn't care that Mom was the one who had won for me, and I didn't care that Frau Taschner's eyes were even colder when they met mine. All that mattered was that Vivien was going to Bulgaria with me, and that it would be just the two of us without any worries for a few glorious days.

We arrived in Burgas, one of the most popular vacation spots in Bulgaria, via an East German airliner. The Bulgarians were friendly, sturdy people, their eyes suggesting a current of passion beneath the surface of their unpolished public selves. We stayed with local residents, renting a room from a family since the tourist hotels were off-limits for practical purposes. It was not that I didn't have the money, but the price of hotel rooms at the official exchange rate didn't allow us enough money left over each day to eat or do anything else. We were only allowed to exchange 30 marks per day, no matter how much we brought along. Any attempt to get black market currency might land us in jail, so we reconciled ourselves to seeing everything on a shoestring. Then there were other local considerations.

"Stay with the group," the tour guide said, "and don't let your women roam around alone. They'll get raped if you aren't careful." I noticed that local men found Vivien particularly interesting, probably because of her blonde hair, fair skin, and blue eyes. I was glad for the tour group, even though it meant we had to go everywhere like a pack of piglets, following the sow in anticipation of the next meal. The tour group ate breakfast and lunch together, and watched enviously from a distance as Western tourists enjoyed unlimited currency exchange and went wherever they wished.

I bought souvenirs for myself and found some small China figures to take to my mother. It was also interesting to watch the local girls hanging around Western tourist hotels, trying to interest the degenerate capitalists in their physical charms. These amateur hookers were East Bloc women on vacation trying to pick up Western currency by free-lance prostitution. They were not Bulgarian; in fact many locals were devout Muslim and were known for their strict moral standards. The city itself was interesting, too. I was told that hardly anyone actually lived there, but that it had been built for tourists exclusively. We spent as much time as possible on the beach and sightseeing, but lurking in the depths of my heart, in its innermost chambers, was the ever-swelling seed of inevitable desolation. In the beginning, I would not admit that the feeling was even there, but gradually I had to recognize what it really was.

Vivien and I were growing inexorably in different directions. The change was as slow as the rain wearing down the mountains, but I couldn't ignore the pieces as they broke off and fell silently around us. Her life was totally focused on career achievement. Mine was consumed by a search for myself, and I was still looking. Vivien had already chosen to consciously ignore most of the surrounding reality and paint her own landscape. I watched her sensitive, delicate hands stacking the rounded rocks into a castle shape on the beach at Burgas and crashed into the ultimate reality of our situation.

We had been together since I was 15. Together we had crossed the adolescent ground of personal discovery and sharing and were on the downhill side where silences say more than conversation. We had never spoken much of tomorrow. Perhaps it had only been alive in my heart. Not once in five years had we discussed marriage. In one heart-piercing instant, I knew that the oncoming tide of years would wipe our love away just as the tireless wearing of waves would obliterate the work of her hands on the beach. She would soon start pre-university training and would have to go to another city. Her dream of achievement was only just beginning, while mine, a primitive vision of what I called freedom, had grown into a strong desire to leave my own country. It was impossible for me to seriously believe in a tomorrow with us together. Nursing those leaden thoughts, I arose early every day and plodded through as many museums and tourist attractions as we could afford, wearing as much enthusiasm on the outside as I could paint on. Then the days were spent, and we flew back home. On the plane she was unusually silent, aloof.

"What's bothering you?" I asked. "Did I say something?"

"Nothing really. Well, just that the architecture was so fascinating." She turned suddenly and looked intensely into my eyes. "You didn't like it did you?"

"What are you talking about? Of course I liked the vacation."

"I don't mean the vacation. You didn't like the museums, the buildings, all the history and the art, did you?"

For a moment I was not sure how I felt. The hours in line and the long pauses while she studied a facade or decaying cornice were tiring. Like the architecture?

"I don't suppose I would ever have looked at some of those things if I hadn't been with you, but being together made everything worthwhile."

She nodded, then turned back to the window. I stared at the back of her head, trying to think of something to say, but the resonance of the aircraft's engines blotted out my mumbles. There was nothing but a droning, mesmerizing hum, counterpointed by the background whistle of rushing air.

Then Vivien turned back and faced me, her hard blue eyes searching mine.

"We are very different, you and I."

I smiled weakly, but could not find my voice. My hand touched hers and I squeezed tenderly. An answering perfunctory pressure told more than any words. We were already dead. The funeral was only a matter of time.

Vivien's pre-university training began, and she, like I, had to move away in order to attend the special school. For the sake of facility efficiency, the government had established specialty schools in different parts of the country. Engineering candidates went to one place, managerial students to another, art candidates to another, and so on. Though functionally practical and cost-effective, the training schools were correctly reputed to be insensitive environments.

Vivien was firmly on the path to her future. Her training cycle was similar to mine in that she had weeks of instruction interspersed by occasional visits home. Once every three months or so, our time off would coincide, but other than that we were out of touch. She was not a letter writer, and there was no way to phone, except to leave emergency messages. There were nights when Bear's snoring and Hasford's fitful tossing wouldn't let me sleep, so I lay awake in the dark, my mind roving over the places and people of the past. Vivien was one of my anchors, but she was breaking away, spinning off into an uncertain tomorrow, guided by her own stars. When we were together, she was effervescent, crackling with enthusiasm for her progress. I listened and was glad for her, but she could smell my fear, see it clouding my eyes no matter what mask I wore. Our conversations became more tentative, uncertain as to what was funny, hesitating in normal conversations until the silence became unbearable. I began to wonder how it would feel when it was finally over, and my mind played endless scenarios of the final confrontation. Instead of a scene full of yelling and accusation, the silences lengthened and deepened. My guts contracted involuntarily, and I stood helplessly watching what I called love dry up and blow away before my eyes.

Graduation from Burg was anticlimactic; like high school we sat in rows, wearing our suits and listening for our name so we could receive our ticket to enter the economy in the right place at the right time. The certificates were passed out following a brief speech by the director, accompanied by a perfunctory handshake and nod, the standard non-emotional ritual. After the meeting, there were no parties, no celebrations. Some young men went home with their parents; others simply went home. The graduates were not filled with anticipation and wonder because we all had contracts. No one told us to go out and save the world, and there was no sense of mission other than trying to find a way to make our respective lives as pleasant as possible. School was simply over, and with the turning of that page, my attention focused on the next dilemma.

All of my former worries faded before the next great hurdle — service in the armed forces. Our four weeks of basic training at the Baltic camp had confirmed my forebodings of military life. From my earliest recollections, my country's main goals were simply an expression of unrelenting opposition to the Western way. Our society was built upon the often-repeated presumption that the rest of the world wanted what we had; our customs, our science, our industry, our whole way of life, and as soon as the oppressed masses found a way, they would throw off their chains and create a replica of our socialist society. As I grew older, it became obvious that while the West had its share of problems, even its lower classes had a basic opportunity to fulfill their dreams. What did we have to defend? Who wanted to possess our way of life? No matter what they taught in class, I knew that if there was war, it would either come on purpose from our side of the border or by some tragic, stupid accident. It was illogical to believe that any other industrialized nation would risk the destruction of their nation for the possibility of conquering our backward land.

I wasn't willing to die defending a lie.

My problem, therefore, was simple. All I wanted was to minimize my military service, but since I had no party connections nor anything to trade that might buy my exemption, either induction or enlistment was inevitable. But I would delay it if I could. Yes, there was a way to slow things down, but it required immediate action. In order to delay entry into the army, I had to break my employment agreement. There would be all kinds of fallout from that action and I was sure to get on all the wrong lists, but I didn't care. The army would have to wait on possessing my carcass.

After checking discreetly with other businesses in Falkensee, I came to the conclusion that successfully making a change was going to require significant risk. If I quit Radio & Fernsehtechnik, I would be reported to the government. And if I simply stayed unemployed, my name would then go on a special list, and I might not be able to stay in any technical field. I might be summarily forced into some other menial job. But in East Germany, you didn't need money, you needed connections. None of my other efforts had been fruitful, and that left the only possibility that I had been saving for last.

My natural father had visited me three times in the 19 years of my life; he never called or otherwise communicated. I walked into the Polymath plant and after a couple of inquiries found him leaning on a machine drinking a cup of coffee. I remembered his face from our last meeting, but he had gained a little weight and his eyes had dark circles. Wolfgang Grossert looked sick and sallow. He noticed my approach and studied me for a moment before his recognition was complete. No smile crossed his face, just mild surprise and puzzlement.

"I need some help with a problem and I want to know if you'll consider giving me a hand?"

"I don't have any money," he said quickly. A nervous smile flitted across his face as though he was trying to make me think his comment was really a joke.

"That's not it. I know you don't want anything to do with me. You never bothered to visit or write."

"I was doing the best I could." He stiffened, but his face showed no emotion. "What do you want?"

"I need work."

"What happened to your regular job?"

"I broke the contract and I'm not going to work there. I just need a job. Will you help me?" It was hard to ask this man, not because I hated or even disliked him; I knew he was my natural father, yet I felt nothing at all. That made my insides cold. A son should feel something for his father, but this was a man whom I didn't know.

"Well?"

"I'll see what I can do," he said. His expression never changed, but the eyes softened just a little at the corners. "I think we can work something out ."

The date approached for me to report to work at Radio & Fernsehtechnik, but I had made a special appointment with Herr Doktor two weeks prior to that time.

He appeared precisely as I remembered from our first meeting, still peering out on the world from behind the brown, plastic-framed glasses, still sitting in his perfectly neat office looking like he was in control. His long fingers held a perfectly sharpened pencil, rolling it back and forth as he watched me with unblinking brown eyes.

His voice was cordial, but not warm. Doktor had never been warm.

"What can I do for you, Herr Kaaz?"

I took a deep breath, hoping that my fear would not be too obvious.

"I am here to tell you that I will not be coming to work as planned."

His brow furrowed, his eyes narrowed to slits, and his lips pressed together tightly. Radio & Fernsehtechnik was a successful enterprise, and he was not used to personal agendas complicating his business goals.

"What are you talking about?" His voice cut the air like a dagger.

"I've decided that it's not in my best interests to work here, so I'll be looking for another job."

Doktor's hands slammed down on the desk top as he jumped to his feet.

"You can't do that! You signed a contract, and you have to come to work here unless I release you!" The word "I" carried an especially heavy inflection.

"Nevertheless, that is what I am doing." I stood, preparing to leave.

"I don't know who you think you are, but you aren't going to do this to me! We haven't settled this matter, and I'll see you soon to resolve it once and for all." His voice carried the expected threat, but I had already planned what I was going to say.

"Herr Doktor, I was 14 years old when I signed that contract, and I've changed my mind. There isn't anything more to discuss." In one movement I turned, opened the door and left his office, taking special care not to slam it behind me. After his initial reaction I wasn't nervous; I had predicted his reactions correctly. I had already lived that scene a hundred times in my own mind trying to decide how to handle it, and some of those mental versions were a lot worse than the reality I had just experienced.

On the way home, I went to the Poliklinik of Falkensee.

"My stomach has really been giving me trouble," I said to the physician.

"Where does it hurt?" he asked without lifting his eyes from the paper.

"All over here," I said, touching my navel lightly. "It may be something in my family. My father has stomach trouble."

"Sure," he said. The pen made scratching sounds as he wrote the medical excuse. "Get some bed rest and come back in one week."

I returned to Radio & Fernsehtechnik and turned the medical excuse into the business office so they wouldn't be able to penalize me for unexcused absence.

The game had begun in earnest.

In a week, I didn't "feel" any better, so the indifferent Poliklinik doctor extended the medical excuse. That brought me up to the day when I began work at Polymath, my father's factory. By breaking the contract, I had cheated Radio & Fernsehtechnik, but if I were to retain some control over my own life, there was no other way.

As planned, I began work at Polymath and quickly fell into the standard training sequence.

Uwe came by the plant one night at 10:00 p.m. to ride home

with me. Enveloped by the warm summer night, we rode to my house, then stowed the bicycles and went for our usual neighborhood walk.

Heading West down Calvin Strasse without an agenda and scuffing our shoes on the hard packed gravel surface, we passed the Siedlereck Bar. Just outside the bar, we saw two men talking in loud voices, their words slurred by alcohol. I began to feel a little nervous by their appearance, so we turned back toward the frontier sign and began to walk at a brisk pace. Siedlereck had the reputation of being the worst bar in town, and we wanted no part of the frequent fights and constant surveillance by police.

Their voices took on a new and more insistent tone and their shadowy forms moved in our direction.

"Let's go for it," I said. "If we can get past the frontier sign, they'll probably leave us alone."

Uwe and I broke into a run, and the men did likewise. With arms and legs pumping in fearful flight, we approached the red and white signs. Then Uwe fell back suddenly, and I heard the sounds of curses and the thuds of fists hitting flesh as they caught him. I could see one hold him and the other raise some kind of stick high; he brought it down on Uwe's head with an audible crack. The broken piece went flipping away, landing on the street with a bouncing, hollow, wooden sound.

After lingering a moment to inspect their work, the men walked away laughing and slapping each other on the back. One was loudly promising to buy the next round of schnapps.

As I approached, Uwe struggled to his knees and groaned. Even in the dark I could see the black dripping stain. He sniffed and spat, his own blood falling from his nose and lips in stringy globs, breath coming in short gasps, punctuating painful twitches.

"Where did they get you?" I asked. He couldn't stand alone for a number of minutes and leaned heavily on my shoulder. Finally, we stumbled slowly to my house. Using an antiseptic, I cleaned his cut scalp as we discussed what to do. The wound oozed blood and lymphatic fluid, but Uwe never flinched.

"Now here comes the ointment," I said. "It probably won't hurt like the alcohol." He went on talking in a curiously soft voice, eyes streaked red from strain, but they were fixed on the wall as his mind put everything into precise concentration.

"Don't call the police," he said. "They'll just give us a lot of trouble and probably won't do anything because there weren't any other witnesses. It's just our word against the drunks, so we have to take care of this ourselves."

"What do you mean?"

"I have to go home and get something. Then you'll see."

We slipped through the gap in Detlef's fence and I waited on Pestalozzi Strasse in front of his house. Returning in a few moments carrying something shiny, he held the object up so I could see.

"This will do the job. Bernd Riebisch got it in the Ketzin landfill and traded it to me. Neat huh?"

It was a steel bar fitted with finger holes, and sharp studs on one edge. The Western movies called them brass knuckles. If we were caught with this illegal weapon, there would be real trouble.

"I want to do this myself," he said. "You stay a little behind, and I'll take care of business."

"Keep it out of sight. They may have another stick, or worse."

He nodded and smacked his palm with the knobby metal thing, and smiled grimly. "They'll never know what happened."

We were about 30 meters from Siedlereck when the men stepped from the shadows again.

"Looks like our little friends want some more," one said. His voice was louder and more slurred than before. Maybe a few more drinks made them overconfident. We let them get within six meters, then turned to run away, Uwe being the slowest, and closest, to them. As they closed in, he stopped abruptly, pivoted about-face, and slugged the nearest one in the stomach. The man dropped immediately like a flattened sack. His companion approached, fists at the ready, but Uwe swung once, his fist arcing past the man's clumsy guard, hitting the left cheek. I heard the grinding snap of broken bone and teeth. The man collapsed in agony, whimpering and gagging as blood filled his torn mouth.

"Hold onto this for me," Uwe said. He passed the red-stained weapon to me, and I dropped it into my back pocket. "Now I'm calling the bullen." That was our slang name for any local police.

In a few minutes, the police arrived and Uwe gave them his version of the story. The two men made no effort to dispute the details, and in truth, probably didn't even know what had put them down so hard. One sat in a pool of his own vomit, hugging his stomach, while the other lay where he had crawled, next to a small tree at the roadside, crying and holding his face.

One of the police snapped at the men, ordering them into the patrol car. They complied slowly, but were in such pain that the police didn't even bother to handcuff them. The other officer walked back over where Uwe and I were standing.

"We've seen these two before. You should have given them another kick or two. Call the station if you have any more problems, and we'll lock them up for a week, after they get out of the hospital, that is." He turned and walked back to the car, boots crunching dirt, and laughing like he had just heard the best joke of the whole day.

"Real tough aren't you?" the officer said to the men. "You couldn't even handle a couple of kids."

Uwe was thoughtful now that the adrenaline had subsided. "It's funny. I can't ever remember seeing a policeman before tonight and not being afraid for myself."

"Me neither."

"We need to remember this," he said with a satisfied sigh. "I don't think we'll always be on such good terms with our protectors."

The eleventh-hour employment at Polymath bailed me out of one problem and into another. Although my computer machinery repair skills were needed, the only opening was on the night shift, so that's where I ended up. Aside from the basic problem of adjusting to the unnatural work hours, it was awkward because I could see my father from a distance. Nonetheless, there was not much to discuss other than work, so we seldom spoke more than would any other two employees.

One night, things were particularly slow and nothing broke down, so I settled into a corner and tried to understand what I was feeling.

No matter how hard I tried, there was just no relating to Dad. Was it an irrational bias planted in my own mind? Probably not, because Mom had never spoken harshly of him except to say that he used to drink and yell a lot, and even when she obliquely mentioned his habit of physical abuse, it was not spoken as condemnation. It was more like she was speaking of a sick person whom she pitied, but could not help. I could never remember a time when she assailed him as being a bad person. I was trapped in the emotional no-man's land vacillating between indifference and a wish to feel affection. My mind knew that I ought to possess, or at least go in search of, substantive feelings, yet another part knew that if I did it would just be going through the motions.

I didn't love Dad, but neither could I hate him. He had done me a favor with the job, but any man might have done the same for another he called a friend. Putting it in perspective, I concluded that I was fortunate to have a job so soon. In a country where finding new employment was virtually guaranteed, I could always find something, but it might be a job I didn't want. Although I knew that he had been a key to success in that effort, at least he never bragged about connections. When we passed in the corridor, he would simply nod, not changing expression and never breaking stride.

Being around Dad was like looking through a telescope backwards; I knew that the people there were physically close, but they appeared so very far away that I would never bother to reach out, since actual touching was impossible. I put my relationship with him back into that untended place inside where it had languished for so many years. There was nothing to be gained for either of us by worrying about it now. He had come through once when I needed him, and maybe that was a good place to leave it.

About that time, I was able to make a deal that put me into a select social class, especially since I was so young. Automobiles were precious items in Eastern Europe. There were no hulks rusting in junk yards or behind the storage shed. Instead, all the junk was nurtured, patched, coaxed and forced into running

137

condition until so little was left that it was completely consumed.

Reiner, my real father's brother, worked as a mechanic in Falkensee and offered to help me fix an automobile if I could find one that was affordable. Since the state regulated almost every other aspect of life, it was no surprise to find that one of their agencies also set the price of used cars. Real life, however, was still governed by the principle of scarcity, and since cars were so hard to get, they were much more valuable than their official price. To sell one for more than the state allowed or pay more than official value was a criminal offense because it was black marketeering. On the other hand, there was no other practical way to buy a car, because if a person only offered the official rate, the seller would either laugh out loud or withdraw the offer to sell. The waiting list for new cars was more than twelve years then, and I couldn't imagine waiting until middle age before owning one. The sellers and the buyers all knew the score, and the only way to get a car was to break the law and pay dearly.

During high school when most of the boys had bought motorbikes, I took a lot of ribbing and kept my bicycle in order to save money. With a promise of mechanic's help from Uncle Reiner and ten thousand painfully saved marks in my pocket, Uwe and I eagerly boarded the train to East Berlin.

The car lot was a potpourri of vehicles, from decaying two-cycle Trabants to a gleaming Mercedes Benz sedan. Owning a good car on the East side was like owning waterfront property. Unless you wrecked it, or set it on fire, it grew in value. Everyone knew these simple truths. There were no clever signs with slogans about excitement or quality, no colored flags or flashing lights. The car lot was as well known as the meat market. There were no salesmen, but various owners were there to answer questions about their merchandise. One of them noticed us inspecting the older cars, and he must have become curious. Window shopping wasn't a tradition in East Germany, because people went to the store to buy, not to look.

"Do you like that one?" he asked. He was a stocky, plain-looking man, slouching, with hands thrust deep into his trouser pockets.

I shrugged.

"It's nice but I don't know if I can afford it. How well does it run?" I touched the white Lada's hood. Dents? Yes. Seat covers torn and faded by the sun, noted. Leaked oil beneath the engine, yes. All of that was expected. It would have given new meaning to the Western term 'used car.'

It rattled to life after pumping the accelerator and a lot of grinding on the starter. The engine ran roughly and blue smoke rolled from the exhaust pipe when the man revved it. The fire wall was greasy and the crankcase filler cap had oil spattered around it on the rocker arm cover. Lights work? Yes. Even the dimmer cycled as advertised. Turn signals? Yes. The floor mats were gone. White paint faded and chipped. Of course. That, too, was expected. A 1972 Lada, a Fiat made under license in the Soviet Union. The seller's voice faded into the mutter of Berlin, and I feasted upon the vision of the Lada. It was on its last legs and would take major repairs to make it really serviceable. Perhaps it was even unsafe to drive. Did the windshield wipers work? I had forgotten to check. Yes!

There in the dashboard was a radio! What a bonus! I had seen better-looking ones than this being cut up for scrap metal because they couldn't be fixed any more. Rust around the wheel wells. No surprise there either.

"How much?" Was I going to act cool and disinterested? No. In the East you can always sell a car. Walking away would be a joke on me, not him. He knew that I was a kid with not much money, and he knew that I couldn't afford much of anything.

"Nine thousand marks," he said smoothly.

The car was the next thing to a wreck, but it was the most beautiful thing I had ever seen.

"I'll take it," I said.

His eyebrows went up when he realized that I actually had the money in my pocket.

He filled out a bill of sale showing the sale price as 4,500 marks, the official rate. I gave him the 9,000 and he gave me the paper and the keys. We both lied when we signed the documents, and we both would have to remember to lie in the future if anyone asked about the transaction. That was the system. To do business most of the time you had to lie. That day, it didn't bother me a bit.

Uwe and I might have been kings as we drove back from Berlin on the F-5 Highway. At 53 k.p.h. the front end shook, and I wondered if our blue exhaust plume was breaking some law. In a few minutes that didn't matter because the radio worked well and the AFN station in West Berlin came in clearly. We rolled both front windows down and drove with our arms braced in the window openings like we saw the Westerners do on TV, only we were being passed by everything with wheels instead of being out in front.

Arriving in Falkensee, I drove immediately to Uncle Reiner's garage. As I pulled up to the door, I revved the engine, and smoked up half the block. He came walking out slowly, wiping his hands on a greasy rag. Seeing me at the wheel, his expression showed initial amusement, then shock as he realized that the automobile was mine.

"Carsten," he shouted over the rattling engine, "it's so smooth! Is it even running?" Reiner cupped his hand to an ear as though attempting to hear some subtle sound. "And it's so clean! Where did you find such a jewel? I want the man's name who sold it to you so I can personally thank him."

After the engine was switched off, he walked slowly around the whole vehicle, not speaking at all, alternately wringing his hands and wiping them on a rag. Finally, he stopped next to my window.

"Well?" I said. "What about it? Got us here didn't it?"

"I can see that." He sighed, then nodded as though in resignation. "I can fix it, but it will take all of my connections to get the parts. It might have been easier just to start buying pieces and make a new one."

"But it runs, and I got a deal!" I waved my arms, delineating something very big and wonderful, but he remained unimpressed.

"Good, because once we get it repaired, you're going to sell it and trade up. Whatever I can do for this thing is only going to be a temporary solution." Then he laughed, "You're going to find out what it means to get dirty, Carsten. You get to help!"

He laughed again and walked back into the garage shaking his head.

Since there was an open interval in my schedule before fulfilling my contract work obligation, I spent some time with Vivien planning another vacation, this time to Prague. Once we had agreed on departure and return dates, her preparations consisted of setting up a minutely detailed itinerary for the whole trip, even noting the time of day for visits to local attractions. Her art interests figured heavily into everything, and we were scheduled to visit every museum and historical monument in that storied city. She didn't discuss the plan as though it was subject to modification, rather, she finalized and presented it to me one afternoon shortly before our departure.

"This will be great," she said, "we'll get to see all the museums. Wait until you see the buildings, Carsten. They're really old, just dripping with extinct architecture and one-of-a-kind decorations. It will be great!" Her blue eyes danced and glittered with anticipation. I reflected how not so long ago, she had looked at me with the same excitement animating her gaze.

I nodded passively, and thought that there was nothing now to do but follow through and make the best of it. We had drifted so far apart that I felt this would be one of our last times together. It seemed that her feelings for me had permutated into a residual, but distant affection that was cooling with each passing week. My perceptions were confirmed when I learned her mother's reaction to our planned excursion.

Vivien's parents made no protest whatsoever of the projected fifteen day trip with me, and for a few days I didn't understand why. When the truth finally dawned, I was amazed at my own blindness. Her mother began treating me politely, almost cordially, because she knew that soon I would be nothing more than an object lesson in who not to hang around, something for Vivien and her mother to remember and laugh about. She knew that school and time and the vagaries of a young woman's interest would soon finish our relationship. This was not at all like the trip to Bulgaria. There would be no more need for her to actively attack when our relationship was already in its death throes.

Personal Ausweis - Personal ID that had to be carried at all times.

Carsten's father's permit to enter the frontier area; this also had to be with you at all times

Carsten Kaaz
and
Jurgen Gaertner
at the
Baltic Sea
— 1985

Carsten
Kaaz
— 1985

143

I was no longer a threat to their daughter's success, and they were sure I would soon disappear. They were like smug vultures, waiting for the last twitches of our dying love. Frau Taschner gloated politely over our impending break, but it didn't matter anymore what the woman thought. I knew that I had given my best to establish a warm relationship with Vivien's parents, and the fact that we hadn't made it wasn't my problem. In the back of my mind, a new and comfortable feeling was beginning. Losing Vivien meant losing the girl I had loved since my heart became capable of that feeling. But maybe my spirit was stronger than I had originally thought. It felt good to be strong, and even through the pain, I could feel the survival instincts becoming active. No matter what the future, I was determined to do my part.

After the short flight, our stay in Czechoslovakia was much as I had anticipated — an endless repetition of cased and sequestered art, ornate and polished furniture in rooms that had miraculously survived two centuries of existence in a part of Europe that had never really been at peace. The old couple from whom we rented our room were like Prague itself, accommodating enough, but patronizing, solicitous and simultaneously insolent. The fundamental absurdity of our situation was inescapable. Since we were from an Eastern Bloc country, we were only allowed to exchange 30 marks per day. If we were to pay for our room, there would be hardly anything at all left over, and definitely not enough for meals. The solution to that problem was a five-day supply of food, packed like a massive picnic lunch and brought along on the airplane. All around us swirled the Western tourists, spending with apparent abandon. East Bloc greed for their hard currency was so consuming that they were required by local law to pay upon entering the country, like admission to a side show or zoo. I put on the best face I could and strolled in Vivien's wake, adhering to her schedule with apparent interest about the old buildings. Inevitably, she noticed my lack of enthusiasm. We stood for a moment on a street corner, and through the rumble and honk of the Czechoslovakian traffic, her voice sounded unusually harsh.

"You don't like this do you?"

"It's not that," I said. "I just don't know very much about this stuff so it's hard for me to appreciate it." It was a lie, and I was sure that she knew it. Should I have said that I took her to those places because I was happy when she was happy? It was too late for that answer because our common interests were no longer what mattered. In the end, it was differences that had captured center stage.

Her enthusiasm for the sights continued undiminished through the rest of our stay, and we returned to East Berlin sharing nothing but the unspoken feeling of our estrangement. At the end of each day, she had feigned fatigue and gone to sleep immediately. She hardly held my hand during the last few days, much less had any sexual interest. The trip was a sad confirmation of my gnawing fear. It would be over soon.

One evening, a few days after we returned, Uwe came over and we took an evening walk through the pine thicket. We had passed through a particularly dense part when we heard the murmur of nearby voices. That meant there was either a team of border guards or police, or someone else had discovered the pleasant privacy of that place.

Vivien was standing in the shadows near a bush with Hans Porzich. He was the father of one of Vivien's school friends, and she had just leaned over to kiss him.

I looked away like a child who is frightened at a horror movie.

"Uwe," I said, "please tell me if that was Vivien."

He walked quickly and quietly back down the street and returned in a moment.

"You don't need to go back down there. It's her, with Herr Porzich. They didn't see us."

My body felt suspended, frozen, non-functional, with a cold vacuum where my heart was supposed to be. My mind knew that our love had died the common death of silence long ago. When? Who could tell the moment when it had ceased to breathe. There had been warning enough, the ever-growing silences between us, the words that might have been spoken but never made it to our tongues. There had been no funeral because the passing had been silent, almost merciful, an unannounced

145

end to the awkwardness that had bound us together for so long. Vivien's life had been intertwined with mine for more than six years. Now that the reality of our parting was upon me, I could only try like a hiker buried in an avalanche to dig myself out as best I could.

The next day, my mother could see that I was upset, but I avoided her questions and tried to disguise my shaking hands at the dinner table. I was not in need of the sympathy that mothers give so well, but perhaps a dose of philosophy from an objective observer would help. I went to visit Frau Kubicki and explained everything.

"You knew that this would happen, Carsten," she said. "You and she were so different. It was as though you were on separate roads that ran together for a while, but now must move apart forever." She sat relaxed in her chair, not observing me out of curiosity but reflecting the compassion of her heart.

I nodded.

"Focus on your goals."

I nodded again.

"You have goals, live your life."

"Yes," I said.

"Carsten, don't pity yourself. You've done enough of that already."

The last words slipped past my wounded emotions to where they could be considered for their value. They were the voice of one calling to a comrade who had been cast into the sea. They were words of life. Swim! Swim for yourself or you will drown. No one else can save you!

A few days later I stopped by the Konsum to buy some chewing gum and nearly ran into Vivien as she was walking out the door.

"Hello," I said. It was a timid, tentative greeting, full of indecision and trepidation. I had to say something, but what, and how?

"Oh, hello," she said without inflection.

I stammered something, and she frowned.

"What's the matter with you?" she asked curtly.

"Uwe and I were walking Friday night, and we went

through the pine thicket like always."

She stared without reaction, not moving a muscle.

"I saw you with Hans Porzich."

The expression changed, and anger came up in her eyes. "Don't you have anything better to do than sneak around in the bushes at night with your strange friends?"

"I wasn't …"

"Herr Porzich has troubles with his wife, and I was just walking with him so he could talk a little. You take walks don't you?"

"But you were kissing him."

She stamped her foot.

"I'm not going to stand here and listen to your whining. If you don't like what I'm doing that's your problem. There is nothing going on between Herr Porzich and me anyway. Mind your own business." She turned without further comment and stalked out the door. An old woman slowed as she passed me on her way out, the old eyes registering interest and practiced curiosity.

I stood silently, and for a moment wondered if it had all been a mistake, a misunderstanding, but then I realized that I was only fooling myself. I knew what I had seen, and I knew what it meant, but I didn't know if I could actually make the break. Could I simply tell her goodbye? Could I have the courage to formally end it?

The next night, Uwe and I leaned on my front-yard fence, staring in silence toward the brilliantly lighted Wall. The mirrored windows of the distant guard towers reflected dull bronze. Five hundred meters away, across the border, we could see tiny warm lights in a 20-story West Berlin apartment building. The double-decker buses came and went their way, trailing dark, smoky diesel tails. It was a surrealistic portrait pasted against the silent blackness of the night.

I turned to Uwe.

"There's just one way for us to get out of here. Do you think that we can somehow make it?"

He smiled a quiet, confident smile.

"Yes," he said. "We can make it."

147

Sometimes a person has to be told that things will be all right, even if the outcome is still unknown. Uwe's words pulled me back from my tottering walk along the edge of despair. The dream of a better tomorrow took on its own life at that moment. The dissolution with Vivien remained an informal non-event, and although I knew that it was irrevocably over, I could not gather enough courage to say goodbye to her with my lips. In the inevitable hours of introspection and self-recrimination that followed, the desire to regain control over my life reasserted itself. I resolved not to go out with her, but to remain civil out of respect for our long association. The emotional drain of parting from her had obscured the frustrations of daily life, and for a time I had forgotten about wanting to leave East Germany. Now unencumbered, the old dream could live again. A little reading gave me the general information I needed to revive it.

There were laws. There were legal ways to do things.

Dad was in the front yard trying to start our two-cycle lawn mower. I approached and stood in silence until he looked up.

"Hi, son."

I shifted uncomfortably.

"Dad, I need to talk to you about something really important."

He wiped his strong hands on his T-shirt to clear the sweat and gasoline away. The lawnmower was spotless. He always cleaned it before putting it away and insisted that I do the same whenever I cut grass.

"Sure." Looking at me more closely, he could see that it was something serious. "What's on your mind?"

"Dad, I've been thinking things over for the last couple of years, and I have decided that I want to leave East Germany."

"I'd like that, too. Where do you want to visit?"

"Not travel. I want to leave for good."

He squinted against the morning sun and his lips twitched. Dad had always given me a lot of room to be myself and have my own ideas, but this was clearly something else.

"Carsten, have you really thought this over? If you were to do that you could never come back."

"I know."

"Why do you want to leave anyway? Mom and I love you a lot, and Roberto would really miss you."

"I love you too, but everything weighs upon us here. There is no freedom to grow. Somebody's either watching or taking care of us from the day we are born to the day we die. Do you remember how you and Mom took Roberto and me to the zoo in East Berlin, and how we loved to look at the animals? Well, I've been thinking it over, and it seems to me that there are just two classes of people in our country, the zookeepers and the animals. Sure, we get fed and protected, but we can never grow up into what we were made to become. No matter how nice things get, we're still behind bars. This will always be a cage."

He looked at his feet, then up and away as though trying to see something in the sky.

"They'll put you in prison if you try anything."

"I've thought that over, and there are emigration laws. I'm not going to do anything illegal that will get me into trouble."

Dad looked into my eyes for a long moment.

"You're nearly a grown man and you can make decisions, son, but this really worries me. Isn't there some other way you can work your feelings out?"

I shook my head, and braced for the next comment.

"This is going to kill your mother."

"Please don't say anything to her for now. I'm only going to do some research and find out how it can be done. I'll discuss it with you both when things get a little clearer."

"OK, but you really need to be sure. Once it begins, there will be no going back, and there will be people in the government who won't like it at all." He squinted again and wiped his face. I couldn't tell if it was sweat at the corner of his eye, or a tear. His voice changed as though there was something in his throat. This was the man who never raised his voice, and hardly even cursed when he bloodied his knuckles working in the yard.

"Do you understand what I'm telling you? They'll remember this for the rest of your life. You have to be sure that you are making a good trade, because you'll have to live with the consequences whether or not they let you go."

Two days later, I stood at the reference shelves in the library looking up regulations on emigration. Yes, there were the references. Go to this volume, that page, such and such paragraph. With care and focused purpose, I studied and referenced, but even as I saw some progress, it became apparent that the game was only beginning. As I looked for the actual statutes governing legal exit, I found the pages and paragraphs missing from the law books. The pages weren't torn out, just not there, never published, never even printed.

"Excuse me," I said to the librarian, "but I'm looking for this reference." I indicated the page and paragraph with my finger. She smiled and took the book from the my hand, stopped, flipped pages back and forth, then looked up.

"It's not available."

"What do you mean?" I asked.

"It just isn't available. Do you want anything else?"

"I'm talking about a law and you are telling me it isn't available?"

She looked very steadily into my eyes.

"If it isn't in this book, it isn't available." Then she looked away.

I knew that she didn't understand what I wanted, and the urgency of my desires wouldn't change a thing. There was nothing more to be said, and she wasn't wasting her breath.

Arriving back home, I stewed about it for a few hours, then walked over to Uwe's house.

"Uwe, we need to go find out who has applications. I know that someone has them, because I've heard that others have applied to leave." There was a real danger. In my searches for emigration laws, I had noted some other things as well. It was a crime against the state to try to get someone else to leave the country. Conviction on that charge could get me three years in prison.

"Uwe, when they question us, you can't say that this was my idea. Tell them that you thought of this on your own and that we just happened to discuss it one day and find that we had the same interest. If you tell them that I persuaded you, I'll go to prison."

He smiled and shrugged.

"You're my best friend, so you don't have to worry about me."

He was right; I wasn't worried about him. In fact, I was beginning now to worry more about myself and how I would behave under the yet-unidentified stress that was sure to come.

We went to the Rathaus, to the office of the local Stasi. No one visited that drab place for recreational purposes, and since the state security police had no public law enforcement functions, normally guests only came at their special invitation. The door knob was old and the steel shiny from a thousand sweaty clutchings, numberless contacts with hands that held the rod of authority in an unyielding grip.

"I'd like to apply to leave the country," I said to the man behind the desk. His bald head shown like one of the polished marble balls in Alexanderplatz. He scratched his nose and pushed the chair back, regarding us with interest, then without comment sauntered into a back office.

Uwe and I stood trying to appear calm. Dad's words came to mind like an old echo. "Are you absolutely sure? ..."

I couldn't live as half a person. Half a person. Yes, we were all half-persons, groaning under that dead system. I had to leave, or I could never grow. Like a tortured sprout, groping, clutching for nourishment in the crack of a gray sidewalk, I would grasp after fulfillment. Stepped on again and again, I would either be bent to the shape of the system or just lie down on the gray concrete for one last time to die.

The bald man shuffled back into the office.

"We have no responsibility for that in this office. You have to go to Nauen."

That was an anticlimax. There in the den of the Stasi themselves, the request had not even raised an eyebrow. There were no menacing, faceless men, no trouble at all. We didn't know what to think, so we followed the little man's direction and drove to Nauen to locate the Stasi headquarters. Entering the city, we had to ask directions because the building had no sign.

"I want to apply to leave the country. To emigrate."

The dark eyes studied my face, clothing, and posture with

practiced professional interest.

"Me too," said Uwe.

The dark eyes flicked over him, cataloging with the same interest.

"You need to fill out these forms and bring them back. Then your request can be considered."

"We'll just do them here. How about letting us borrow a pencil?" Then we sat on the hardwood bench and scribbled away. About a half hour later, we brought them back to the desk.

The papers disappeared in the moist hands and into the rear office. In about ten minutes, a tall hefty man came out and directed us to another office.

"So, you want to leave," the next official asked casually. His eyes signaled only a passing interest. No alarm. No anger.

Very strange. Totally unexpected. This wasn't what I had figured at all.

"Why do you want to leave?"

This could be a trap. If I said I wanted to change the system, I would be breaking the law. One wrong word could land me in jail.

"I just want to see some of the world," I said. I clarified the statement. "I want to go to America."

I might as well have pulled a gun and pointed it at his mother. His head jerked up and his chin jutted out as he glared at both of us. Spittle sprayed involuntarily as he exploded, his voice rising in pitch and intensity.

"America! They're our worst enemies! What's the matter with you?" His breath came in short exhalations, and he licked his lips. "Isn't your own country good enough?"

I felt his breath upon my face and I was afraid.

"The law says that I can apply to leave."

He settled slightly and fixed Uwe in his unblinking gaze. "Do you also want to go," his voice hesitated, mouth working as though the word was a foul tasting piece of meat, "to … America?"

"Yes."

"Well, you can leave the forms if you want, but don't hold your breath." He threw the two papers at the desk, but they only

152

sailed sideways, jerking in short back and forth arcs onto the floor. He let them lay. "You punks are all alike. Nothing is good enough for you, is it? You have to have blue jeans, and your little lives aren't any fun unless you can have some American rock record screaming in your ears."

I started to answer, but he stood abruptly.

"Watch your mailbox. We'll be in touch." He left the room with heavy clumping footfalls.

Uwe and I looked at each other, then simply stood up and walked out the door.

"What do you think?" Uwe asked.

"Who knows? They have to reply, I guess." That wasn't true. They didn't have to do anything. I knew that by now.

"Sure they'll reply," he said, "but they can just deny it and never say why. You know how it goes."

All I could do was reluctantly agree that we had done what we could. As we drove back to Falkensee, a dark depression covered me like clouds before a storm. Zoo keepers and animals. The men in charge wouldn't have a job unless they had someone to harass. If they let us go, there would be two fewer inside their little kingdom.

It was never going to work, and I knew it. I could sense that Uwe knew it too, but each of us was afraid to speak defeatist words. We were encouraging each other with brave exteriors. For the moment, that was all we had to share, but somewhere deep inside I felt a new motion, the genesis of an iron determination that was to become the new center of my life.

It was like being in a bag of some kind. I smelled the stupefying sullen air that remains trapped in an old car when it is parked for the last time. I saw the rut, no the chasm, into which I had been forced. I had become just like the others, just one of the multitude who wandered in search of grass tufts in a mediocre pasture. I, like my parents before me, had eaten from the trough because there was no other food to be had. I had felt the rough, cold bars against my face as I searched for some way to let my life grow. It was a zoo. The keepers were well practiced in their art, and I had become just another in the endless stream of beasts as they filed through the chute into what would be their final corral.

It seemed as though we were trapped.

Over the next two weeks, Uwe and I had more long conversations trying to sort things out.

"If our government won't explain the laws, we'll see what the Americans have to say," I told Uwe. "Today I sent a letter to their embassy in East Berlin."

"What do you think will happen?" Uwe asked.

"They'll answer," I said confidently. Once again, I was anything but confident; I had no idea how their embassy would react to the request. In the letter, I had introduced myself and told them of my training, background and desire to get information on emigration. It was a tiny, fragile hope, a lone point of light flickering among the gray clouds covering my life. I was desperate for help and had no other sources.

Two weeks.

Every other day, Uwe would make it a point to stop by the house and ask about the mail. Then he quit asking with words and just said hello and stopped, inquiring with a respectful silence.

Nothing.

Three weeks.

How could I do anything if no one would help? The numbness crept ever higher inside, and I was torn between dread and anticipation of tomorrow.

"Carsten, there's a letter here from Berlin." Mother's eyes got bigger in surprise. "From the American Embassy."

I could hardly believe it. Nothing else could have at once lifted me up, but held me at the same time dangling over a bottomless pit. Hope and fear were madly intertwined into that instant of time. I held the envelope and carefully inspected both sides. The return address was in small but elegant blue lettering, and the letter appeared to have been opened. As anticipated, the post office Stasi had taken an opportunity to read it first, and had not done a very good job of resealing. I didn't care. Someone had heard my request and at least had the courtesy to reply. My eyes devoured the paragraphs.

Polite greeting. Yes, there were emigration laws, but my

government would help me with that. Sincerely, then a signature. Huffman, Consul General. Someone in authority. Mom's inquiring looks were too much.

"I just wrote them a letter asking about how I could visit America," I said. "This is the reply." I waved the letter at her and bounded upstairs to my room. For the rest of the day I read and reread it. Her lips were silent, but her eyes were full of questions that I wasn't prepared to answer.

There was a phone number on the letterhead. I recalled Dad's words again: 'This will follow you. ...' Things could never be the same anyway. Besides, this wasn't the end of the world. I was just an East German kid who wanted to go to America to see how the rotten capitalists lived. What could be so bad about that? Would they believe that was all I wanted? What did I really want, anyway?

I shook away the doubt and resolved that to act immediately was more important than to understand right now.

The next day after work, I stopped at the public phone on the way home. I put the money in the slot and dialed the number. After an operator and a secretary, I reached the man whose name was on the letter.

"Huffman here." The voice was cordial and clear.

"I am Carsten Kaaz. I wrote you a letter recently about coming to the United States."

"Yes, Herr Kaaz, how are you?"

"Could you give me some more information?" Surely my voice would crack from the strain. "I want to come and visit if that is allowed."

"You're welcome to visit the embassy, but you should think about the consequences."

"Please explain."

"The Volkspolizei may very well arrest you if you don't have government permission. You already know that don't you?" He paused. "And you can only visit. You cannot stay under any circumstances. Do you understand?"

"Yes, thank you." I had not really considered trying to become a political refugee inside the compound. My mind was totally calm. The act of placing the call had transformed me and

155

displaced fear. "Do I need to come at a specific time, I mean do I need an appointment?"

"No, but it needs to be during business hours so there will be someone here to talk to you."

Hanging up the phone, I knew that I had to go. That evening, I stopped by to tell Uwe.

"When do we leave?" he asked with a smile.

"They'll arrest us, my friend," I said. "And who knows what else."

He laughed.

"As long as they don't have two drunks beat me up. That really hurts." He chuckled repeatedly at the jest.

From that moment, we thought only of going to Berlin.

If ever a city could grow a soul, it would have to be Berlin. East Berlin was dressed up in her best, waiting for a boyfriend, but she was hiding massive scars and deformity. A concrete and barbed-wire corset circumscribed her sagging waist like a tourniquet, barring the loss of human resources to the West, but choking her own life as well. She was decked with jewels, but they were poorly cut and shabby by Western standards. Her shops and stores were stocked with more goods than any other East Bloc country, but the failures of central planning still alternately choked or flooded her arteries with both wanted and unwanted goods. Other East Bloc visitors drooled because their countries offered even less. She wore makeup too, thick and heavy, covering more than a minor blemish. Beneath the powder and the moisturizing fluids, there was a face dulled by pain. It was the scarcely understood agony of a generation that had not dared to hope for too much. It was the 40-year-old grimace of the pauper camped out next to the rich man's estate, the contorted visage of one drying up on the inside, left barren in a desert to bake under an unfriendly sun.

For every man or woman who died on the Wall, a thousand more died a silent, prolonged death. Their spirits eroded particle by little particle, until nothing was left but living in wait for the end.

Their imaginations were squeezed dry without them even knowing it. We had resolved, as only the young can, that we would not meet the same fate as our predecessors, and in the faces all around, we saw evidence of the truth we had come to know in our hearts. Our country was dying, rotting to death from the inside. Even though we were young, we were starting to smell the same, and we were afraid of tomorrow, terrified to the depths of our souls of what kind of men we might become if we didn't do something.

Uwe and I made our journey by train, hoping only for an opportunity. My dreams and his were circumscribed by the same threats, and bound by the same thin hopes.

We stood on the Strasse and watched people coming and going with hardly a glance at the American Embassy's three-meter-high walls. Our own Volkspolizei were stationed at ten-meter intervals around the building, but it was obvious that their attention was directed to the street, and not at the building and grounds. The embassy was a fortress and couldn't be approached from any side without passing at least one guard.

We walked around the whole compound once.

"There are Vopos at each gate."

"Yes," said Uwe. "What do you think?"

"I don't know yet." I was scared, but it wouldn't help to discuss that.

We circled the building again, stopping here and there like tourists looking at something really interesting. The guards were bored blind, and didn't appear to notice us. People passed us up and down the street, this way and that, singly and in small groups.

We walked around the whole complex a third time. Inside my heart was a rising sickness. It was right in front of me. Would I have the courage? Could I force myself to move?

"Let's do it," I said in a harsh whisper.

With hearts banging wildly, Uwe and I walked as casually as we could up the sidewalk near the main entrance. A burly Vopo wearing the dark green uniform was planted at the opening next to his small guard shelter. His eyes were dulled by the hours of uneventful waiting, the aching feet, the blur of unconcerned faces that flowed past in an endless river. He never noticed our intention until it was too late. We walked past him, picked up the pace and simply turned sharply through the embassy gate. I listened with dread for a guttural command to stop, but none came and I dared not look back.

That little piece of ground was like a grotto, a shaded grove where the outer world fell away allowing a piece of what I thought was America to bloom. Flowers and neatly trimmed bushes punctuated the open spaces; the air even smelled different to my nose. I knew that was only my imagination, but I savored it anyway.

"We made it," Uwe said.

"This is great," I said.

The covered walkway led to a large door. Behind the door was a desk; next to it, a large American flag and a picture of Ronald Reagan.

"We have come to see Herr Huffman," I said to the small man behind the desk. His eyes moved over us with analytical precision, capturing every detail. Was he from the C.I.A. we had heard so much about?

"While you're waiting, please fill out these visitor records, then just sit here." He indicated to chairs along the wall.

In a few moments, a tall man emerged with the receptionist from a door along the corridor. He was wearing a three-piece gray suit and a large gold Seiko watch. He introduced himself. "I am Mr. Huffman, Consul General, and you are Herr Kaaz and Herr George?"

It was almost like being in a movie, while looking through the cinema camera at the same time. We were inside America, but still inside the gut of the Communist state. Mr. Huffman asked how he could help, surveying us all the while. I imagined that by the time we left, he would know much more about Uwe and me than was written upon any form. The outer door flew open and another person entered. He was oddly dressed in a checkered sport coat with pastel pants; oversize green-framed sunglasses obscured part of his face. Not like I thought a diplomat ought to look. The ambiance of the place was overwhelming, and I was intoxicated. The embassy was an official piece of ground, but it was devoid of the frowning, oppressive atmosphere I had experienced since childhood.

I heard laughter somewhere in another room. I tried to remember if I had ever heard laughter in one of our government buildings.

Huffman studied the forms for a full minute in absolute silence, then smiled.

"So, you would like to visit America?"

"No sir," I said without hesitation, "I want to live there."

"That's why I'm here too," Uwe said proudly.

Huffman's eyebrows arched, betraying human concern behind his officially molded face.

"Do you have any family or relatives in the U.S.?"

"No, sir."

"That makes things a lot more difficult, Her Kaaz." His head was shaking from side to side. I was crumbling. "Under the circumstances, there is really nothing that I can do for you."

The sentence was pronounced, but I refused to believe that it was over. There had to be something else, some way around the diplomatic blockade. I knew that we could not live inside of this little piece of transplanted America, and I thought that the Stasi were waiting patiently for us to emerge. Somehow, my heart resumed its normal rhythm and hope remained alive despite the words he had spoken.

His face softened and his brown eyes met mine intently.

"You were very courageous to come, but you must understand that once you leave these grounds, I can do nothing to help. You're a citizen of East Germany, and my country's laws have no power over your fate."

"I know."

"You have to have their permission to leave, Herr Kaaz. Perhaps if you will apply. ..."

"Yes, sir. Actually I have applied, but I think they aren't going to let us go." I could feel that he cared, but I could also feel his wariness. He couldn't know for sure why we had come, and for all he knew, it could have been some trick to embarrass America. Yet, even with all of the uncertainty, I felt the part of Huffman that really cared about me. The eyes said it all. If I were thirsty, he would have shared his water. If I were hungry, he would have shared his own bread. But I was getting up to leave, and leaving America. I would once again have to feel the weight of my chains. Back to my cage in the zoo.

After a few more moments of pleasant conversation, again he shook our hands and wished us a good day. Another man appeared to escort us to the exit.

The door clicked shut and we were on the street again. I hardly dared to look around. It seemed just as before, moderately busy with small knots of people scurrying by. A guard was three meters away, but his back was turned. Uwe and I began to walk briskly and our breath came easier with each step. Perhaps we had somehow not been noticed?

Then there were two Stasi. They had quietly slipped in behind us as only they can, one on either side, and flashed ID. "You have to come with us." One reached out and gripped Uwe's right arm while the one on the other side held onto my left arm.

They simply guided us in much the same way that a son would steer his aging mother through a crosswalk on a crowded street. There was the grip, firm, without variation or adjustment. There was the pressure, a little left, a little right, until we were herded without haste to a nearby unmarked doorway. There was no struggle, no pulling away. They knew that we wouldn't run because there was nowhere to go. We were all inside the cage together. Once we saw where they waited for us to go, we simply went. There was no reason to resist.

As we reached the opening, I said, "If you want to know why we went into the embassy, call your headquarters in Nauen. We're well known there."

There was no visible reaction. It was against the rules for us to talk without permission, but I didn't care about rules.

Fear followed the Stasi like a foul smell. It wasn't necessary for them to beat prisoners or otherwise put them to physical harm. Being taken off the street meant being dragged away into the unknown. They knew that a prisoner's mind was as much of a weapon as electric shock or wooden clubs when fear was properly nurtured. There were laws against mistreating prisoners, but who was going to enforce them? Most of the time they didn't beat people because the authorities truly feared hardening a troublemaker by excessive mistreatment, so if he were finally free, he became an implacable enemy, resisting everything — a man with nothing to lose. In their own way, the Stasi also hated publicity. A story of injustice always sold newspapers, and political reverberations from such events could continue for months, even years, embarrassing government figures in international forums. The Stasi liked to take care of things quietly, using just enough of the right kind of force at the right time to show the offender who had the power. Fostering a subservient populace was the goal of the State Security Service.

Uwe was led off down the hall, and I was shoved alone into another room. The door slammed shut. In the company of two wooden chairs, a table, and a pad of writing paper, I waited and turned inward. I didn't wonder what Uwe would say when they interrogated him. As long as he didn't tell them I persuaded him to come along, there would be no charge of conspiracy, and therefore probably no prolonged jail time either, but then again the Stasi were never entirely predictable.

Perhaps they were calling Nauen. The headquarters there knew who we were. Or maybe this Berlin branch had already known all about us. Maybe they were waiting for more instructions. Maybe the people in charge were out to lunch or off for the day. Maybe the underlings didn't know what to do with us. Whatever, whomever they were, someone, somewhere was deciding our fate.

Two hours.

Only the occasional muffled noise of some activity elsewhere in the building. In the hall? In the next room? Somewhere. No sounds at all unless I moved. Gray walls. Cobwebs in the corners. No windows. Dust in the corners where the broom would not go without a special effort. Nothing much on the wood floor. A few dark spots. Blood dries black. No, it wasn't blood. Ink maybe. My wandering mind tried everything to stave off the creeping boredom mixed with a fear that wouldn't subside.

Three hours.

The initial terror gave way like a tired tree lying down for the last time on the forest floor. I thought about sleep, but there was still enough nervous tension to keep me awake. Should I go and try the door? If it was unlocked and I walked out, they might charge me with attempted escape. That would be jail for sure. Doing nothing was still the safest thing.

Four hours.

I checked my watch incredulously. Was it possible that so much time had really passed? I didn't even have to go to the bathroom. That was curious.

Five hours.

Had they forgotten? That was hardly conceivable. No, they just wanted me to sweat and get really worked up, so they could wear me down. I thought of Uwe, but there was nothing I could do. I reviewed the story silently to myself. We were friends, that was all, and we had been talking one day and I said I was going to Berlin to visit the American Embassy, and he wanted to go too. Just a coincidence, nothing more.

The door opened and a tall thin man stepped briskly into the room. His gray suit was neat. Probably had it cleaned yesterday.

"So, Mr. Kaaz, tell me what you did in there." He wore a mask. Warm smile. Warm words. The eyes didn't smile at all. More gray than blue, and showing no feeling.

"You probably know about my applications to leave," I said. "You also know about my letter to the embassy, the reply too. What can I tell you?" All of a sudden, the fear was gone. He was just another man, another official purveyor of irritating questions. Even at my age I had seen a thousand like him. "I discussed the letter with the Americans. There really isn't anything more to say."

Suddenly I realized that he was the one who was afraid. It didn't show on his face, but why else would he be asking me, a 19-year-old kid? I was a nobody.

"Ask them if you want to know anything else," I said.

He dropped his friendly manner like dirty underwear. The eyes narrowed and burrowed into me like needles. He was intense. "Do you understand what you're doing? Do you understand that you hold your whole future in your hands?" His features were immobile, frozen, sharpened to a razor's edge, but relieved with tiny tracks and folds like a creased and wrinkled knife, and aimed at me. "If you don't cooperate, we'll break you." His hands made a gesture like snapping a twig.

"I know why you're worried," I said softly, "but I'm not a spy. The only thing I want is to leave. I want to live my life the way I want to live it. That's all I can say. I didn't break any laws. I made a legal application."

The man straightened his coat, stood abruptly, and left the room without speaking.

What now? At least my nerves were manageable. Speaking out made me feel like I had some control.

The scrape of footsteps sounded suddenly outside and the door opened abruptly.

"You can go now," the man said, "out in the hall."

"What about my friend?"

"Shut up." One of them stood a few meters away watching impassively. Uwe emerged from a nearby door and looked around, trying to get his bearings.

I looked steadily at him, trying to see something in his face, but he looked sleepy.

Without another word, one of the agents motioned us up the hall, opened a door and pointed out onto the street. The door slammed roughly and it was over. We just stood there for a moment, then walked away. Life continued uninterrupted all around us on the streets, and I could even hear birds twitter above the traffic's heavy rumble. Uwe and I were both exhausted mentally, but otherwise our visit with the Stasi might have just been a bad dream.

"How did you feel?" I asked as we sat on the train.

He smiled.

"At first I was so scared I couldn't think, but later they left me alone, and I got tired and fell asleep. It reminded me of the fan club trouble, except I knew that you were there too, and that helped me to be strong. As soon as I saw they weren't going to beat me up, it got easier." He looked at me with a half smile in his strong features. "Do you think I'm getting used to being arrested?"

Houses blurred past as the train gathered speed. He was silent for a long time, then half turned in the seat to look directly at me.

"Did we handle it right, Carsten? Did we do the right thing?"

My head was nodding automatically before his words were finished.

"Of course. We just want to live as free men, Uwe. I think men are meant to be free to choose what kind of lives they want to build, and I think that if a man wants freedom, he has to do something to earn it. Maybe this is what it will cost us."

The train rocked and rumbled across the fields. Houses, cars stopped at the crossings, people in their yards were frozen pictures in the windows, sliced from time and flashed before our eyes. We had been in the enemy's merciless embrace, the hug of death, the caress before the final darkness. But we were all right. We had emerged alive, and more committed than ever to our goal. I decided we were better off by far than our captors.

The house was empty when I returned home, and a note from Mother was on the dining room table. Gone to Gittie's house, it said. She and Gittie were close friends. I drove in the car with Uwe. He waited outside while I went in to see Mother.

She looked as though she had been beaten. Her eyes were puffy and red, makeup gone, washed away by the torrent of tears. Her eyes filled again when as she saw me. The Stasi had called her at work to tell her I had been arrested, but wouldn't say why or when I would be released.

"What have I done wrong? You're destroying yourself and I can't stop you" The crying intensified. "You don't realize what you're doing!" Gittie frowned at me, but focused her attention on comforting Mother. This was not the place for explanations.

We drove home and I felt badly for Mother. Clearly she had suffered much more than I.

That evening at dinner, everyone was quiet, and Roberto picked sullenly at his food.

"What have I done that you should behave like this?" Mom finally said. There were no tears this time, but her pain was obviously undiminished. "Your father and I have always been good citizens. We haven't taught you to do these things."

Now was as good a time as any to let it all out, so I did.

"We live a lie," I said, the color rushing to my face. "From the first moment we wake until the instant of sleep, we must live two lives. It's like being one of those insects we catch for biology, and then pin to a board so we can get a really good look at it. We satisfy our curiosity, but the poor bug dies. They watch us all — me, you, everybody — until we're so old our lives are all burned out, then they don't care anymore. If we don't think the right thoughts, we'll end up on a list somewhere in a government office. We can't go here, we can't read this or that. We can't buy the wrong books or go to the wrong movies. We can't be real people, and we can't grow up into anything because we aren't allowed to choose!" My face was burning. Didn't they understand? Didn't they feel it too?

"It isn't all that bad," Dad said. Then he dropped his gaze to the plate and sighed heavily.

"Yes it is, Dad. You got used to it but I can't."

"What if you do emigrate, Carsten," my mother said. "We'll be separated forever."

"Oh, I've been thinking about that too, Mom." I outlined a plan to visit another East Bloc country and meet them sometime.

Mother's shoulders squared. I understood then that she thought I would simply disappear from their lives.

Dad relaxed somewhat and laughed.

"It might work," he said.

Roberto's eyes darted back and forth, then seeing a resolution of sorts, he too relaxed, and all around the table there were smiling faces. At least I had been able to say the basics. There were other thoughts in my heart that were far more dangerous, though, and I didn't dare speak of them, even to my own family.

Aeriel view of Falkensee, East Germany, taken from the West

166

(Arrow shown points to home where author lived)

# CHAPTER SIX

From that day on, Uwe and I each had two shadows. One was cast by the sun, the other by the Stasi. They weren't really trying to follow secretly. I imagined that the animals of the African plains must feel about the same when they get a faint whiff of lion around sunset. Their skins would crawl and twitch, and they would glance nervously into the fuzzy darkness. Somewhere in their simple minds was the half-conscious truth that an evil presence had come to visit, its gaze following their walk, looking for clumsiness or weakness, licking its lips in anticipation, watching their habits, and sizing them up for a quick snack if the opportunity arose.

But Uwe and I weren't skittish zebras. We had seen the enemy up close, and we weren't going to run away with the swirling, panicked herd. It was time to think and to plan.

It was late and we were on one of our customary evening walks. The talk was of life and how we could solve our dilemma, what we would do next.

"Somebody's watching us," said Uwe quietly. He nodded his head in the direction of the Litfass Saule, the ubiquitous round poster-covered pillar found all over Europe.

Sure enough. This was a known uniformed policeman who no doubt had been pressed into service by the Stasi to provide surveillance during the less convenient hours of the day. He wore civilian clothes, but his obese profile was impossible to disguise. The harsh white light of the street lamp glinted off his thick glasses.

"Hello," I called. "Hello!"

Uwe and I waved.

The corpulent silhouette moved quickly behind the pillar.

"Nice to see you!" we laughed, but not too loud. We were walking and talking as friends, and as friends we were also walking the edge. To openly insult a policeman could land us quickly in jail. We couldn't call him Schweinebacke to his face, but we could use the pejorative label for our own enjoyment.

We were followed to work, and on the job I encountered other complications. Word had leaked out at Polymath of our embassy adventure. Co-workers would stare at me for no reason and shy away as though I had a communicable disease.

Two days later, the director, Peter Schreiber, invited me unexpectedly into his office. He was the highest official in Polymath, and although I had never before met him, his manner was unpretentious and friendly. I liked him immediately.

"I like to travel, too, Herr Kaaz, but there are just some places where I can't go," he said. No pen or paper was in his hands. This interview was probably not his idea, but he had a job to do.

"I understand what you're saying, but there's more to it than that," I replied.

"Perhaps," he hesitated, then went on tentatively, "there's something else. If you want your own apartment, no problem. We can get one for you."

For a moment I was stunned. It was a calculated bribe, not an insult. One of the most sought-after commodities in East Germany was private space. There were many who pleaded for the privilege that was being offered to me so easily. Were they that afraid of me? How was that possible?

"Herr Schreiber, I've already told everyone else. I just want to be free to live my life, to decide where I want to go, what I want to do."

He was nodding, lips pressed together, eyes attentive.

"What right," I asked, "do they have not to let me go? I was born to my mother. She owns me if anyone does. Does she have the right to say I have to stay in my yard for the rest of my life?"

"There are things you have to live with, Carsten."

I shook my head. He was only a reluctant messenger. There was no point in trying to persuade him.

My mouth moved again before I could think it through.

"I understand how a country can decide not to let strangers come in, but how can anyone justify making a prison out of our own land?"

He looked down at the desk, eyebrows arching as he thought that over.

"It's the same way for all of us, not just you. Remember why they built the Wall, Carsten. Our country needs us. All of us."

"Herr Schreiber, if they want people to like it here, to stay here, they need to make the country different. They need to change it!" I met his gaze and said it as sincerely as I could. He deserved sincerity. "They can change it if they want to, or they can leave it the way it is. I'm not going to wait."

He nodded and searched my eyes. A thoughtful, sincere gaze probed by character. In a moment he spoke.

"Well, I just want you to know that we need you here, and I hope you're really thinking clearly. Your future depends on making the right choices. You haven't passed the point of no return, but your recent behavior has upset some powerful people." He watched for a reaction, but seeing nothing encouraging, thanked me for coming. "Have a good day, and remember that you can come talk to me any time you want."

While most of the other Polymath workers found my behavior a good opportunity for ridicule, Jurgen Gaertner was different. He was an engineer, and we had recently struck up a friendship that was more like a resonance of personality. He was seven years older than I, and married. Jurgen and his wife lived in the town of Staaken, also inside the frontier area. After visiting him on several occasions, I found that we had a great many interests in common. As our friendship developed, he expressed an understanding of my frustration with our life in East Germany.

"It's as though we're criminals," he said. "We've worked hard, we've succeeded in education, yet they lock us up like animals."

There was nothing I could add to that except to tell him how I had been trying to find a way to leave legally.

"Maybe I'll apply too," he said.

"No," I said, "that would be a disaster, particularly since we work together. They'd accuse us of conspiracy. They'd make it stick too!" I looked intently at him. "It would be prison at Rudersdorf. There are so many laws nowadays that they can find one that we've broken any time they want. All they need is the excuse to look closely."

Jurgen fell silent and dropped his gaze to the floor.

"You must realize that they'll never let you go."

A few days later the police came to my house.

"You have been in Staaken, have you not?" It was not a question.

"Visiting my friend."

"In the frontier area, Herr Kaaz?" That was not a question either. They obviously knew everywhere I went, everyone I saw.

"I have a pass for the frontier," I said.

"Ah, but that is only valid in Falkensee and you know it."

"Where does it say that?" I could see him scrutinizing my face. It must have been starting to turn red. Every time I got excited or mad, it was like a beacon light. He was enjoying it, that much I could see.

"You've broken the law. Is there anything you wish to say about it?"

"Yes, what kind of country is this where I can't even visit my friends? Are we in some kind of jail?" My insides were boiling and I saw a vision of the rest of my life. It would be a never-ending sequence of move, countermove, move, countermove, then stalemate. This was just the beginning too. They were slowly tightening around my life like an insidious snake. My soul was clotting, coagulating like milk left in the sun.

He made a few notes on a pad and excused himself with a smirk and the inevitable 'Good afternoon to you.'

A week later, the letter came from the police headquarters in Nauen. "You have broken the law by entering the frontier area in Staaken without proper authorization." They even quoted the number and paragraph so I could look it up if I wanted to. "You will pay the fine noted below."

My visit to Jurgen cost me 80 marks; they made him pay 50 marks for letting me enter his house.

Not long after that, Jurgen and I decided to drive to Berlin for something to do. I had traded cars a few months earlier, and my newer green Lada hummed smoothly. For a little while, I felt free. The wipers cycled endlessly back and forth across my windshield, pushing the rain into little ridges that were instantly stripped away by the air pressure. Other drops took their place instantly. If I were gone, no, when I was gone, another drop would instantly take my place. I'd either be swept away into oblivion, or find my way out across the unforgiving landscape that offered no shelter to my soul.

In Berlin we strolled the streets, window shopped the stores, and ate coffee and cake. The rain came and went and the city was slick with water.

I looked upward to the sky, and sang somewhat off-key. "Singing in the rain, I'm singing in the rain. ..."

Another voice joined in.

"What a glorious feeling, I'm happy again. ..." It was behind me and much more melodious.

The small group said hello.

"You speak English?" The young man's eyes were alive with delight.

"Sure."

"I'm Kyle Peterson, and this is Gloria Torbati and Christine Maugans."

"American?" I asked.

"Of course." They laughed and poked each other as though their nationality was some kind of little secret. They were so alive!

"We're students at American University in Washington, D.C., on exchange to Brussels."

What a stroke of luck. Americans! Young Americans right in the storefront window, the showcase of the East German Republic.

Chicago, Atlanta, Fort Worth. Their home towns were names I had read before. I knew where they were from maps.

Jurgen and I offered to show them the city and they instantly agreed. Into my customized green Lada with its rear spoiler and black-louvered rear-window sun shades.

172

One of a kind in East Germany. As common as field mice in the West. The day was cold and damp, and people on the street bundled about in their coats. The Americans rolled all the windows down and stuck their elbows out on the window ledges. They gawked at every park, building and monument in the city, sucking up our public culture like so many sponges.

"So," Kyle said, "your city is very clean and orderly. I really feel safe here."

"There's not much serious crime," I said.

"Our country isn't this safe," he said. His tone was odd. What was he getting at? "Maybe we can take some lessons from you."

"Not too many, I hope."

"You don't like it here?"

I studied him for a moment. Did he really mean what he implied, or was it a word game? Jurgen talked with the girls. Kyle and I began the debate.

"There is order here. People know what to do. Their lives all seem to fit into the larger picture of things. It all seems very organized," he said.

"We live our lives the way we must," I said. "Can you imagine having to get official permission to have your friend visit just because you live close to the border? Then even if you apply, you know that they're not going to grant such a simple thing?"

"There must be some reason."

"I'll tell you the reason." Emotions crowded behind my lips, demanding a voice. "They rule us through fear. The government chokes the personality out of its people, and then it fears their reaction. They can never let us be free because they'll be out of a job in a minute."

"I don't see any slums. No drunks on the corners."

"True, but come away from your hotel and see the everyday people. The average man and his family live now like yours did fifty years ago." My face had turned red and I could tell that he had noticed.

"Can you tell my why that is? Everyone is taken care of. I don't see the very rich taking from the very poor." His tone was somewhat less confident.

"Wait ten years for permission to buy a car. Wait ten years to rent yourself an apartment. You'll never own anything more than a stereo, car, and the clothes on your back. Kyle, the state owns everything and everyone! We're just so much dirt under their feet." I locked eyes with him. "They own us like so many cattle. The people are the servants here, not the masters."

"You aren't telling the same story that the other kids told us yesterday," he said. "That youth group sounded pretty content."

"They were probably members of Free German Youth. It's a Communist youth organization. What did you expect them to say? I used to belong to it myself. They'd have been in big trouble if they had said anything critical in public."

"Aren't you stretching things?" His tone had softened. It was the voice of a man who had lost an argument and was trying to find a way to back down gracefully.

"I'm speaking from my own experience, Kyle. I've applied to leave the country, to emigrate to America."

The effect of my statement was immediate. All other conversation ceased.

They wanted details, so I told them of the letters, the call to the embassy, the visit, and the arrest. Without rehearsing my complete life's history, I told them of life without hope in the iron cage. Their faces were solemn, and mostly they were silent. A question came here and there, to clarify this or that detail, but mostly there was only respectful silence.

United States Armed Forces Network radio came in clearly, and I turned the radio up. The theme from "Dallas" blasted our ears.

"How would you like a copy of the New York Times?" Kyle shouted over the barrage of noise.

"That would be great. I'd like to compare a Western paper to the junk we have to read in Neues Deutschland." Another morsel of the outside world would soon be mine!

We parked the car out of sight of the main entrance and walked into the Metropol Hotel. A neatly lettered sign near the entrance reminded the reader that the hotel was restricted to foreign visitors. Kyle approached the desk.

"New York Times, please."

The clerk studied us through narrowed eyes. Jurgen and I kept quiet while the girls chattered at us as though we were carrying on an English conversation. They were dressed like Americans, and we like Europeans, and it was still hard for the clerk to be sure who was who.

"Are you registered at the hotel?" asked the clerk.

"My father will be checking in tonight," Kyle said.

"I'm sorry. You have to be registered to get a paper." He was staring intently, so he could make an accurate report later. Kyle's repeated requests brought a blank expression and shrugging shoulders. The official mask had slipped into place, and nothing could penetrate it.

Kyle made deprecatory comments about the man and the hotel management, but the mask never wavered. The clerk's eyes took it all in, while the facial muscles never reacted at all.

On the girls' suggestion, we passed the doorway without challenge and bounded lightly upstairs to the restaurant. Prices were high and Western currency required. American paper preferred. I ordered a Coke. At $2.50 it wasn't cheap, but it tasted wonderful. It was like the ones that Vivien had given me years ago, the ones I would save for weeks before sharing with Uwe. It was another tiny reminder of the other possibilities of life.

I sat casually in the restaurant, but felt my intestines churn with anger. The whole thing was inside out. I was an East German citizen in my own country's capital city, but inside this hotel I was lower than the janitor. On my own, with my identity known, I couldn't even buy a foreign newspaper. I resented the faces around me, the ones from West Germany, from France, from all the other places, speaking all the other languages. They could enjoy my land in a way that was forever forbidden to me. What kind of men, I wondered, could do such a thing? Who could construct a society that denied the best to its own sons, while giving strangers an open invitation so long as they brought the right lucre?

It was time to go. Each of us prepared to return to our own world. Jurgen and I had been deeply touched by the chance meeting with these young people.

The girls were teary eyed. Kyle was earnest.

"Maybe you can work things out somehow," he said. "Don't give up. We'll write to you. Please write back!"

Christine said, "I work for a Congressman. Maybe I can help somehow."

We all hugged and wiped the tears away.

Then they were walking away down the street. Gone.

Back in the car, Jurgen and I hardly spoke for a half-hour.

"They're the same," I said.

"The same as what?"

"The same as I had imagined. The man in the embassy showed that he cared even though he was trying to be official." I sighed heavily at the loss. "They're warm and kind people," I said. "Sure, there are some who are stupid and greedy, but there must be many good ones. Jurgen, what do you suppose our people would be like if they were free?" Jurgen didn't answer, but turned his face to look out the side window.

The Lada's motor churned on, and the tires made their hissing buzz. East Berlin disappeared in the rear-view mirror and familiar reality grew ahead of us. Its massive stultifying presence filled our minds as we returned home.

Home? This was hardly my home anymore. Perhaps my heart had already left, and all that remained was getting the rest of me out.

"You have to be careful," I said to Jurgen as we parted company that evening. "You have to be quiet about how you feel until you see how things go for me. No point in both of us being put into prison."

"Yes," he said, looking toward his house where Gabi, his wife, waved a greeting from the steps. "There is more to consider in all of this than just my feelings."

Mowes the policeman had come to my house while I was away. He had risen in rank since that day some eight years ago when he came to investigate my transgression with the homemade arrow and note. Now he was the highest-ranking police officer in our district. A personal visit from him was very unusual, because he was no longer involved in day-to-day enforcement. Herr Mowes was now a minor administrator in a land ruled by administrators. He had a green Wartburg now, instead of the ridiculously small scooter that carried him to my house so long ago. On this visit, finding that I wasn't home, he told Mother to have me report to his office on Saturday morning and left an official police postcard with the date, time, and place noted. It wasn't a social call, and I could see Mom's fear rising up to choke her. Mowes wasn't exactly a family friend.

"Did you do something, Carsten? Are you in some more trouble?"

My voice was a bitter whip cutting the air with practiced sarcasm.

"Living here is always trouble, Mom, but no, I haven't done anything else. I just made a legal application to leave, and visited the American Embassy. Mowes probably just wants to harass me."

She stood silently in the kitchen as I left.

There was nothing to be gained by driving my customized Lada, so I rode my old bike. Whatever Herr Mowes wanted of me, it wouldn't help his dogmatic sensibilities to see a 19-year-old appear in a better car than he could ever afford. The humble profile would be most prudent today.

His office was on the first floor of an old house on Schoenwalder Strasse, not too far from the cemetery. It had no cells and was an administrative office, not a jail. The beige carpet was cheap, worn to the point where the thin jute backing showed through. Paper. A plague of paper covered with typed or scribbled notes, reports; a wrinkled, dog-eared impending avalanche of paper. There was paper everywhere. On the beige filing cabinets. On the large metal desk. Some in neat piles. Some just lying in stacks. The curtains had well-maintained cobwebs here and there. The room was like an old car that had just been parked for the last time. It was worn out, not abused or torn up, but ready to expire from fatigue. It smelled like the air in the basement when you come back from a long vacation, or the lifeless rubber stench from inside an automobile tire. Tinged with the odor of coffee brewed too strong, it was utterly dead. Erich Honecker looked sternly down from his dust-edged frame, and beneath him sat Mowes the note-maker, legitimized in his little sphere by the man in the dirty frame.

"Have some coffee, Herr Kaaz." My father might have used the same tone of voice. Friendly. No tension. Something important was up. He waved me to sit in a wooden chair in front of the desk. Always on the fat side, his form had rounded and filled out over the years, more than I would have guessed. He didn't convey an impression of laziness, but one of inexorable purpose, like a hungry snail eating its way across a broad leaf.

He studied a pencil while twirling it in his fingers.

"Can you see the problem you're causing?" It was not a question really. He continued in the same matter-of-fact voice. No tension. Still no anger. "Your parents and Fraulein Taschner are really suffering because of the way you are behaving."

So that was it. More questions that were really statements. More showing the badge. More intimidation. Why had he brought up Vivien's name? Surely he knew that these days we hardly saw each other at all.

"Let's forget about all the trouble you've been involved in. Wouldn't you like that?"

I had heard the standard threats before, but this was somehow different. He was setting the stage for something. Maybe a little counterpoint would help.

"My closest friends can't even visit me. I just don't want to live this way."

His manner never wavered as he handed me the paper. I could see that it was completely covered on the front and about one-fourth of the back with typewritten words. He resumed the lecture.

"This trouble affects many people. Your parents cannot continue to live in the frontier area with such problems in their household." He sighed heavily. So relaxed. "Fraulein Taschner is sure to be influenced by your behavior, too. She's receiving a special education and has a bright future. We can't allow you to corrupt her. ... Her family might have to move to another area. ... She might not be able to study anymore. ..."

The voice faded away as I went into shock. I had heard with my ears and now my eyes saw. Hardly believing, I read the typewritten words.

"I, Carsten Kaaz, have changed my mind about leaving the country and withdraw my application to leave. After discussion with family and friends, I realize that I have made a mistake. ... There will be no further attempts by me to have contact with officials of the American Government. ... I no longer have the desire to leave. ..."

"What is this?" I stood abruptly and threw the paper onto the desk.

He didn't flinch. All the time that we were talking, he held the rope in his hands. It had been ever so gently placed around my neck, and now there was no way to get it off. I snatched up the papers again and finished reading the statement. On page two there was a blank where I was supposed to sign.

I looked directly into his eyes. Hazel. No blinking, just a penetrating, interested stare. Like the snake that sways before the bird. Interested in the prey.

"You can't make me sign this!"

"Relax, sit down." His face was calm, no creviced features, smooth and shiny like the lake on a windless day. "Like I said, you've already made too much trouble for your parents. We might have to move them, and you know how bad the housing shortage is. There's no telling where they'd end up." He shrugged. "And we can't risk Vivien turning on us. After all, the state has invested a lot in her education."

He slowly took the paper from my hand, then carefully matched it with carbons and two other copies. His hand held them out. Mowes said nothing, but watched me through his interested hazel eyes.

The exit had been blocked by an immovable object, and I had been forced to remain among the dead. Another application or contact with the Americans would give the police legitimate grounds for imprisonment. The innuendoes, the softly spoken threats against my family and Vivien were not empty words. They had done it before, retaliated against family and friends of troublemakers. This was no threat of torture or imprisonment, but something in a way much worse. It was the assured protracted destruction of the lives of those whom I loved.

What would my parents' lives be like if they were forced from their home into one of the gray four-story mausoleums they called apartments? What kind of hatred would I earn if Vivien's family were forced to leave their home, or if her schooling were interrupted? No, it wasn't an idle threat at all. The government would without compunction reach out and crush everyone I loved if I didn't comply.

I hesitated for just a moment, then signed the papers with a scrawl. The carbon paper had slipped sideways. How odd that something so insignificant should make an impression.

I threw the paper down upon the desk, and the black ballpoint pen made a harsh slap on the debris. The interested hazel eyes didn't even blink. The green-suited bureaucrat was only a hired messenger. The real masters had no face, no name, were nowhere to be seen so they could be cursed in person. The master was the strangling fog, the inexorable grayness that crept ever more thickly around my flickering tiny life.

I took a step toward the door, then turned slowly. Interested eyes met mine.

"The last word hasn't been spoken yet," I said.

He shrugged an official shrug, a practiced twitch of the shoulders that meant it was a trivial matter, and that he didn't care. My desire for life was of no consequence to him, nor to the faceless thing for whom he was authorized to speak. I tried to slam the door on the way out, but there was a piston closer, and it only sighed politely back into correct position.

The bloodless execution had taken about one-half hour.

I saw Uwe on the way home. He too had been summoned for a conference.

"What did he want?" he asked.

I explained the conversation and told him about the letter.

His desperate eyes silently asked another question.

"I signed it," I said.

His eyes widened.

"What? I don't believe you? After all we've done, you signed it? Was all this for nothing?"

Hurt, angry and guilty all at once, I snapped back, "Listen Uwe, your family relations are different from mine. Your father turns off the heat to your room in the winter. He slaps you around and your mother tells you that it's your problem, that she has others of her own. Mine love me, and they've sacrificed a lot. I couldn't allow my parents' lives to be destroyed! He even threatened Vivien!" My heart felt like lead, as though it would sink through my stomach. "Try to understand. We're nearly split up now, but I can't be the cause of her destruction." Uwe didn't understand at all. I had been his friend, his hero, his leader, but I had been broken by an overweight police officer on Saturday morning who held no weapons except pen and paper.

Uwe mumbled something and pedaled away to his appointment. His visit with Herr Mowes was a very short one. He simply looked at the letter and signed. I didn't wait so he went home alone.

I was broken. The incident replayed over and over in my mind until I thought I'd go insane. Such failure! I had retreated at the moment of truth, abandoning our dream. Sitting around the house was like being imprisoned, so I stalked out the front door and jumped in the car.

Gravel popped and crunched beneath the Lada's wheels as I pulled out onto the dusty street. Acceleration. Radio on. Curses on my tongue, in my mind, down to the depths of my heart, curses. Accelerate again, 90, 100, 110 kilometers per hour. Radio on with the music taunting me, coming from a place where I could never go. Coming from the place where people lived to the place where I was dying. I had to get it out somehow or it would devour me. Perhaps Jurgen was home. I turned the green Lada toward his house knowing that he would understand.

The story of that morning poured out like blood from a severed arm.

"I feel like my life is over," I told him.

Quietly listening, Gabi pressed her lips together and shook her head sorrowfully. Jurgen said things, now forgotten, but things that helped me calm down and get back in control. We watched TV and talked through the afternoon until after midnight, when Gabi offered me the couch so I wouldn't have to drive home in the middle of the night. Knowing all the risks,

181

they never once mentioned my coming unbidden into the frontier area nor the trouble it might cause them.

In the days that followed, I spoke to Uwe several times, but a barrier of pain separated us. At that point, he didn't have much to say. Whether it was out of depression or anger was impossible to tell.

Maybe I would see things more clearly if I took a holiday. Jurgen had some ideas.

"The Baltic Sea?"

"Yes," said Jurgen. "Let's go to the Baltic for the day. We can catch the ferry to Ruegen Island. It's a popular spot."

Kartoffel salad, schnitzel, and coffee in a thermos. The Lada's tires rumbled over the road. Four hours later, we were wading in the cold waters. I wore my cowboy hat. Just moving around provided a much-needed distraction so I wouldn't indulge in too much self-pity.

A few days later, Jurgen and I went to Berlin to the used car market. Nothing much was there, and I wasn't in the buying mood anyway. On the way back, I stopped in Rangsdorf to introduce Jurgen to Lutz. These two best friends ought to know each other.

"Take care of him," Lutz called to Jurgen as we were leaving. "He needs a big brother sometimes."

After the diversion, I still felt like a condemned man. Vivien and I still saw each other occasionally, but that was only because I couldn't summon the courage to just say goodbye. I felt like both a fool and a coward, because I couldn't make a formal end of things. When we were together, her touch was remote, like a tap on the shoulder from a stranger asking for directions on the street. It could have been the same touch she used for anyone at the beauty shop or the meat market. Our deepening estrangement remained unspoken by us both, and the acute pain I had felt for so long subsided to a gnawing cramp that never quite went away.

On the brighter side, Uwe's depression over Mowes victory began to heal, and we resumed our evening walks. At about nine o'clock that evening, we ended up at the place on Calvin Strasse where the red and white signs marked the beginning of the frontier area.

"I'm sorry about how I've acted," he said. "I just saw everything disappear when you signed that paper. Then there was nothing but mere survival here, without hope for freedom. I just couldn't cope with the feelings."

"It's all right."

I was just now able to look myself in the mirror every morning, because of my own guilt. "I just didn't know what else to do. He had me and he knew it."

"We were both trapped. I probably would have signed if I had been the first one in his door." He stared at me intensely. "What now?"

"That's what we have to consider. Let's get together like always. A long walk every other day will help us sort it all out. They might not be too sure that I've given up wanting to leave, especially after my last words to Mowes. It's just too risky for you at my house anymore. You've been warned and fined so many times for entering the frontier area that if you're caught again, they'll throw you in jail!"

He nodded.

"It makes sense. They need to just forget about us."

"Yes!" My insides animated with sudden energy. "Their guard needs to drop so we can find some kind of opening. Then we can make our move! You can't visit here at home with me, but we can still take walks at night. We know the neighborhood and all the hiding places. I don't think that they could possibly overhear, so our conversations will be secure."

Once again, we began to stroll the dirt paths through the pine thicket, among the trees that had finally grown up like all the children in the neighborhood. We were careful to stay only on the edge of the frontier area and legal, in case someone might still be watching. We were not disappointed.

"There's Koch," Uwe said.

"In his yard pretending to water flowers."

"What time is it?"

"Five minutes to midnight," I said.

Koch slowly coiled the garden hose and sat down on his steps just below our line of sight. Devoted as a dog, he would sit for hours hoping to get a look at something incriminating. We laughed and congratulated ourselves. The regular Stasi agents had been withdrawn and our surveillance assignment passed to the local spitzels, the informers. That was a sign that we had passed to a lower level of priority.

"We'll bore them to death," Uwe said. "They'll get so tired of seeing us that they'll begin to wish we were gone."

"Yes, we'll wear them down." I enjoyed the laugh, too. The forbidden thought had come and gone many times in my mind, and I felt sure in Uwe's too, but now it was time to ask the question directly. "Uwe, what would you say to trying to figure out a way to escape, you know, over the Wall somehow?"

He looked at me for a long moment, then nodded almost imperceptibly.

"A lot of people have died in the wire, but some of their plans were really hare-brained. Maybe we could think of something." He paused again, then spoke with great emotion. "I'm with you! Let's do it!"

From that time on, our goal was established. We walked, and we talked. Same paths, same pauses to lean on the same sign-posts. We discussed and dissected all possibilities one at a time. We leaned on the frontier warning placard for hours at a time talking about how we could get out. How they must have yawned, watching our deliberations. Now and then as we strolled, a face would flash pasty white as someone peered through bushes. Then there was Herr Mohn who took up the habit of sitting out late on his front porch. We laughed at his clumsy attempts, but now it didn't matter who was watching. We'd put them all to sleep by doing exactly the same things again and again and again.

Unfortunately, my work place was not so uneventful.

"Well Carsten," the janitor said. "Do you still want to go?" His face was streaked with dirt, but it was adorned by his best sly smile. "You know, to America? ..."

I stared at him without expression. He was a sort of mental tick, one who has almost nothing in his own existence except what it is able to take from the lives of others. I turned away.

"It's history. I don't want to discuss it."

His muffled laughter reached my ears, and I wanted to crush his ignorant face.

Everyone at Polymath knew of my abortive attempt to emigrate and being the object of continuing amusement was not exactly a pleasant prospect. The personal irritation was bad enough, but more importantly, I wanted the recollection of my adventures to fade in everyone's mind. Something had to be done. Perhaps finding another job would be best.

It was Saturday morning, and I was knocking on a neighbor's door.

"Herr Dittschlag, my name is Carsten Kaaz. I live up the road on Zwingli Strasse."

He rubbed his eyes. Sleeping late? By 9:00 a.m., everyone ought to be up. I was doing him a favor. A man of his physical stature probably needed more energy just to keep moving about every day. Almost two meters tall, 110 kilos. I had seen him in the convenience store many times over the years. Apparently soft-spoken and kind, his smile came from the inside. His yet-unshaven face showed a beard gray like the few remaining hairs on his head.

"Good morning," I said, mentally noting that he ought to lose weight. Perhaps 60. Ready to retire? "I'm now employed at Polymath and am looking for a position with another company. Do you know anyone who is looking for a man with good electronics training? I can fix any analog control device around!"

Dittschlag rubbed his eyes again trying to focus on my face. He really seemed to be thinking about it.

"Send me information. Your schooling, experience, you know." He was the director of maintenance at Plastikwerke, a state-owned company that made a variety of plastic and fiberglass products. He supervised the other supervisors. We parted with a friendly farewell and I walked home. If this worked out, I'd be able to get a fresh start and have a lot less attention from nosy peers.

Two days later, mother came home with good news.

"I saw Herr Dittschlag at the Konsum today. He said for you to come for an interview on Monday."

Genuinely excited, I made sure my shirt was freshly ironed, and arose early for the appointment.

Dittschlag and his assistant Krueger ran the factory-maintenance programs. They were as alike as nice and nasty. There couldn't have been many men who shared less in common. For every kind word and act of encouragement from Dittschlag, there was a paragraph of sarcasm and belittlement from Krueger. The actual interviews were little more than a formality. They asked about my grades and extent of technical education, but in the land where employees were expected to make career choices for life, not a word was spoken about my reasons for changing jobs. Phone calls had been made. Information had been passed. The management at Plastikwerke knew who I was because the Stasi had told them. The company had been told to give me the opportunity in the hope that it would encourage compliant behavior. They were slipping me a tranquilizer, a distraction, something to occupy my restless mind until I slipped into the placid rhythm of acceptance and my rebellion died.

The Stasi placement service worked just fine, and I was hired after a cursory interview.

Krueger assigned me an office in the back part of the plant, but since I was the only numerical-control expert in the factory, he could only supervise my attendance. He had no idea what I was doing with the various machines, or why.

"What about the control circuit repairs for the mixers?" Krueger asked. "What are you doing about it?"

"It failed only this morning, but we have no spare parts. We can put it back in service within an hour when the parts are here." I paused and rubbed my chin. "Of course if I drove to Berlin, I could pick them up and be back by late tonight."

"Impossible," Krueger shook his head and sneered. "You already know that we have no money in our budget plan for automobile travel. You'll have to take the train if you go at all."

"What's the difference? I can drive to Berlin just as cheap as I can take a train."

"The difference is that if you take your car it will be at your own expense. Don't bother trying to argue about it either."

"I'll take the train then."

"If you don't bring back a receipt, that trip will be on your own money, too."

Later that day, I picked Uwe up and we headed for East Berlin.

"How are you going to work this out?" he asked. "You said they wouldn't pay for car travel."

"If I do it their way, it will be nearly two days before the machines can go back into operation. I'll get a receipt at the train station when we get back. I just want to get enough to pay for the gasoline."

The car vibrated to the sounds of the Armed Forces Network's Western rock, and the road unrolled before us. For another little while, we felt free.

"Krueger's a real pain," I said. "He doesn't know anything about my work, but he's always trying to tell me how to do it. He's always looking for something to criticize." Krueger was a tightly wound spring, quivering impotently with impatience and indecision.

Uwe laughed easily.

"You take it all too seriously. If you don't ease up, you'll get sick."

"Oh, I have that worked out already. If he wants to talk to me, I listen, but when he starts to yell and curse, I just walk away. If he fires me, the machines will go down, and they'll fall behind in their quota. It's like everywhere else; nobody takes pride in their work because they're working for the state." I slapped one hand on the dashboard. "We're supposed to be the state, my friend, and we're working for ourselves, right?" Then I spat out the words, "This is all a stupid joke!"

The "parts maneuver" worked well, and I had the opportunity to make an evening run to East Berlin at least once a month. My hopes for satisfaction at work were satisfied a little more with each success at circumventing the system. It was all beginning to seem like one magnificent game.

Our plan for distracting the watchers also seemed to be working. January through May we discussed, planned and evaluated escape contingencies with tireless energy. By then, we noted only occasional nocturnal observers near the dusty paths of our neighborhood. Yawns had replaced inquisitive stares, and then an important bit of good luck came our way. Herr Schirmer, the Grenztruppe officer, remodeled his house. He hired several of the local young men in order to save money.

I found a way to help on his roof several times. This was particularly important because Schirmer's house was ten meters from the inner Berlin Wall.

Between strokes of the hammer, I looked up and down the security zone as far as possible. There were no dogs tethered between the towers. The notch-shaped anti-vehicle ditch was a brown slash mark, three meters inside and parallel to the inner barrier. The rumors were true. Even a tank couldn't cross that area; if it somehow managed to find a way through the concrete and steel reinforcements, it would be unable to climb out of the ditch, which must have been nearly three meters deep.

A series of carefully masked actions allowed me to stay on the roof for a long time, and pretending to evaluate my work drew the time out further. Then there were the wires. From the roof, it was so hard to tell. ...

"Hey, what are you doing up there?" Schirmer stood in the backyard, hands on his hips looking up at me. Had he seen me studying the Wall? "I'm not paying you to daydream. Come on down here and help clean up this scrap wood."

According to the government, the Wall was built to protect us. Protect. Only an idiot could believe that. The wire, the ditch, the broken glass embedded on top of the Wall all faced one way, inward toward us. I had heard a lot of talk, too. Electrified wire? Not true. However, the top strands were connected to a system that set off alarms at the slightest touch. Land mines? Not true. The earthen surface of the inter-wall area was clean and neatly raked. Men and guard dogs traversed there, and if there were really mines, no one would be taking that stroll.

I drove another nail and leaned back pretending to check the board. Making a little noise would give me a few moments more. Another nail. Some banging on the roof itself as though working.

"Kaaz! What are you doing?"

"Just finishing the wood on the edge of the roof. I want to get it on straight."

"Don't fool around. Do it right."

I could see the narrow asphalt road where the vehicle patrols drove between the inner and outer barriers. Perhaps we could time the patrols somehow. Automatic machine guns? Not any more. In the beginning when the first wall was constructed, there had been machine guns connected to trip wires, but the Western governments had put up such a commotion about it that sometime later the emplacements were removed. The midday sun gleamed off alarm wires ankle-high off the ground. Wires both on the Wall and on the ground in-between. Lots of opportunity for a frightened escapee to make a mistake.

"Well?" It was Schirmer again.

I drove another nail and leaned back to inspect.

"Looks good from here."

Schirmer grumbled under his breath and stalked away barking orders to the other helpers.

That night, Uwe and I walked as usual.

"We have to know more. I could see a lot, but there may be other things that I missed."

"Agreed," Uwe said. "I know someone who might be able to give us the information if I can pay him enough."

"Don't tell me his name," I said. "It will be easier to avoid talking about that if we're captured."

He turned suddenly at that.

"They aren't going to catch us, are they?"

Then seeing my apparent confidence, he relaxed.

"I'll get to work on it. How much have you got to contribute?"

We decided to set up an escape budget and began saving for it like a vacation. Five hundred marks should be enough. After Uwe got the information, he and I would again compare notes to be sure things were correctly understood.

A few days later, I was sitting on my front porch drinking coffee. Frau Kosa shuffled up to the gate and rang the bell.

"Good evening, Carsten. You are looking tired. Have you been getting enough sleep?"

The years had beaten upon her terribly, and those eyes that now sparkled with grandmotherly interest had seen much hardship and pain. But even two world wars and the death of her husband had not quite worn Frau Kosa out. I assured her that sleep was not a problem.

"My television is not working," she said. "Can you come look at it?"

"Sure."

"I will pay you of course."

"No way! You gave me enough candy when I was little to cover a thousand repairs!"

"So the young man remembers his childhood." She laughed a sweet, kind laugh and shuffled back into the street. "Don't be too long. I have no one but the TV to keep me company most of the time. There are no more little ones around here to spoil." She laughed again and shuffled away.

Since the television antenna ran through her attic and the mast was mounted on the roof, I decided that it was necessary to climb out onto the roof for a closer inspection.

Frau Kosa's house was only five meters from the inner wall, and the view was perfect.

In the attic was an unexpected treasure. Her husband had saved the periscope from a German tank, and she had left it in an open box balanced on the ceiling joists in the attic. With the old device, I could observe the inter-wall area through an upper window without fear of being seen from the street or one of the guard towers.

This was even better than Schirmer's roof, and I knew that an elderly lady wouldn't worry if repairs took a long time. There were the ground-level alarm wires. No wonder there were no dogs in this section of the Wall. The wires were different heights and spaced one meter apart. It would be hard to cross them at a run without contact, even if their position was known. Initial surprise would be no good if an automatic alarm was triggered. Our keepers were full of surprises.

Twenty minutes later I came down.

"I think it will be all right now, but I need to come back in a few days to check it."

She murmured thanks and took my hands in hers. How cool her fingers were against my sweating palms, how fragile her skin. Almost transparent.

"You were always so nice. Have some candy." She offered a small piece wrapped in cellophane.

It had never tasted so sweet.

Two days later, Uwe went with me for the follow-up visit.

She squinted at him. "Uwe George?"

"Yes, Frau Kosa. Do you remember me?"

"Oh, how you have grown. How is your mother?"

After a few moments of polite conversation, Uwe and I climbed into the attic. "Hold this thing and look through it like this."

The attic air was heavy and hot, but neither of us cared as the sweat silently soaked our shirts in ever widening V's. After fifteen minutes, we had memorized the details and descended.

"You boys have to have another piece of candy before you go. I gave you one already didn't I?" She clucked over us for a few minutes and then we left.

We re-examined the possibilities for escape, one scenario at a time. We had to be careful and thorough.

"All right," I said. "Let's start with the most improbable ideas first. How about blowing a hole in the Wall and running across?"

"Getting explosives is impossible unless you know some trick. I've heard that you can make chemical fertilizer blow up, but I don't know how."

We laughed. The only fertilizer we had ever seen came from the rear end of animals or our own septic tanks. We had heard that a few years earlier, two East German soldiers had stolen a Soviet tank and tried to crash it through the Wall but failed because the concrete was so heavily reinforced. If a tank couldn't penetrate, we certainly could not hope to force our way through.

Balloons? They had been tried. Some arrangements had worked.

"Hot air requires bottled gas and burners. I have no idea where we'd even begin to look. What about helium? How many would we need?" Uwe asked. "Can you work out the math?"

I did work it out the next day, and the answer was unbelievable. I performed the calculations again to be sure. "About 1,000 each," I told him.

"You can't be serious."

"The only balloons we can get are the small ones like they sell at the Volksfest. Each one has to lift its own weight and have some buoyancy left for the payload. We'd have to inflate at least a thousand for each of us and contain them inside some kind of net."

"I can see them at the store in Falkensee. May I please have 2,000 party balloons so we can sail over the Wall?" Uwe acted the impossible scenario out. It would have been really funny if the reason had been different.

"I could get a Moskvich sedan with plenty of ground clearance. Perhaps we could jump the Wall," I said.

"No problem for me to build a wooden ramp, but putting it in place would be risky," Uwe said.

"Let's see what the pencil and paper have to say about it." I made the estimates and worked the formulas. Once, twice, three times. Each time I finished one set of calculations I put it away and redid everything from scratch to recheck it. The next day the answer was ready.

"No way," I said.

Uwe nodded, but his eyes asked why not.

"A Moskvich could be tuned up to run that fast just once, but we'd have to go 150 k.p.h. to clear the second wall."

Uwe laughed.

"If we could get someone on the West side to film it, we'd be millionaires."

"Dead ones, I think. The car would be totally destroyed by the impact on the other side, and that's only if the ramp didn't collapse as the car hit it, and provided we got onto the ramp just right without having a wheel slip off. Even if everything went perfectly, the car would still be demolished, and we'd be dog food." I carefully and completely burned my notes, taking care to stir the ashes to a fine powder.

What if we used a ladder? A very long one.

"A fire truck?"

"Yes," I said. "The volunteer fire department has one with an extension ladder. Maybe it's long enough to reach over to the second wall. We could steal it and drive up to the first wall, then go across on the ladder."

Uwe looked skeptical.

"Let's check it out," I said.

That night about 10:00 p.m., I parked my car on a side street and slipped quietly down Schoenwalder Strasse to the squat building where our town's fire-fighting equipment slumbered. I peered intently through cupped hands to shut out the reflections on the station window. It sat patiently in the darkened garage, a red and silver beast that rolled on impossibly large wheels. As a small child, I had seen it in parades and wondered where they got those enormous tires. There were the ladders, neatly interlocking like folded grasshopper wings. Observations on Frau Kosa's roof showed that the inter-wall area was at least thirty meters wide.

"Impossible," I told Uwe the next day. "Even if we could get the truck through town without being spotted by the police, we'd still have to tie the steering wheel down and crawl out on the ladder while the truck was moving."

"Sounds like a good way to get killed. I'd prefer something a little less dangerous."

"What about sliding across on a rope or maybe a wire from Kosa's tree to the second wall, then slipping over it."

Using the same method as the car idea, I made three sets of calculations. The verdict came with our usual nightly walk and discussion.

"We'd have to shoot a small-diameter nylon rope over using a bow and arrow with some type of hook that would catch on the other side. The rope would sag when we put weight on it and would therefore be below the top edge of the outer wall. We'd have to have some kind of device with wheels that would ride on the rope that we could hang onto."

"There are lots of opportunities for something to go wrong."

"Yes, then there's the speed."

Uwe's lively eyebrows arched again in the request for

clarification.

"I figure that with the angle from her tree to the top of the second wall, we'd probably reach 20 k.p.h."

Uwe made a clicking sound with his mouth and moved his hands to signify something breaking. The speed of our passage would give the guards little time to shoot, but our legs might be broken by the impact with the outer wall. Not too promising.

The conversation died and Uwe's impassive face remained imprinted in my mind for the rest of the day. Things were not looking very good. In order to escape, we had to do something different, something unexpected, or else we'd end up hanging in the wire full of holes, or thrown into Burg Prison with the rest of the political offenders. I had heard stories about what happened inside the massive walls of Burg. Unless the West German government ransomed us from prison as they had with others, it would be an unrelenting hell for as long as we had to stay. Rumor was that the government kept special violent prisoners in Burg who would make things especially bad for political activists and social troublemakers. Beatings, mental terror, rape, and who knew what else were supposedly available as "unofficial" punishment for those who were on the "list." Bullets would be better.

The escape possessed my whole mind. I thought of it while at work, driving in my car, going to the bathroom. I even dreamed escapes.

In my dreams there were many voices calling as we dragged our slow feet through deep mud. I couldn't see anyone else with me, but somehow I knew that Uwe was near. In the dreams we always got to the second wall, but I could never quite see the other side.

One evening after midnight, I was sitting on the front porch. The darkness had an edge of coolness and moisture. It had the feel of space, of liberty. If the physical sensation of freedom could be described, it would have to be equated with the caress of the night air. Incessant thinking about the Wall had made it so familiar that my fear was subsiding. It was becoming more of a problem, more of an intellectual challenge than a thing of terror and death. I had to get to know it better, to touch and feel its physical being, so I'd be able to keep everything in perspective. I walked impulsively from the yard across Zwingli Strasse and into the vacant lot next to Jerke's house. It was a good thing the Jerke family had no dogs.

Moving boldly nearer, I touched it for the first time. Smooth here. Rough there. Ripples like the folds of human skin. Ridges where the forms had been separated as the slabs were cast in a factory somewhere. Cracks. There were cracks between the joints where the concrete sections were dropped in horizontally. Uprights every three meters held slabs in their steel embrace. Light stabbed through the tiny spaces, as though the sun itself hovered just on the other side of the obstacle. I looked through, and fear surged horribly from the deepest reaches of my heart. This was the place of annihilation, a desert place where hearts without pity ruled by day and night, where the truncheon and the bullet decreed order in their awful majesty.

The putter of an approaching motorcycle echoed and reverberated between the walls. It was a mounted patrol moving slowly, about 23 k.p.h., as though on a Sunday drive. Closer. Suddenly it was almost impossible to breathe. My throat contracted involuntarily. The machine was even with me now, close enough to touch if it had not been for the Wall. In a horrible paralytic flash, I could see the soldier's face, burning into my memory as I stood on tiptoes like a child trying to get a look at a walled-off construction site. His eyes were dots of hard black set into a fleshy white countenance punctuated by angry acne.

Then the machine was gone, the exhaust echoing a diminishing frequency into the distance. My heartbeat slowed with the fading noise, and all at once I could breathe again. Directly above, hanging in their diagonally braced struts, were the insulated wall-top wires. Four strands. One barbed, three alarm. How sensitive were they really? It was said that the slightest touch was sufficient to summon all kinds of unwanted attention. If discovered going over the first wall, surrender was still an option if the escapee stopped and didn't offer resistance, but making it all the way to the second wall put things in an entirely different perspective. The border troops at each tower were totally responsible for their section of wall, and any successful escape was presumed to be the result of someone's criminal negligence. The guards were under the very real threat of prison if an escape succeeded. That was plenty of incentive for them to kill anyone who tried to go over, and that fact left no room for possible leniency by a secretly sympathetic sentinel. Who would risk prison to give some nameless stranger a break? While standing there, I discovered by accident that pressing my back against the Wall in that particular location almost completely hid me from the north tower, and only slightly exposed me to the south. If the guards weren't looking, it might be possible to move into position and maybe set up some kind of ladder. But what kind could we use to clear the wires? The overhang seemed impossible, and my heart sank again.

June arrived. White legs were everywhere as people got out their shorts, and vacation once again became the focal point of all Europe.

Maybe we could escape through Hungary. I turned the idea over and over. If we got a tourist visa from our government, it might be possible to slip across the border into Yugoslavia. Their borders were more open with the West.

During this time I also realized that it was necessary to make an emotional break with my parents. If I failed to do so, my eventual leaving would be much harder on them. Also, if I were known to be estranged at home, the authorities would be less likely to suspect that my parents had any knowledge of my illegal intentions. I used my own behavior to set the stage.

At every opportunity, I was rude and inconsiderate. I parked the car on the grass where it would be in the way. Coming and going at all hours of the day and night disrupted my family's sleep, and if anyone said anything about it, I would reply with the most cutting remark that I could find. Some of mom's friends began to look at me with disapproval when we passed on the street. The tension escalated until one day when I arrived home, Dad was waiting in the front yard.

He was not even pretending to be busy with something else, just standing there with arms folded across his chest.

"Before you go in, I have something to say to you." His eyes had a peculiar, staring look, with the lids compressed into tight folds; his forehead was deeply furrowed. "You're going to destroy yourself by your behavior, and if you don't straighten up, you'll end up in Rudersdorf with the rest of the troublemakers."

I stood in defiant silence, sullenly refusing to meet his eyes.

"But worse than all of that, you're killing your mother a little at a time. Our marriage is being torn apart by the way you are living." He paused and took a breath. Great effort was required to speak these last words. "I don't want to see you again until you've changed." Without waiting for a reply, he turned and marched inside. How I longed to tell him, but it was unthinkable. My parents were honest people, and if they knew anything of my plans they might eventually break down under hard questioning and reveal their knowledge. That would cost them both some time in jail, and no matter what, I didn't want the authorities to have any grounds for that action. Since our relationship was so strained, my mother would show it, and everyone would find out. The inevitable investigation by the prying Stasi would reveal a genuine background of problems. Dad was more private than Mom, but his closest friends would have already heard some hints here and there. That would be enough to keep them both out of serious trouble. If I was to go, it would have to be alone as far as the family was concerned. There would be no room for mistakes and no second chances.

The mind reasons and understands what is to come, but the experience is incomplete until the heart has heard also. My insides went cold at the realization that my plan was indeed working, and to have all things fit into place, I would have to follow it through and remain a callous stranger to the only people on earth whom I still really loved. I still talked to Roberto, but even there I didn't show the former level of interest and warmth. One Saturday while leaving the house, I almost tripped over him coming up the front steps.

"Hi," he said tentatively. "Where are you going?"

"Out."

His gaze averted, and I realized that I had snapped with my eyes as well as my voice.

"Maybe you could take me for a ride sometime. I remember when I was little how you'd go for bicycle ..."

"Roberto, I know you don't understand this, but you just can't hang around with me anymore. You can't go where I'm going!" Could he sense my meaning? No, all he knew was rejection, but it would just have to be this way.

"Oh." His 14-year-old face fell in an embarrassed frown.

"See you later." My feet hit the bottom step, but my heart kept going down. I felt lower than at any time in my life, and the things I was doing were like daggers in my heart. I hated myself.

The weeks passed, and this piece of the puzzle was snapped into position, lubricated by unnumbered private tears. Now all I had to do was carry the plan to its logical conclusion, an open break with the family.

As we considered the "Hungarian Option," Uwe decided that it would be a good idea to first take care of his eye problem. The operation to correct the congenital muscle imbalance came with an automatic ten-day hospital stay, and since I visited him every day, I got to know one of his attendants. She was an attractive girl named Christel, and we began to date even before Uwe's hospital stay was over. Our relationship quickly became serious, and we spent time together nearly every day. As I got to know her better, it became obvious that she was the caretaker type, a person who was at her best when helping others, and from the first she was interested in making me happy. She was a fairly good cook, and went to some trouble to have her apartment neat and orderly when I came over.

In a short time, Christel and I had grown more serious. She was obviously pleased with my attentions, and really liked to be seen in my latest car, a red Polski Fiat. Her apartment was part of the hospital complex, and convenient to town. She had a mild temperament, and was usually willing to do whatever I suggested, so I made my move.

"Since we get along so well, why don't I just move in? Think you'd have room for me?"

Her large dark eyes flashed with mischief.

"I'll have to put you to work if you stay here. Take out the garbage, go shopping with me, you know. ..." She laughed and threw her arms around me.

I felt guilty knowing that, more than anything else, I needed a roof over my head, and hers was simply the most convenient. The needs of the moment overpowered the guilt, though, so I made plans for the transition.

Uwe and I continued our planning as well.

"Budapest is a good distance from the border. I don't know. Suppose we got that far, then what?"

"Think about it. If we could just get to Budapest, we could take a train to some small town within 50 kilometers of the border. We'd look like students on vacation. Then all we'd have to do is walk into Yugoslavia, then into one of the other Western countries. Maybe Italy."

"Let's give it a try." His eye was looking red around the edges, and I noticed how he rubbed it. The operation had not gone exactly as planned, but he was not eager to go back for further surgery.

"Get some money ready. The airline tickets are going to be very expensive," I told him.

I was home packing my things that afternoon, when mom came upstairs with an armload of laundry.

"What are you doing now?" she asked. "Are you packing your clothes?"

I nodded in silence and kept folding, organizing, making a show of being neat.

"I can't understand why this is happening. Have I done something? Where will you stay? Why are you so determined to live a difficult life? Roberto will want to know why you are going. What can I say to him?" I could hear her voice change as the tears started. Inside my heart slowed to nearly nothing, dragged down by unspeakable grief. There was nothing to do but keep up the show, never let on that I had other sentiments.

"Look," I said, "it's time for me to have a life of my own. I appreciate all you have done for me, but I can't live here anymore." I had looked her coldly in the eye, and right before my eyes she crumbled further. More tears, falling fast. My heart was saying to go to my knees and beg her pardon, beg forgiveness for all the ones who had loved me so dearly, but my will was iron, welded to the ultimate goal. When I left, I would be going without family, and the more distance between me and loved ones, the better for them, no matter what happened.

Travel to other countries required permits, so Uwe and I set about the final details. Our visit to the Falkensee police station was routine, and they asked neither of us any unusual questions when we completed the travel request papers. So far, the plan seemed simple and workable. There was plenty of time for the police to decide whether they would allow us to go or not, and there was no complication with the Hungarians about entry visas. Perhaps they figured that if the East German government would allow people to leave, Hungary should be pleased to welcome them. The police clerk reviewed the forms, stamped them with the date and tossed them into a rectangular tray. It was a lot more orderly than Mowes' office. My insides churned with humiliation and anger as I involuntarily remembered his final shrug that day.

"Is there anything else?" I asked. "Do we need to fill out anything?"

The clerk shook his head and yawned.

"The request will be considered, and you'll be notified." From the next room, I could hear muted laughter and the slow slap, pause, slap of typewriter keys. Someone was filling out another form, making another report on someone or something. The officer silently stared us down and we left.

The next day, we drove to East Berlin and purchased two airline tickets for Budapest for a date about four weeks hence. The tickets had a 48-hour cancellation clause for a full refund. Christel arranged for vacation time and would accompany us. Her presence made the trip seem even more normal. Nobody seemed suspicious of two young men and a girl preparing to go on holiday.

If our trip was approved, we would receive permission forms in the mail. If they decided against us, a different form would come, but there would be no explanation of the refusal. Unexplained denials did not reflect secrecy. They simply reinforced the truth that everyone in East Germany already knew; explanations were not required by regulation, so no one was going to tell anything unless they had something to gain. Approvals were given and denied in abstract as if by a cold and distant parent who always knew best, but rarely felt the need to elaborate. Just do as you are told, my foolish children. Leave the thinking to me.

A week passed and no denial appeared in the mail. That was a good sign. Usually, if a refusal of any kind came from the police, it came swiftly. With every empty mailbox, my excitement grew. Time seemed to crawl, but my growing hope was still mixed with dread. Our plan was very simple and very likely to succeed, if we could just get into one of the neighboring countries. We stocked our back packs with light food rations and washed our underwear. Nothing came.

Nothing at all.

Sometimes no reply was really good, but now the silence became ominous. Something was very wrong. If we visited the police a second time, perhaps they would look the applications over more closely and deny them. If we said nothing, perhaps we would be denied anyway, and lose our ticket money. We decided to do nothing and hope that we were approved, but simply not notified in the usual way.

Departure day arrived without any word, so Uwe and I drove to the police station on Koch Strasse to pick up the permits.

"We don't have any visa for you. We don't issue them here anyway." The tall cadaverous officer stretched his green sleeved arms and leaned back in his chair. "You'll have to go to Nauen if you want anything else. It's not our problem."

I felt my face getting red, and control was slipping.

"I want to talk to the chief," I said.

In a few minutes, the local police chief appeared. His gait was slow, mirroring an overpowering inner weariness born of pursuing endless details, and his eyes were dull with negative expectation. He already knew that someone was going to complain about something, and he didn't want to hear it.

His hard voice preempted the complete repetition of my protest.

"Look," he said, "they told me what you want, and I'm telling you that it's not our problem. Go to Nauen if you want to talk it over with someone." His hands folded across his chest as a final punctuation.

A curse exploded from my lips and I jumped to my feet. Uwe yelled something and sprang up, knocking the chair over behind him. The eyes of all the green-clad brotherhood turned hard upon us, and we had their complete attention. I was no longer in control. My face was twisting with rage, and we were walking on the edge of real trouble. Everyday citizens were expected to treat police with deference; any overtly outrageous behavior could easily become a chargeable offense.

"You knew," I rasped through clenched teeth. "You knew all along that you weren't going to give us a visa!"

The Polizei all stared in silence, faces painted with the same stony expression of contempt.

"You did this to us on purpose."

The airline tickets had 48-hour cancellation refund provisions, but now it was too late. We had no visa and couldn't use the tickets, and we couldn't get a refund. They knew all of it! It was just the kind of joke they enjoyed.

They stared in silence, although I could see one of them flexing his meaty hands.

"Come on Uwe, we're going to Nauen."

I made a point of slamming the door as we left the station.

We made the 25-kilometer drive to county police head-quarters wrapped in curses, and I pushed the car well beyond the speed limit. As the kilometers clicked along, our hot anger was replaced by a cold resolve mixed with the inescapable knowledge that we most certainly had been defeated. We couldn't win this part of the game. In East Germany, the most common behavior when confronted by official refusals was to slink away and take it out on someone else at home or work. This time would be different. This time we'd make some of them pay for their fun. We decided that they'd have to suffer something, even a very little, for tricking us out of nearly a month's salary apiece.

The secretary behind the headquarters reception desk at the Nauen headquarters looked genuinely surprised. Perhaps the

Falkensee station hadn't called. She acted flustered and puzzled by our questions.

Lodging the complaint, my voice was loud, like a woman who has been given incorrect change at the Konsum.

"This wasn't an accident! It was done on purpose!" I said.

"No. We sent the denial notice," she said.

"I don't believe you!"

Her incredulous expression showed that she was not used to being given a hard time by civilians.

"I'm sure that we sent the notice if we were supposed to. We are very efficient."

Now two uniformed officers approached and stood, arms folded like monolithic big brothers on each side of her.

"Something must be wrong with your head," I continued, making eye contact with each of them in turn. "It doesn't take four weeks to decide if you're going to give us a visa. If you mailed it on Monday, we would have had it on Wednesday at the latest. You're just covering up your incompetence!" I paused, then asked the question I had really come to ask.

I asked in the same way it had been asked in the days of the cavemen when the head brute told one of the tribe he couldn't do something. I wanted someone in a uniform to go on record as to why I could not go on holiday like so many others.

"What kind of people are you anyway? Do you get some kind of thrill out of messing up people's lives? I want someone to tell me why I can't have a visa!"

"We don't have to tell you anything," the tall one said. "Try calling Schoenefeld airport and explaining it to the ticket agent."

Uwe snorted.

The officer eyed him for a second, then returned his attention to me.

"Maybe they'll give you the money back."

"I ought to sue you for it," I said furiously. That was a laugh and the Polizei knew it. The other officer smirked.

"You can do whatever you want, Herr Kaaz," the tall one said. His arms never moved, remaining folded across his barrel chest, but he took a step toward me. "Right now, you'd better get out of here."

We had lost and we knew it. They had beaten us again, and it stung with a bitterness I had never before felt.

Uwe and I drove home in silence. Perhaps the authorities were only now inaugurating their long-term strategy; deny us everything. Deny, deny until one day we would quietly break and quit asking. Our spirits felt the ever-growing weight of defeat. Whether they understood our ploy or whether they simply acted out of dumb indifference, it was the same. We were beaten and there was nothing to do but retreat.

Christel went to Hungary anyway.

East German guard tower where soldiers fired at the author
and the other two men he escaped with

# CHAPTER SEVEN

If our effort to work out an escape plan were to keep up its momentum, Uwe and I had to have more time. Since my vacation was over, I was supposed to return to work, but the very next day I took off and visited the doctor in the local Poliklinik.

"I have this wart on my hand," I told him. "Sometimes I hit it on things and it bleeds, and it really looks ugly."

The doctor looked at my hand then at me.

"Hmmm. We can burn it away, but you will have to take off work."

I left the office later that day with my hand wrapped in an extra-large white bandage, and an excuse to be off work for two more weeks.

Back at Plastikwerke, Krueger was furious.

"You're taking advantage of us, and you won't get away with it." He puffed and sputtered with unvented rage. Someday he would have a heart attack in the middle of an outburst, but I was sure that event wouldn't be a cause for grief at the plant.

Dittschlag was also visibly distressed. He could see perfectly that I was playing with the system, but said nothing to me about it.

Uwe was still on medical leave until May in order for his eye to have time to heal from the muscle operation. By now it was very red and painful, and I didn't like the idea of trying an escape with him in that shape. Time was running out.

For the hundredth time, we reviewed the options.

"It won't work and it's because of me," Uwe said. "If it weren't for this eye infection, we could get on with it."

207

In a way he was right, but in another way I began to feel relieved, thinking perhaps it was all for the best. Sure, this was a delay, but nothing had changed. Extra time would help us plan better. We were still going over. But even if we had the time, we weren't ready. We had to do it exactly right, and we really weren't yet sure of all the details. That was an understatement. Our plan was poorly developed, perhaps fatally. I wondered if the delay might be a life-saver.

Our thoughts were brave and rational, but no matter how we fought the feeling, in the following days a cloud of depression invaded our lives. As tangible as the morning mists, it clung in wisps and swirls to everything we touched, following us wherever we went. People started to notice and ask us what was wrong.

"This depression is killing me," Uwe told me. "We have to break out of this and find some way to function."

His words reminded me that though our hearts were elsewhere, for the time being our bodies were mired in East Germany. Why not make the best of it? Hearing him say that cleared my thinking at a critical time. Whatever we did about escaping, we had to stay sane in the meantime.

We returned to an everyday routine, trying to fit into the slow meander of local life.

Then one day, as Uwe and I were in the local electronics store, my interests took an unexpected turn.

"Look at that one," I said to Uwe. A girl was examining a stereo.

Uwe appraised her thoughtfully.

"She's something."

I sighed.

"There's no point in trying, I guess. Even though I have a nice car, she can still get someone better than me any day of the week." She had a figure that most models would envy, and her face was delicate and fine-featured, dark hair attractively falling on her shoulders. "I thought I knew all of the local girls, but I never saw her before. Who could she be?"

"Why don't you go ask?" Uwe urged.

For that moment, I was paralyzed by self-doubt, and I

208

watched, immobile as a cobblestone, while she walked out the front door and disappeared into the crowd.

Uwe jerked his head in the direction of the door, and like a couple of cowboys on the late-night movie, we headed out onto the street.

"Which way did she go?" he asked.

Then I saw her drive away on a motorized bicycle. She gave it the gas, and its tiny motor made an absurd whine as it accelerated. We followed in my car as fast as possible, but the moped was nimble and quick on the narrow streets. Down a side street, into an alley. She had observed us and realized that she was being followed. Accelerating and looking nervous on the strange whining contraption, she darted into another alley more narrow than the first. Suddenly our way was blocked and she disappeared around a far corner. Gone.

"Too bad," Uwe said.

Throughout the chase I had been wondering what I would actually do if we did catch up to her. It was sort of a relief.

That weekend, Uwe and I made our weekly visit to the Sunday youth activity in Staaken, about five kilometers from Falkensee. The dance was good, with a lively crowd and a new selection of Western records. As 9:00 p.m. approached and we left for the parking lot, a young man approached.

"You guys are from Falkensee aren't you?"

"Sure"

"My friends took off and left me here. I can't get back to Falkensee unless someone gives me a ride. How about it?"

"O.K.," I said. "I like to drive around anyway."

During the short drive home, I learned that Mario Kruger lived at home with his mother and sister, Yvonne, but as we turned the corner in front of his house, it all took on a new meaning.

"Look," Uwe said, "there she is." He pointed spontaneously at the brown-haired girl we had seen in the store. She was standing at the gate talking with another girl as we pulled up.

"That's Yvonne, my sister," Mario said.

During the introductions, I had trouble not staring, but then my mind finally went into action. It was late in the evening, but we were young and looking for something to do.

"I have an idea. Let's go to Berlin," I said.

Gasps.

"I'm serious. We're ready, right Uwe?"

"Right."

He was appraising Yvonne's girlfriend.

"We go there all the time. It can be a lot of fun."

What seasoned voyagers we were, like Tom Sawyers pretending to be mightily bored by the whole business of traveling around in a nice car with money in our pockets. By the time we arrived in East Berlin, the stores were closed, but we walked around Alexander Platz and gawked at the window displays. The drive back to Falkensee was long enough to impress the girls and plan another trip to the big city.

The next weekend Uwe, Mario, Yvonne, and her friend Martina made the drive with me to East Berlin during regular hours. Still enjoying the profits of my last automobile trade, I decided to buy clothes for everyone.

Mario reminded me of a child with his simplistic viewpoint and unconscious optimism.

"You shouldn't spend like this, Carsten. You won't have anything left for yourself." His fingers brushed the sleeve of his new jacket.

"I have a good reason for doing it. Besides you're all my friends. You'd do the same for me." It was not possible for me to give any hint of my real feelings in this situation. I couldn't spend East German marks when we escaped, so why not get some good mileage out of them now? As the excitement of East Berlin unfolded, framed by the blossoming of my new romance, I felt my focus being divided, but ever present was the knowledge that my life was not to be of this place and these people. I was enjoying existence as much as possible, but it was not a deep-seated joy of life, just a make-do transient happiness. Even if we didn't escape until next summer, I would have to work hard to spend the extra money I had made from successful buying and selling.

Yvonne, like her brother, possessed an almost primal innocence, and as she clung more and more to me, I became captivated. After that trip, we dated regularly, and while she was away on a trip to Leningrad with her Oberschule graduating class, I decided to play Kris Kringle by buying a new motorbike to replace her old and rusty one. After returning home, she unpacked and gave me a brief summary of the sights and sounds of the U.S.S.R. Then, like a child, her attention soon wandered.

"I'm going to see my friend Martina," she said as we walked together to where she usually parked her motorbike. At the shed door she stopped abruptly, stared for a moment, then looked at me, her eyes wide with delight.

"What's this?"

The burgundy and chrome of the new motorbike illuminated the windowless gloom of the interior. She whirled like a nimble dancer and threw both arms around me. I felt like the legendary Kris Kringle on Christmas morning.

A few days later with her mother's permission, I moved into her house, nominally sharing the room with her brother. My life usually did not have too many loose ends, but there was the problem of Christel, who would soon return from vacation in Hungary. I needed a way out of that relationship of convenience, so I turned to my best friend.

"I feel bad asking, Uwe, but I need your help."

"Just ask."

"I moved into Yvonne's house, but Christel is coming back from Budapest. I just can't get up enough courage to face Christel and tell her that it's over between us." It was an understatement. My insides were aching with guilt. I knew that I had used Christel's attraction for me in order to fill in part of my overall plan. That was that though, and there was no going back. I had to live somewhere outside my own home, and housing was nearly impossible to find.

"Uwe, would you go for me? Talk to her?"

He agreed with a simple nod.

The next day I saw him on the street.

"Did you see Christel?"

He smiled the solid, simple Uwe smile.

"I moved into her apartment today. The hospital where she works needed a carpenter, so now I have a job there, too."

Uwe was an excellent messenger.

Christel was a survivor.

For a few days it seemed that life was settling into a pleasant routine, but one evening Mario asked me to come sit in the living room.

"There's something important I have to tell you," he said. "Yvonne has another boyfriend."

"You've got to be kidding! She has spent all of her free time with me for the last two weeks. How can that be?"

"You don't understand. He's been away."

"So? Is he coming back?"

"Before long." Mario paused and his eyes shifted left and right like a child, trying to avoid speaking some dreadful truth.

"Peter Zimmermann," he said simply.

"You can't be serious."

Mario nodded. My pulse and breathing seemed to cease.

Peter Zimmermann was a well-known persona. A little less than two meters tall, he lifted weights. In court ten times for assault, he was never convicted because no witnesses would come forward. He liked beer and could consume it in large quantities. He was known to throw empty bottles for sport. The uncontested leader of a loose group of 12 or so other toughs who were all well known to the police, he was said to be responsible for the high demand for plaster used in making casts in the local medical clinic. Peter's father had abandoned him and his mother when he was very young, and just recently his mother had died. He lived alone on the first floor of a two-family house in Falkensee.

Peter Zimmermann was as well known for his violence as I was for my odd, now well-known obsession to emigrate. He had no emotional attachments. None, that is, except Yvonne Kruger.

My whole life flashed before my eyes. Mario's voice was distant. I tried to concentrate.

"Are you listening? He's working as an ice cream vendor at a Baltic Sea tourist resort. I think he'll be back soon, and I don't know what you are going to do."

I did not know either, and the next few days were filled with apprehension as the new crisis consumed my waking hours.

I was eating breakfast with the Kruger family at the kitchen table when a knock came at the door.

Yvonne got up and let the caller in. It was Zimmermann. He glanced at Mario and Frau Kruger, then fixed his dark attention upon me. He wore a T-shirt that clearly revealed his physical strength. I smiled and tried to look like a friend of the family, but my pale face surely revealed my fear. Without speaking, he followed Yvonne into her room; she closed the door. I sat for a moment, fork still in hand, then made the only reasonable decision.

"Excuse me," I said, dropping the silverware and pushing away from the table. "I have to go now." Frau Kruger mumbled something in protest. As I walked out the front door, there was only one possible destination — up Berliner Strasse, past Pestalozzi Strasse, and left onto Zwingli Strasse, back to my parents' home.

Standing in the living room, I began the lie and watched their faces reflect a mixture of joy and reservation.

"It's over," I said. "I won't be trying to emigrate to America again." Mother's face reflected a great relief, while frank skepticism remained in my father's eyes. They agreed to my request to move back in, and although no particular conditions were attached, I was still determined to keep my emotional distance. That night I tried to sort out my feelings. Yvonne had already become a strong focus in my life. She was 17 and I was just 20. I was already graduated from technical training while she had barely cleared high school. She gave the appearance of naiveté, but there was something else hidden beneath the innocence — an unsettled, restless urge that surfaced only occasionally. Then there was Peter Zimmermann. How close had he been to Yvonne? Did he love her? Did she love him? Was it safe for me to walk the streets? I remembered how Zimmermann had come into the Kruger house that morning. Frau Kruger and Mario offered a tentative greeting but obviously without enthusiasm.

Once again, I was still dangling between two worlds. On the one hand, I had real-life interests — like Yvonne, Uwe, Zimmermann, and my job. On the other, the ultimate goal of escape had fueled my basic drive. I had to live in the everyday East German world, and appear to be part of it, while my heart and soul were elsewhere. For the moment, my day-to-day survival was the most important thing to consider.

While I was allowed to live at home, the tension with my parents never really went away, and if my long-range plans were to work out, I could make no effort to repair that painful rift. The distance served the purpose of an emotional screen so I could survive the severe juxtaposition of emotions.

I decided to continue my basic lifestyle. Leave early, stay out late, and hardly see mom and dad for days at a time.

One night, I returned home late to the darkened house as usual and found a note.

"Your real father has died and his funeral is tomorrow at Friedhof Cemetery. You should go."

I hadn't seen him since I worked at the Polymath factory, but I did as mom suggested.

The story was that he died pretty much as he had lived, alone except for the woman who shared his bottles and his apartment. Alcoholism had aggravated his bleeding ulcers until there had finally been an attack that killed him at 44. A few days later, I stood silently by as his burial urn was placed in its receptacle. There was nothing to say. My mother stood next to his brother and parents. The woman with whom my father, Wolfgang Grossert, had been living was too inebriated that day to come to the funeral, so there were only the five of us to see his remains in a little metal container.

How was I supposed to feel? I hadn't even used his name since I was six. Even when we worked in the same plant, he never came to see or talk to me any more than the other men in the factory. In explanation for the years of silence, he had only said he was doing the best he could. Perhaps that was true. He died a miserable death, and for that I was sorry, but it was no use saying that he would be missed.

Looking at the burial urn itself was ironic. How neatly the lid fit into its place. The parts on my automobile engine didn't fit that precisely, and they existed to serve the living. No prayers were spoken. We did not know any. There were only five of us, a strained sense of obligation, and a tidy little meeting to put a tidy little container into a tidy little niche.

The world around me seemed even more frozen and desolate. I had to figure out how I could continue to exist in a vacuum where almost no emotional supports would be available. At that moment, I was really alone. Uwe couldn't return to live at his home on Pestalozzi Strasse because his stepfather had forbidden it as the final entry in their book of parental abuses. But he had Christel, who apparently cared for him.

Did Yvonne care enough for me to risk Zimmermann's wrath? Had he recaptured her affections? With whom could I counsel while the Stasi sniffed at my heels? They had reappeared quickly after the failed attempt to visit Hungary, and even though I now took my evening walks alone, I was aware of the neighborhood spitzels and their curious eyes. I wasn't a promising associate for anyone who disliked the attentions of the Stasi, so I stayed away from other friends, including Jurgen and Lutz.

Living day by day was the only way to make it, so I focused much of my thought on Yvonne. I knew that Zimmermann wouldn't forget that I had poached on private territory while he was away selling junk food to the white-legged tourists on the Baltic. He wouldn't forget the involuntary reaction that had betrayed my fear that morning. Mario told me that Yvonne had made him promise not to harm me in return for getting back together with him. The only other thing in life was the plan, so between dreaming of Yvonne's long brown hair, dark eyes and sinuous physical beauty, I dreamed of the Wall, its wire and the stolid guards with their shiny automatic rifles.

A few days later, I got the news from Yvonne's mother that her daughter had broken up with Zimmermann. She explained then in detail when before there had been only an awkward silence. "After he came home, it was never the same for them again, Carsten. I think the time she spent with you ruined her relationship to Peter because you showed Yvonne that there was more to life. She couldn't forget you, and he knew it. That became an open sore, one that never healed." She smiled sincerely. "We all think a lot of you, and there's still room for you in our home."

It would have been that easy, but for the time being, I decided not to move. Emotionally, though, I walked back into Yvonne's life and our relationship resumed, becoming even more intense for me than before.

As we again spent time together, I was consumed by an inexpressible joy, a lightness of heart that I had never before felt. But somehow in the farthest reaches of my mind, behind all the passionate feelings, there were alarm bells ringing. If Yvonne had left Zimmermann, he was now a very angry man with nothing to lose.

For the first time in my life, I appreciated living inside the frontier area. My residence was the only truly safe place where I could go about personal business without having to look over my shoulder. For things to be ideal, I would have to somehow get permission for Yvonne to live with me. I went to the police station and applied for her frontier area pass, not having any real hope that it would be approved. To my utter amazement, a permit was granted without so much as an extra question. It was noted on the form that she and I were engaged, although I had not said that to the officials. It appeared that someone was still trying to smooth my way in the hope that I would fade away into the background. There was no other explanation. That same day, I saw Peter from a distance in town, and he held up his deadly right hand and made a fist, a living hammer, then waved it at me with special emphasis, showing that it was meant for my face.

I watched my back constantly whenever outside of the frontier sanctuary, but one night a few weeks later, as Yvonne and I were visiting her father at his apartment in town, a new development occurred. Mario came into the living room with a strange look on his face.

"What's wrong with the windshield of your car?" he said.

I went to the door and peered out onto the darkened street. Even in the moonless night I could see that every window on my red Polski Fiat had been smashed. The windshield was caved in and hanging like dead skin sloughing off of a snake. I ran into the hall and up the stairs to use the telephone. This was something that the police would have to deal with, and it was one of the few times in my life I was shocked speechless.

Mario went back out onto the dark front porch in time to see a powerfully framed figure emerge from the darkness. The visitor carried two objects. With the large sledge hammer, he methodically crushed the Fiat's hood. Satisfied with the result, he repeated the process on each fender. The dull metallic thuds reverberated in the quiet night, mixing with the delicate tinkle and crunch of pulverized glass. The smasher then carefully pried open a can of white paint and poured it in a broad streak across my red roof and hood. With a swirl and flourish, he threw the last of the paint and the can itself onto the front seat. The destruction of the car had taken only three or four minutes, the length of a telephone call to the police. By the time I returned to the downstairs apartment, the figure was gone, carried by his weaving intoxicated gait into the deep darkness of that usually quiet street. Mario's father was eager for a closer look.

Breathless with dread and confusion, I found Mario as he stepped back indoors. I didn't venture out, but I wanted to know.

"Did you see what happened? Who was it?"

"It was dark and I didn't want to get too close." He hesitated, eyes searching left and right like the day when he told me that Zimmermann was Yvonne's boyfriend.

"Come on," I said. "You had to be able to see who it was only five meters away. Was it Zimmermann?"

"Maybe. It could have been. It sort of looked like him." He didn't want to talk about it.

We went outside and walked around the wreck. Even in the dark it looked horrible. I dreaded the coming of the sun, when the full extent of the destruction would be revealed.

Then came the Polizei, circling the wreckage, their flashlights weaving all over and following the still-creeping streaks of white paint from roof to seat covers. The district foot patrol officer showed up with his dog, but kept his distance. No point in letting the Doberman get glass in his paws. Their own boots crunched the glittering fragments that decorated the street. One officer began to ask me questions, shining the light back and forth from my face to Mario's as the story unfolded. In the background, I could hear the foot patrolman talking to the dog as they circled the area again and again. Finally, they moved away down the street, the dog snorting, straining and huffing at his heavy leather strap.

"Well," said the other officer, "could you see who it was?"

Even in the dark I could see Mario squirm. He stammered something.

"What was that?"

I cleared my throat. "I've had some trouble with Peter Zimmermann, and whoever did this looked a lot like him in the dark."

"Ah, Zimmermann." He seemed pleased. "Herr Kruger, tell me where you were standing."

Mario indicated with a pointing finger and the officer made notes.

"Did you see him or not?"

"Well, it is dark out here, but it might have been Peter. Whoever it was could swing the sledge hammer with one hand like it was a toy."

He nodded and took more notes.

"Well there isn't anything more to do here; we have to go visit elsewhere now. We'll be in contact with you Herr Kaaz. I advise you not to leave the car on the street. Someone might steal the radio."

In a few days, I received a postcard in the mail notifying me of a date to appear in court. Peter had been arrested for the vandalism and was to be swiftly tried. I remembered the past and the many witnesses who failed to appear when he was accused of a crime, and I remembered the ones who had accidents just before a court date, too. This time I was merely the victim, and the Polizei were the ones pressing the charges. I had little choice other than to follow through, and somehow I hoped to have the car restored. The body damage and upholstery would cost ten thousand marks to repair. As a precaution prior to the trial, the Polizei confiscated Zimmermann's stereo and car so he couldn't sell them and hide the money. Restitution of actual damages was an important feature of East German law, and in most cases victims could expect to have a good portion of their losses made right at the criminal's expense.

The court was a plain, functional place. It smelled of the government, painted official colors, trimmed in books, the costume and ambiance of power, cloaked black in relentless uniformity. The visitors' seating area was crowded with people, many of whom wore the uniform of rebellion, blue jeans and tattoos. My skin crawled and I felt as though many eyes were staring at my neck, sizing it up for breaking. Zimmermann stood silent through the proceedings, like a simmering volcano, speaking only when a question was put to him by the judge. Since neither I nor Mario could actually identify him, our parts were small. The dog had followed the scent to Zimmermann's house, and while the testimony of the police dog's nose had helped convict many men, in this case, Zimmermann had finished himself off. In his state of drunken anger, he hadn't done a good job of cleaning the white paint from his hands.

"Herr Zimmermann, it seems that you are quite unable to control your passions, particularly when you have had a few drinks." This judge and Zimmermann had met before, and the judge was clearly without the slightest sympathy.

Zimmermann stood in the place of the accused, not overtly defiant, but like a massive rock, a monolith of anger charged with the unfathomable energy of self-destruction. He conveyed no sense of regret for his actions, and when his gaze met mine, it was like looking into a void. No, he was not sorry for anything, except perhaps that I hadn't been inside the car when he mutilated it.

The magistrate made notes.

"Do you have money to pay for the damages?"

"No."

"We will sell your own car then. You have a Moskvich?"

"Yes."

"We will sell whatever you own until there is enough money to pay for all of this."

Zimmermann showed no emotion. Impassive as a mountain. I imagined the rumbling of hatred like lava awaiting an opportunity to erupt. I shuddered thinking what dreams he now nurtured.

"One last thing, Zimmermann," the judge said as he leaned forward in his chair. His face was a grim impassive mask, and his stare was deadly. "Once more. I will only see you once more in this court, and that will be the end of you." He paused to allow the words die among the silent onlookers. "Once more for any reason whatsoever, and I personally guarantee that you'll go to prison!" His brow furrowed and his lips lost their color. "Do you hear me? Do you believe that I'll send you straight to Rudersdorf?"

"Yes." The reply was flat, without any emotion or inflection. It was an eloquent testimony to Zimmermann's unyielding heart.

The judge waved his hand to the guard and Zimmermann was led away so final arrangements could be made to carry out the sentence.

Although I knew the car would be repaired, I was uneasy about the rest of my life. I still cared for Yvonne, and Zimmermann was loose. I didn't know if he would stay away from her and me.

Two days later, the question was answered. I saw Zimmermann from a distance in town and he made a fist, holding it high as a reminder.

Complications of life pursued Uwe and me with a vengeance. Twice, three times every week as we drove around town at night, a Polizei would step from the shadows and wave us to the curb with his lighted signalstock. It was happening for the second time in the same evening.

"I'm really getting sick of this," Uwe said. " We ought to tell him to … "

I waved him to silence.

"Let's play it cool. Maybe it's just coincidence."

The policeman's boots scraped as he paced around the car looking for safety violations.

"Ausweis, bitte," he said.

Holding my identity card in his hand, he studied it, as though contemplating some infinitely complicated matter.

"Open your trunk."

"What's the problem?" I asked roughly.

"I'm sure you have all your safety items, but I need to see them anyway," he said, then shined the light directly in my eyes. Without even looking into the passenger's side, he muttered something else. "And Herr George, too. How interesting."

He gave me the treatment, a whole safety inspection right there in the middle of the street. Brake lights. Turn signals. Bright and dim headlights. A look at each tire testing tread depth. First-aid kit in trunk. On and on.

If any of the required items had been missing, he was ready to give me a stiff fine, but all was in place, even to the last emergency bandage in the first-aid kit.

"O.K., you can go now."

I got into the car and slammed the door.

"Have a nice evening," he called as we pulled away from the curb.

A block away Uwe finally spoke.

"I saw him talking into his radio as we pulled out. Probably telling the guys back at headquarters what fun he just had." He slouched down in the seat. "I can't believe this."

"That wasn't anyone I've seen before, but he knew us both by sight. What does that tell you?"

After driving for another half-hour, we decided to call it a night, so I took Uwe by his house, stopping for a few minutes for a final talk in the driveway.

Suddenly he turned in his seat.

"I can't believe it. There's another cop shining his light on your license plate!"

"Let's ignore him."

We didn't look in his direction anymore, but in a moment he was tapping on my side window with his heavy light. I rolled the window down.

"Ausweis Und Fahrzeugpapiere, bitte."

"Give me a break," I said. "Haven't you been talking to your headquarters? One of your comrades just did this half-an-hour ago!" I handed the papers to him.

"Let's see in the trunk. By the way, who's that with you? What are you doing here this late?"

221

"My friend lives here, and is there some kind of new law about talking to your friends? Since he can't come into the frontier area, I ought to have the right to spend some time with him if I want."

Finishing the cursory inspection of my emergency kit, he made a great show of counting the spare light bulbs and looking at the jack.

"Does it work properly?"

"Does what work?"

"The jack, Herr Kaaz. Does it work?"

He looked around a little longer, then motioned for me to close the trunk.

"Did I break the law?"

He stared at me wearing a smirk, but my question remained unanswered. I was about to ask again when he switched off the light and turned away.

"Have a nice evening, and be careful driving."

His boots crunched out a regular, confident rhythm in the crushed rock and in a moment he disappeared into the darkness.

"I've had it for tonight," I told Uwe. "Time to go home."

Pulling into my yard a few minutes later, I switched off the engine and sat for a moment in silence. Across the Wall, I could see the lights of the West German apartment building, but in my mind, they might as well have been the stars, forever beyond my pitiful grasp. My blood congealed, thick with anger. I hated it here! I hated my own country because of what it was doing to me, because I didn't want to be a quiet little robot. Even after I went in and lay down beside Yvonne, I couldn't sleep. This couldn't continue! I writhed in my own pain and wondered how my parents had managed to stay sane after living in the cage for so long.

Between fearing for my personal safety and trying to assess the depths of my reopened relationship with Yvonne, I hardly felt as though a victory had been won over Zimmermann. I understood that even if I were really careful, there was bound to come a time when he would surprise me in a place where I was vulnerable. When that happened, I would be severely injured, maybe even killed. Fitful sleep came only after my fatigued spirit succumbed for the night.

My problems were temporarily eclipsed by a new crisis in Yvonne's family.

"Carsten, I need your help." Frau Kruger's eyes were red from a day of crying. "It's all too much! I can't handle this all by myself. Please help me!" She poured out the story.

Her son, Mario had a history of trouble with the police. A few broken street lights, a smashed electrical transformer, then cars began to disappear from Falkensee only to be found abandoned out of gas in neighboring towns. He was an amateur, not taking any care to cover his activities, not even removing his fingerprints from the inside of the stolen vehicles. The trial had been merely an exposition of evidence. There was no defense except his youth and lack of a father in the home. Repeated offenses had brought down the system's full statutory wrath.

Two years, Rudersdorf.

The prison was overcrowded, so his entry had to be postponed until space could be found. Eight months later without further warning, the official postcard arrived indicating the date and time he was to report for incarceration. His mother packed a few things as though he was going to stay overnight with a friend. I shuddered inside at the possibility of going to that place. If things went wrong, I might be making a trip like Mario. I quickly blocked the thought.

"Mario looks up to you, Carsten. He wants you to drive him to Rudersdorf on Monday. He thinks it would be easier if you went along." Her voice faded, then the sobs began again, heartfelt and agonized, heaving her slight body. "I should have paid more attention to him. I could have … " The tears distorted her words.

It was January, and the earth was sleeping. Our breath puffed white as we walked to the car, while Mario laughed and joked as though we were headed to the ice cream store. Frau Kruger's face was a veil of pain. Mario wore the pants I had bought him in Berlin.

We stopped at a restaurant on the way, where Frau Kruger bought lunch. We ate the broiled chicken between faltering lisps of conversation. Mario's appetite was good as usual.

He was always ready to eat.

"Mario," his Mother said, "you must work hard, and stay away from those criminals. If you behave, they'll let you out soon." She picked at the chicken with the fork. "You're not a bad boy. Don't let them make you into a bad boy." She swallowed hard and grabbed for coffee to wash the food and her tears down.

Rudersdorf rose solitary out of the landscape like a ghastly gray monument trimmed with barbed towers, held sure in the jaws of pacing dogs and watched by grim men with guns. Beholding it for the first time, Mario fell silent, submerging a growing fear, yet not fully comprehending the place that was about to swallow him. I spoke a brief goodbye with a handshake for luck, then sat in the car as Frau Kruger walked him to the main gate. He clutched the cursed postcard in a trembling right hand. For a long time, his mother held him close, then he was gone. I waved once more as the guards led him away like a trusting child into the iron gates of hell.

We did not linger in that sad place. Driving home in silence, I sensed the desolation of Frau Kruger's heart. She sputtered and mumbled through surging recrimination as she struggled to come to terms with unassuagable grief. Yvonne didn't get time off from school to accompany us on that trip, so there was only me as a reluctant, helpless witness. When I dropped her off at home, she took my hand between hers and kissed it, thanking me for being so kind. I felt of no more value than a witness to a fatal traffic accident.

Days passed and I regrouped. It was as though I was some kind of ungerminated seed, borne reluctantly on the vagrant currents of life toward a tomorrow filled with nothing at all. Yvonne was my only real interest.

She and I spent a lot of time together. My parents didn't object to her sharing my room, and we even managed to take a holiday at Ohrdruf, skiing in southern East Germany. It was personally gratifying to have such a beautiful consort who turned heads wherever we went. There on the snow-covered slopes, she was fresh and vibrating with the essence of life. For a few days, we existed in an eternity of pristine white happiness, but when we returned to Falkensee, the magic evaporated, turning into a kind of spiritual slush that once again threatened to cover me forever. Overtly, nothing was different, but inside there was a hollowness of heart, an echo in my soul where fulfillment should have been. I had the things that I had sought for in life, the things that my peers still struggled to possess. I had a car, a nice one. A better one than most men twice my age, gotten by cleverness and willingness to venture, not by conniving or sneaky connections. That was something to feel good about. I had a job, a good one. A better one than many others because I was really the only one in my work place who knew what I was doing. In reality, I was my own supervisor, no matter what it said on paper. My co-workers were generally interesting and pleasant. Getting up in the morning was not a bad thing. Yvonne seemed to be attentive and caring. Music. Food to eat. Stylish clothes. Love. All of that was just fine, except I felt terrible, as though something important was missing from my insides. And to make matters worse, I could feel the disturbance inside growing greater every day. I arose from the bed, leaving Yvonne alone as she drifted deeper into sleep. Something was missing, something I had to understand, something without which I couldn't exist.

I walked alone in the night.

Down the familiar dust of Zwingli Strasse, north toward the unwavering glare of the lights on the Wall, crossing through the trees and onto the paths that I had walked so often with Uwe over the last few years. At first, I'd only walk occasionally, but as the weeks became a month, my restlessness grew. Walks came once a week, twice, then every other day. As I stirred the dust of my neighborhood streets, I met myself face to face.

By every measure that I knew, happiness should have been mine, but I was miserable. There were flashes of fun here and there, things to carry my interest for a time, but no lasting joy whatsoever. The next evening, I stood by the front-yard fence and looked westward, full into the deep, red burning face of the setting sun. Was that how the sun set in the eyes of a free man?

Inmate. For me it was more than a word. I was a prisoner, and no matter how well-appointed the setting, how diverting the accoutrements, how distracting the beautiful women, I was only half alive. If I wasn't happy now, I never would be. It burst upon my inexperienced heart that I had the things that were supposed to make life worthwhile, but if the present course wasn't changed, these things would soon own me, and then I would never be free.

More weeks passed, and things began to change with Yvonne. Slowly, with the utmost subtlety, another presence was attached to our relationship. More and more, she was finding excuses to be gone. Time and again, I pushed the thought away, only to have it steal back again, nibbling at my mind like a persistent mouse. Who could she be seeing? Who else? Zimmermann. She could be followed, but I didn't really want to become a love cop.

"I'm going to visit Martina," she said one evening.

"You just went yesterday, Yvonne."

"What's the matter? Can't I go see a friend if I want to?" Her reaction was instantaneous, like tripping a preset trigger.

"I can't believe that's the only place you want to go."

Her eyes widened, and as the adrenaline flowed, her cheeks took on a subtle shade of pink. Under other circumstances, it would have been exciting to see.

"If you don't trust me, why should we stay together?" she said.

"If you don't love me anymore, why do you stay?"

"Oh," she said evenly. "I'll just go then."

Her answer was so quick and final I was stunned. It wasn't that I was surprised by the answer itself, but by the ease with which it was spoken. Fifteen minutes later, all that was left of Yvonne Kruger was some memories and the sound of her S-51 E motorbike fading down Zwingli Strasse. I heard her slow for the corner at Calvin Strasse, then accelerate. Then even the buzz of the two-cycle exhaust was gone.

I sat heavily on the bed, letting my heart absorb what my head had known for a long time. With a reflex motion, I turned on the radio.

*"I'll do anything for my sweet sixteen."* The Armed Forces Network station was crisp, no static. *"I'll do anything for my*

*runaway child. Someone just built a candy castle for my sweet sixteen."* I
copied the words to Billy Idol's song on an otherwise blank sheet
of paper, addressed an envelope to Yvonne's home address, and
quickly sealed it before writing anything else stupid. The next
morning, I dropped it into the mailbox, and it hit bottom with a
thunk. That sound was the end, and knowing it was over, and
that parting hadn't killed me, I also knew that I'd eventually be
all right.

Late next Saturday morning, I was working in the front
yard, when in a flurry of pedaling and whirring wheels, a green
bicycle flashed in through the gate.

"I was thinking about everything," Uwe said. "It's about time
that we got ready." He was puffing like crazy, having pedaled as
fast as he could down the forbidden frontier streets.

We had hardly seen each other for the last eight months, but
I could tell by his intensity that nothing had changed. We
exchanged hugs and blurted items of news.

"What about you?" I asked. "What about Christel?"

"Oh, I can't live like that forever. She's all right, but life's
going nowhere. I'm starting to look and act like everyone else in
this country."

I told him later of my own narrow escape and how Yvonne's
departure had reawakened my fundamental desire to leave.

For the rest of the day, we caught up on the details, and as
dusk fell, I walked with him back to his parents' house to return
the bicycle before they noticed that it was missing without
permission. Since he no longer lived there, they wouldn't expect
it to be gone. After supper at my house, we walked in our
familiar way, filling in the fine points of personal adventures.
The time we had been separated simply melted away. It was as
though the past months were now held as common experience,
and we were like old comrades again.

"We have to be more careful than ever," I said. "One wrong
move now, and we'll be trapped here forever. Let's go over the
Wall details. Guards. Dogs. Alarm wire. Everything has to be
perfect."

The discussion went on into the late hours of night, then as
was customary, Uwe said good night and slipped quietly through

Carsten with Yvonne — 1986

Author's last car before the escape,
an East German Trabant — 1987

Memorial crosses aligning the then West Berlin side of the Spree River, representing lives lost in their attempts to gain freedom

the hidden door in the back fence and into Detlef's yard. He was hurrying and failed to look carefully both ways on Pestalozzi Strasse, and so didn't see the two border guards until they had already observed him. They strode purposefully north on Pestalozzi Strasse, fingering their slung Kalashnikovs. Uwe had only a split second to decide. His ID showed that he had moved. If his name was called in, it would be instantly connected to me. Could he run? If he doubled back into Detlef's yard, they'd be able to trap him in the yards bordered by the westward curve of the Wall. If he ran straight ahead, they'd catch him in the pine thicket to the west or in the fields beyond. With the Wall behind him, Uwe turned to face his fear.

He meandered toward the Grenztruppen at a normal pace, trying to appear relaxed. The soldiers' interest was high. Fifty meters separated them. Forty. Thirty meters. The soldiers were clearly curious and their step quickened. Another twenty meters and he'd be at the south end of Pestalozzi Strasse, where the buses turned around. He walked faster, they walked faster. Faster. Fifteen meters. With a burst of speed, Uwe sprinted sharply to the right and ran westward down Berliner Strasse, then leaped over a fence, disappearing into the bushes and dark. Close behind, he heard the heavy thud of boots and the unmistakable slide-snap of oiled metal as the troopers charged their Kalashnikovs. Their intent was clear.

"Stop or we'll shoot!" one of them bellowed.

He vaulted another fence, tore his way through the familiar bushes, then hopped over another low barrier. In the distance, hoarse voices thundered for him to stop. A flashlight beam oscillated wildly as its owner careened full speed into unfamiliar shrubbery.

Then they were on the radio calling for assistance; soon there would be more pursuers. Using the key he had never returned to his parents, Uwe let himself quietly into his family's house, and within minutes emerged wearing light-colored clothes. Retrieving the bicycle he had ridden earlier, he then took the only possible course of action. To the left, Pestalozzi Strasse dead-ended into the Wall. To the right were noise and flashing lights. After pulling on a light-colored shirt and a pair of his stepfather's work pants, Uwe mounted the bicycle and turned to the right, heading south on his street toward the commotion.

Two police cars and an army truck were parked near the bus turnaround. Ten, maybe twelve Grenztruppe, five or six Polizei. No dogs yet. Everyone milling around, everyone looking up and down the street, everyone with a gun in his hand. Their muttering conversation was like the baritone buzzing of the blue death-flies around a ripening carcass. The spirit of the hunt was in the air. Soon these men would begin to climb the fences to search the backyards, centimeter by centimeter.

"Good evening," Uwe said to the group. He continued to pedal at an easy even pace.

No one spoke, but a stocky Polizei returned his greeting by a nod and gesture with his flashlight. Sweat trickled down Uwe's back as he disappeared into the night.

A few days later, I made another reconnaissance of the Wall, taking a hazelnut branch and rubbing it back and forth across the broken glass to mark the exact top of the Wall. We needed the precise measurement so there would be no mistakes. Uwe and I met and worked out the final material details.

"There will have to be two ladders. One to get over the first wall, and one to climb down the other side. Then we'll have to carry the second ladder to the outer wall and use it again to go over," I said.

Uwe understood that he would make modifications to the ladder chained to my father's shed. That would carry us over the first wall. In addition, he would build an entirely new second ladder. It had to be strong, light, and made in sections in order to be smuggled into my house in pieces. Light meant able to be carried in one hand by the man who was first over the Wall.

"It better not be heavy, because you'll have to run with it," I said. Then we both laughed. We would really be running! I made the calculations. Vertical height. Overhang of the wire. My father's ladder was a little larger, so it would do fine for the first wall. Our initial approach would be one of stealth, so its bulk and weight wouldn't be a problem. Since it couldn't touch the wire, special removable braces had to be constructed that would steady it in the proper position, but still hold the critical angle.

I rechecked the problems, then transferred the raw measurements to another sheet of paper where they were written without any scale or unit of measure. The calculation notes were carefully burned and the ashes crushed in the water heater fire box. I handed the paper containing the non-annotated information to Uwe.

"You'd better not let anyone else find this. You know how nosy …"

"This is fine. Where is the best place?"

"Next to Jerke's house, about three meters south of his chicken pen. I went to the Wall again last night to look it over. The light is incredibly bright between the walls, and they're sure to see us at some point. But if we can stay camouflaged for just a few seconds, our chances are increased."

"Perhaps we'll be lucky," he said.

Luck would be a factor. The windows on each tower were surfaced with a bronze-colored material that muted the glare of the sun and the nighttime lights. That made it impossible to look at a tower and see whether the men inside were looking your way. If both guards were sleepy, and if there was a hard rain to mask any sounds we might make, and if the tower windows fogged a little, we might make it. But how could we possibly camouflage ourselves in that arena of light?

"It's so bright between the walls that dark clothes will make us stand out clearly. Perhaps light colors will be better."

Uwe considered the question.

"Let's test the idea," he said. "Go change and I'll watch you to see how it works, then we can discuss it the next time we meet. I think it'll be too risky to get together again tonight."

I put on white everything, sneakers, pants, T-shirt, and wind breaker. While Uwe watched from the bushes, I walked eastward on Calvin Strasse toward the point where the street disappeared beneath the Wall. I wanted to appear to any accidental watchers as though I was only out for an evening stroll, so I ambled along, hands thrust deeply into jacket pockets, breathing deeply of the night air.

My heart was pounding with raw fear. This was different from sneaking through Jerke's yard. I was in the open just walking down the street like I had some right to be there. What if a guard suddenly happened along? What if a Polizei had been relieving himself in the bushes and saw Uwe and me talking? What if Koch slithered out in his yard to water his bushes? I couldn't help but notice the guard tower at the end of Berliner Strasse. Were the ever-present watchers glancing my way? I cleared Koch's house, then Krentz's, where I had taken guitar lessons. Then the tower was in full view. What if they were looking? Would they dismiss me as a local walking off excess alcohol, or perhaps getting out of the house after a domestic fight? There was only one ultimate test to our camouflage idea. I had to go all the way to the Wall and lean right against it.

All around me were familiar houses, trees, the motionless forms of cars and bushes. But that night, every object had an ominous life of its own, like the toys in a child's room when he awakens fearfully in the night to see them looming about. Then there was the Wall itself, massive, strangely comforting in its unchanging bulk. For a moment, I pressed my body against it, hoping that Uwe was paying attention. Then I stepped back, looking neither left nor right, and went directly home at what I hoped was the same casual pace.

The next day Uwe reported.

"The closer you got the more you blended, until at the last you just disappeared against the Wall. The light colors will really help. I'm sure of it!"

"At least we have a good chance of approaching without being seen from the street. Buy your clothes Uwe, and hang them in your closet. Soon we will have our vacation." For all of the upbeat talk, there was still a strong possibility that we would somehow fail.

I didn't want to die, neither did Uwe.

Trying to make my life appear normal was a constant challenge. Living two lives was becoming a habit, but it was still a great strain. With such high stakes, a person can never relax, never really be himself, never trust his own tongue without first carefully selecting the words. I had to be on my guard constantly, but it was getting easier, because like most of my countrymen, I had become an expert at concealing true feelings.

Korinna Wieczorek and I dated casually, and one evening while at her house, a few of her friends dropped by.

"After all you've been through, do you still want to go to America?" the blonde-haired girl said.

Her date joined in with enthusiasm born of prying curiosity rather than genuine concern.

"Yes," he said. "How do you feel about it all now? The Stasi had you once, didn't they?"

The girl watched me like a lizard sizing up a nearby bug. One wrong move, one inappropriate statement, even an unguarded look might betray my true feelings and make me the latest hot topic in the local youth gossip circles. If that happened, the few truths that were known would be amplified and embellished until the tales were really interesting. Then the Stasi were sure to hear, and the watching would begin all over again.

"America's real to me," I said. "I have friends there who write, but lots of things have changed in my life." My eyes evaded theirs. "Right now I have other interests. I guess it will make sense someday."

The conversation drifted into other areas as their predatory curiosity was satisfied. I was relieved, but more wary then ever. Reputations die hard in small towns.

The new second ladder had been built, and the extra braces were made for my father's ladder. I painted the second ladder white and thought it through again as the brush wandered to and fro in my hand. They would only have to hold up for a single use. We had calculated a special measurement for the second ladder rung distance, because when we mounted it, we would be leaping, not walking up. The rungs were farther apart than normal, perfect for feet that were in a big hurry. The pieces were concealed in the shed behind my parents' house.

So far, there was no indication that anyone was suspicious.

Other worries were inescapable. The Grenztruppe in the towers would prefer to capture us, because a live criminal is more useful as a deterrent. We also knew how the policy was worded to the troops: 'Capture if possible, but don't hesitate to kill if you cannot otherwise prevent their escape. You are totally responsible for your sector at all times!' The guards were never in the same tower for more than one day at a time, and their companions changed as well. The theory was that if men didn't serve together more than once, they'd never get to know each other and friendships couldn't develop.

Each man stood for about eight hours in a ten-square-meter area with another man he didn't know. Guards were supposed to be already politically reliable, but in East Germany, political reliability in the military was subject to testing at any time. No one could know if the other guard was a genuine soldier like them, or a political cadre whose assignment was to see if they held some aberrant attitude. They shuffled their feet and fingered the large Kalashnikov safety levers. Mostly they just watched in silence. Hour upon hour went by with nothing moving between the walls except for the patrols that came at odd intervals. For the most part, the border troops were hard men made harder by their tainted task. The grinding boredom and unrelenting suspicion left tracks across their spirits like scars on an addict's arm. After years of pretending to protect the East from the West, after half a life of telling the same unbelievable story over and over to their wives and children, some of them actually came to believe that they had helped save their people. These were the worst of all, because they would do anything, betray anyone, to serve the god whom they had chosen. We hated them all.

All was in readiness save one small thing. We needed rain. If I had known how, I would have prayed for it.

"The clock will be set for midnight every night," I told Uwe. "If it starts to rain, I'll come to Christel's place and get you. Have your clothes ready."

It all seemed so simple. What we needed was a good downpour to fog up the tower windows and cover any noise we might make in our approach to the Wall. I'd stay up from midnight until 4:30 a.m. to watch for the right conditions.

Saturday night the sky opened and heavy drops of water began to pock the dusty street. The blessed rain fell; slowly, sporadically at first, in rattling bundles, then in lashing, beautiful, nearly opaque sheets.

Into the car, my heart pounding. Hardly daring to think, to breathe. It was really happening. Through town to Christel's apartment. I beat on the door.

"Uwe, it's me!"

Movements inside. Somebody walking around. Thuds and thumps. The door opened and out he came clothed in white just like me.

Back to my house and into the backyard. Water blowing and swirling in impossible patterns against the brooding darkness. In the distance, even the pitiless lights between the walls were dimmed by the downpour. Rain ran down my collar, into my pants, and dripped from my nose. I sniffed and spat reflexively.

There was no talking as we completed the work, because we

had done it a thousand times in conversation and on paper. Rung by rung, we assembled the second ladder. Uwe had done such a good job. If it had been for school, he'd have gotten an A. Another rung slipped into place, and Uwe screwed it down tightly. He hefted the ladder, testing its balance.

And then the rain stopped as though someone had turned off a faucet.

Abruptly, the only sound was water running and dripping from the house and trees. I stopped sniffling as the last big drops trickled away across my upper lip. We stared at each other, blobs of white against the mottled shadows of the bushes and shed. The Wall lights seemed to brighten in the distance.

"We have to have rain." My voice was a rasping whisper. "The rain is critical! We have to have it!"

Uwe's indistinct form moved, shaking his head in disgust. Then I heard the click of metal as he began to disassemble the ladder screw by screw. At 2:00 a.m., I dropped him off at Christel's front door. He dragged inside squishing with every step, leaving my car seat with a wide and darkening circle. Was Christel still a sound sleeper? What lie would he tell her? Would she believe it? Would it matter what she believed?

Sunday, Monday, Tuesday, no rain. I slept late and ate my meals while mom and dad were at work. By the time they returned home, I was long gone. We saw almost nothing of each other for days.

Wednesday, I made it a point to stop by and speak directly to Uwe at work.

"I'll see you at the youth club in Staaken tonight. Korinna and I are going to come over for a while, I guess." It sounded strange to be speaking of Korinna, because if it rained tonight, I would be gone from her life, like a switched-off light. The effect that might have on her was not something I had worried about too much. There wasn't much room for concerns other than basic survival. I figured that there was no way my leaving would be of any harm to her.

That evening, she and I sat at a table near the door, talking of casual concerns as the music from the stereo swirled and flowed in delicate eddies, echoing from the wall and the bare ceiling.

We sipped Quick Cola, a tasteless excuse for a soft drink that was only slightly better than nothing.

He entered the door easily, like a hungry tiger slipping through the bush, and took in the room in one predatory sweeping glance. His eyes locked on me, and I knew why Peter Zimmermann had come. My mind was blank with surprise as he crossed the few meters between us. Only once before, in court after he smashed my car, had I seen him up close. Muscles bulged beneath his new Levi's jacket, nearly rupturing the T-shirt beneath.

"Come outside," he said. The words were spoken quietly, but in a simple, direct command with a big grin; he knew he had all the advantages and was about to beat me into trash.

I moved, my eyes involuntarily fixed upon him. Now it's going to happen to me, I thought. Vaguely, I realized that all conversation around us had stopped. Uwe approached from across the room, but I waved him away.

"Let it alone."

He stopped, but did not withdraw. My legs were boneless, twitchy, as though imperfectly connected to my brain. The door closed behind us and I felt the soft night breeze. No rain tonight, but how sweet was the darkness, how … the fear came in a wave, almost blotting out all thought. I struggled to maintain control, but my imagination could already feel the blows from his hammer hands.

"Before you start, I want to say a few words." What did I have to lose?

"Make it fast." There was no emotion is his voice. He had done this sort of thing so many times before it was routine.

Behind Zimmermann, I could see faces pressed against the club's window panes, peering through cupped hands, hoping for a good look at the event. When it began, Uwe would come out, but even the two of us would not be able to stop him. After Zimmermann got through with me, he'd probably work Uwe over to make sure we got the point.

"I loved Yvonne Kruger," I said. "I met her one evening standing in front of her gate with Martina."

He flexed his hands again, making and unmaking a fist.

237

"I didn't know anything about you until I had already moved in with her." My mouth was dry, but I wanted to swallow. "When Mario told me, I didn't really know what to do." I took a breath. This was something anyway. He had not attacked yet. "Everyone in town knows who you are, and I don't need any trouble in my life right now."

"Everyone knows you too, Kaaz." The voice was flat, devoid of feeling.

"I really thought Yvonne loved me, too. It was a good time in my life. She was really sweet and good to me, you know, like a child, naive."

"Some child." His hands had stopped flexing. What did that mean?

"Sure, I know that now, but I gave her a lot of things, expensive things."

His stance shifted slightly, and for the first time, his gaze drifted slightly away and down.

"I never understood that part, Kaaz. You and I are so different. What did she see in you anyway?"

"I'm not sure I know about that, but it's for sure that I spent everything I had trying to keep her happy."

He had definitely relaxed, and a reflection of human pain moved across his hard features.

"I lost everything because I loved her, too," said Peter.

"I think we need to talk some more," I said. "How about if we take a walk?"

He nodded and looked around, not focusing on anything in particular. For the first time since leaving the dance hall, I took a real breath. It was not like feeling safe exactly, but at least there was hope. Behind us, the gaping people strained at the windows with their face pressed and comically distorted against the glass. From that distance, they really couldn't see what was happening in the unlighted parking lot.

"She told me it was over with you," I said as we shuffled our feet along the gravel road.

"Same for me," he said. "Yvonne told me you were really bad, mean to her."

"Me, mean? She'd stay with me for a few days, then get

really restless and tell me she was going to see Martina."

"Same here. Well, we'd fight sometimes, but she always seemed to win. I never had any defense against her tears. The last time she came, I knew it would never work. She was different after being with you, never the same girl I knew in the beginning."

"Well, I saw her change, too. Now that she has finally left ..."

He stopped abruptly and faced me.

"You mean she's not living with you anymore?"

"With me? Not for weeks." I suppressed the urge to smile. Perhaps now wasn't the time to ...

Zimmermann laughed a deep rolling laugh.

"Now that neither one of us has her, I wonder who does?"

"Oh, I can tell you that. It's Mario Seifert."

"Seifert? That little cripple," he said. More flexing of the hands, making fists over and over. Then, he breathed deeply, getting control. "Well, it was fun to watch you going down hill with your cars. From Fiat to Moskvich to Trabant is quite a distance." He smiled for the first time, almost kindness in his eyes. "What did you do with all the money you got from selling cars?"

"How about making a guess."

More laughter.

"What a joke. We're both dummies. Smashing your red Fiat made me feel a lot better for a while. Sort of got rid of my frustrations, you know." He called Yvonne a few names, then lapsed into silence. "I've really had it with her!"

"She took us both for a ride," I said. Then my courage was rising. "How about if we forget about our disagreement?"

He stopped like a statue and faced me, leaning forward in an aggressive posture.

My heart fibrillated.

"On one condition," he said ominously.

"What?"

"That you let me buy you a drink!" He slapped me on the shoulder. It felt like being struck by a mallet, but I felt only a rush of relief. We reversed our steps and soon the dance hall came into view. Approaching the club was like getting ready to actually eat a pie that your mother has been baking all day. It was something to savor, an experience over which to linger.

Peter opened the door roughly and for one eternally triumphant moment he and I paused side by side on the threshold. We each had the other's arm around our necks, like comrades coming home from the wars, like brothers who had been torn apart in their youth and reunited in one glorious nostalgic moment. I loved it! Eyes widened, then widened more. Lips ceased to speak, and the odd laugh, the mindless giggle drifted into silence. For the second time that evening, the only sound in the dance hall came from the stereo.

Uwe was a wide-eyed watcher, too. He was the first to walk over and ask what everyone was thinking.

"What's going on?"

"We just decided to have a drink," I said easily. Then in a lowered voice added, "I'll explain later."

Peter was generous with the Schnapps, and it was only the second time in my life that I had tasted alcohol. It burned my tongue and throat. Why in the world did people drink this garbage? Those thoughts were eclipsed by the simple joy of existence itself. It was as though I had been to the edge of death, then snatched away by a miracle. Perhaps I had also found a friend unlike any other I had ever known.

Elbows on the table, staring into foamy glasses, Peter and I got acquainted.

"I think I know how Yvonne got away with fooling both of us at the same time," I said.

"Let's hear it."

"She had it figured out from the beginning. Yvonne could stay with you, then me, because our friends were completely different and we never socialized. You know, we swam in different ponds."

"Like dating two guys from different towns." Peter's eyebrows arched as another thought was forming. "If I catch that Seifert creep …"

It was my turn to reach out and slap him roughly on the shoulder.

Uwe's face wrinkled in disbelief. Other people continued to

gawk.

Peter nodded and ordered more drinks.

After midnight, he had enough drinking and small talk, and though he had far outpaced our consumption, his walk and speech were still steady.

"I have an idea," he said. An animated, excited state bloomed in a moment. "Can you drive me home, Carsten?"

"Sure. Uwe's riding with us, too."

As we drove along, Peter was jovial and light, as though he knew a wonderful secret. Arriving at home, he told me to wait and was gone only a few moments. He emerged carrying something bulky in a sack.

"Remember this?" he said, patting the bag fondly.

The can's outline was obvious. Did I remember my red Polski Fiat, the one that would turn heads when I drove by? Did I remember the can of paint Peter had slopped over the hood and inside? It was almost amusing to think about it now. If that was a can of paint he had in his lap, what would he do this time?

"Yeah, I remember. You're not going to pour it all over the inside of my car again are you?"

Laughter.

"This will be a lot better. Let's go."

I put the car into gear. "Where?"

Uwe was silent, wondering, probably worrying about where a ride with Peter would take us.

"Seifert only lives a few kilometers from here," Peter said. "I have a message for him and a letter takes too long."

I revved the engine and engaged the clutch. Gravel splattered and smoke flowed behind in a rolling cloud. Carried along by Peter's eagerness, I drove recklessly.

Mario Seifert's house was a small one bedroom, set in a meager yard, surrounded by a one-meter-high fence that was topped by a single strand of barbed wire. After parking far down the darkened street, we scuttled up the sidewalk amid snickers and whispered jokes. There was no thought about consequence, only adrenaline, excitement, daring to do something outrageous in a society where order and outward propriety were universal standards. Over the fence. It creaked and shivered at our transient weight. Peter pried the can open with his pocket knife.

"I have brushes, see?" he said, offering them.

"No, thanks," Uwe said. "I'll just watch."

The house was dark brown and the white paint would stand out well. Without further conversation, Peter selected a spot on the siding and began to paint. Dip, stroke, dip again. The letters were about a meter high and clearly formed. He began to laugh.

"Shhh," I said. "Quiet! Someone's going to catch us."

"Ja, Ja," he said. The brush made a distinctive slap-swish as the message was completed.

It was one thing to call Yvonne those names in a private conversation, but quite another to see them slopped across the side of a house.

"What a mess," I said. Still, it was funny, and I tried to suppress my laughter. Even in the dark, the contrast of the paint against the dark house was dramatic. The message could easily be read from a block away.

Peter spoke. "I'm going in."

"Isn't this enough?" asked Uwe.

"Don't give me any trouble. I am going inside." There was an ominous edge on his voice, and his glance silenced Uwe.

What would I do if Peter started to destroy the inside? I was totally involved, but could think of nothing to do except go along. A wave of outright fear had replaced my irresponsible reverie. This could take a bad turn for everyone if it went out of control, and no one could control Peter.

Uwe's experience in carpentry and maintenance was valuable when it came to getting through doors.

"You don't have to break it. Just give me a minute," he said. A few clicks, some scraping with a small blade. The door swung silently open and we all went in.

Peter grunted his approval and strode into the living room.

"Don't get carried away," Uwe said.

"I know what I'm doing. Mind your own business."

I looked at Uwe, who shrugged and shook his head. Nothing we could say to Peter would matter. His intent was irreversible, like a locomotive going down grade with a mile of boxcars pushing it ever faster. Peter stood very still for a moment, then entered the bedroom in three giant steps.

Dipping his brush for the last time, he painted a figure on the wall directly over the head of the bed itself. The letters were a facsimile of a particular old German script, not the kind of lettering you'd find just anywhere. "P.Z.," his own initials exactly matched the shape and style of the tattoo that had been needled onto the inside of Peter's left forearm years before.

"That's enough," he said. Turning to me, he nodded seriously and pointed at the wall with the dripping brush. "I didn't want you to get blamed for this."

Uwe's relieved sigh was audible. If Peter had started to destroy the house, there would have been no way that Uwe and I, even together, could have stopped him. We stepped back onto the front porch and Uwe re-locked the door, wiping the handle clean of any fingerprints.

As we drove the short distance back to his house, I recalled the words of the judge when I had faced Peter in court after he destroyed my car: "I will personally see to it that you go to prison." The man had stared with such intensity at Peter that there was no doubting his meaning.

"This is liable to cause us a lot of trouble," I said over the motor noise.

Peter's head was tilted slightly to the side, as though he was listening to something far away. He was disheveled, fingers spotted with white paint, and Levi's torn where he had caught them on Seifert's fence. Sitting still and stiff like a corpse, he appeared as though all the life had been drained away.

"What have I got to lose?" he said. The voice was tired, longing for rest.

No more words were spoken until the simple goodbye when we dropped him at home.

The next day, Uwe and I met briefly.

"I really feel bad about Peter."

Uwe studied my face for a moment, then shook his head almost imperceptibly in the negative.

I continued. "We have our goal, our dream. What does he have?"

"That's true, but there's nothing we can do about it now."

Uwe's expression made it clear that he knew that I had left something unsaid. He knew me too well. Anyone could see that Peter's life was simply drifting toward ultimate disaster, but his path had curiously intertwined with ours for a brief moment. What could we do with that opportunity? Uwe and I parted with the question still unspoken.

Over the next few days, I visited Peter regularly. We decided to talk again about Yvonne, life, everything, just like we were old friends getting reacquainted.

"What do I have, Carsten?" He wasn't feeling sorry for himself, just analyzing the situation. "There's no one who really cares for me. After Mom died, there was no one who really looked after me in any way. Life's no good when you're alone."

I had no idea what to say, so I mumbled something conciliatory. Then the impossible began to happen. It was like seeing a glacier die where it meets the sea at the end of its slow grinding journey. It snaps and groans along, moving, yet appearing not to move at all. Massive and dangerous, it is secretly shot through with hidden crevasses and faults. In an instant, unbidden, gigantic pieces break off in a whirl of splintering ice and rushing sound, to be inevitably reabsorbed into its ancient home, the eternal ocean. How could something so powerful ultimately be so fragile?

Peter began to cry.

As the grief spilled out in a crescendo of groans and agonized tears, I gained a profound perspective. I had felt what I thought was the hollow echo of loneliness in my own life, but I had just been feeling sorry for myself.

Peter Zimmermann was truly alone. His had been the universal hope of having someone who could understand and appreciate him for the person that he was and for the one he might become. He also knew that with Yvonne Kruger, it could never come to pass. He had loved her so completely, given his heart over so fully and without reservation, that when she was gone there was nothing but a ghastly vacuum, a terminal emptiness and ennui of spirit.

She was a lovely girl in the beginning, and that was the person whose absence he mourned. Even before I had arrived on the scene, he knew that someone would come and take her away. Even as Peter tasted the sweet fruits of their love, he knew that it couldn't last, and the bitterness of its passing was rending the fabric of his very existence. With her, he had lived for the day and had risen for a time above the fundamental agony in his life; knowing that he had been cruelly used heightened the pain.

I believed that I had been in love, but my tearful times were totally eclipsed by the depth of his genuine suffering. No matter what Peter said with his mouth about it being over between him and Yvonne, it would take a long time before that would be completely true. Until then, whether he liked it or not, his heart was still branded with her name.

Tuesday, Wednesday, and Thursday passed quickly, and we drove around after he got off work just getting acquainted. When Uwe could manage, he was with us. As I got to know Peter better, I began to think the problem over seriously, and Uwe had seen my question coming.

Friday.

Since I was on vacation and Peter was still working, I waited until the afternoon to go over to his house. As I turned onto Zeisig Strasse, I noticed the car in front was an old black and beige Moskvich, Mario Seifert's car. Yvonne was with him. He turned, and I turned the same way. Another block and I saw Mario glance once into the mirror, then double-take and stare. They must have just come back from their trip and seen the house's new paint job. Yvonne turned suddenly in the seat and saw me only a car length behind. Her eyes were impossibly wide, utterly blank with surprise. Peter's house came up on the right and I slowed. Mario braked slightly, then as I turned at Peter's, he gunned the stuttering Moskvich and accelerated in a cloud of blue fog and unburned gasoline. Yvonne continued to gape as they disappeared down the street. I switched the ignition off and waited. Within a few minutes came the ringing, bubbling song of Peter's little motorcycle.

"Guess who I ran into on the way over today?"

He shrugged and motioned for me to come into the house.

"Seifert and Yvonne were right in front of me as I came

245

down the street. They saw me turn in and stop."

"Sorry I missed that."

"We were a few meters apart for the last half-mile. You should have seen the size of Yvonne's eyes when I stopped here." I made large circles in the air with my hands. "This big. No kidding!"

"I'm going to get a shower and change, then if you're in the mood, we can take a little ride up to Bergman," he said.

Bergman was two places with the same name. The official location was the Eisdiele store on the Strasse Der Jugend where they sold candy and ice cream. The vacant lot across the street was also called Bergman by Falkensee's youth, and was a favorite place for evening fun. On almost any night, it was the best place in town to see who was driving what kind of car or motorcycle, wearing what clothes, and going out with which girl or boy.

That Friday Bergman was full of people. As I pulled into the lot, I could see Mario Seifert's car parked with him at the wheel and Yvonne beside him. Shifting into low, I accelerated, throwing gravel from the front wheels, and jerked to a stop next to Mario's. Peter's hands were flexing again, repeatedly making fists. He stretched ominously, then opened his door and stepped out into the night. Mario stood and walked toward me with purpose in his step. He stopped about three meters away.

"So." He spoke loudly, directing his speech to Peter, then staring at me. "Do you know that Kaaz is trying to get you into trouble?" His voice wasn't a shout, but still loud enough to be heard all over the lot, and nobody else was making any noise at all. No one wanted to miss even a line of this ugly little play.

"What are you talking about, Seifert?" Peter said. His voice had the edge I had heard when he invited me outside to fight the week before at the youth dance. There was no humor in him tonight, and his big hands kept up their nervous motion.

Mario's face was a pattern of anger and frustration. Perhaps he had come to Bergman to avenge his honor, or Yvonne's. Perhaps he had already boasted publicly about what he was going to do to me.

"This whole thing is your fault, Kaaz. You're the troublemaker. You think you can do anything you want to anyone, don't you?" He stepped toward me, clenched teeth clearly visible in the failing light. Taller. Heavier by 20 pounds. He didn't have a reputation for being tough, but I was no street fighter, either. I stood silently and shifted slightly to face him squarely. His anger gave him the advantage, and if we got into it, I was surely going to get hurt.

"What are you talking about, you idiot?" Peter took two steps toward Mario, then stood with feet apart, his torso turned slightly, like an enormous spring ready to snap. Slowly and deliberately, Peter turned his left forearm upward until the tattoo was clearly visible. "It wasn't him," he said.

Mario glanced fearfully at Peter then at the tattoo standing out like a sign on the muscular arm.

"Well," Mario said as he swallowed involuntarily, "I never would have thought that of you." His tone was tentative, uncertain, as though he and Peter had once been close friends and his feelings were hurt.

I heard Yvonne start to speak, but Peter's voice cut her short.

"Shut your mouth," he said. "You're nothing but garbage anyway!" She sat back in the seat, looking suddenly very small.

Mario was trembling with anger.

"Kaaz, this is all your fault. You're the cause of it, you're the trouble-maker!" He moved toward me, fists ready, eyes telegraphing his intention to hit my face. The whole youth population was witness to his humiliation by Peter whom he could not beat in a fight, and me who denied him the pleasure of an argument, viewing his accusations with silent contempt. He had to do something to someone! At least Uwe's name hadn't been mentioned so far.

Another step. He wasn't kidding.

Peter's voice was not particularly loud, but in the silence of that minor battlefield it flowed smooth and eloquent, like a famous phrase to be remembered, yet sharp and deadly like the hiss of a bayonet ripping rotten cloth.

"If you so much as touch him," Peter said, "you'll be driving a wheelchair instead of a Moskvich."

247

Mario stopped like a toy when its batteries are plucked out, gagging on his anger and shame.

"Get you," he sputtered. "Your fault Kaaz, get you both!" One gasp, then another, and he turned back toward his car, drowning in humiliation.

"Come on Carsten, let's get out of here. This makes me sick." Peter's voice was tired again, flat, without a trace of anger.

We left in silence, not possessing the victory we had come to gain. There was nothing but emptiness. The game wasn't worth playing anymore; there were no rules, and no prizes for winning. We both felt it. We were beholding our futures. Peter had stood up and admitted his guilt in front of the whole town, and thus condemned himself. His intervention had saved me from personal harm, but virtually finished his life for the foreseeable future. He knew that he had bought his one way ticket to Rudersdorf and punched it with some white paint and old German calligraphic letters on a bedroom wall. Why had Peter done these things? Was he just a defiant young man, unflinching in the face of authority?

I saw in his eyes the mirror of my own unrest, and his unspoken horror at the prospect of living out his life without hope, numbed by loneliness and a past that would follow him forever. In my limited experience, I knew that there were not many men who had the fortitude to take responsibility for their own actions when their freedom was at stake. Peter Zimmermann was, in my eyes, an exceptional person, and I was sure that I had found a true friend.

East German guard helping child escape through barbed wire

# CHAPTER EIGHT

How long did we have before the police came down on us again? Uwe and I figured the probable sequence of events. The encounter at Bergman was on Friday. First thing Monday morning, Mario would go to the local police to make the complaint. They would hear the names Zimmermann and Kaaz and immediately become interested. By Wednesday — Thursday at the latest — they'd get around to mailing the summons to Peter and me. The post office would take a day or two to deliver the documents, so that meant by the middle or end of the following week, we'd have to visit the Polizei at headquarters on Koch Strasse. At that point, they'd know that they had enough evidence, and a trial would be a certainty. Between our visit with the Polizei and trial time, we would each be closely watched. Then at the very latest within two weeks, we would be tried, marked, packaged as enemies of society, and scheduled for respective punishment. Depending on how the judge was feeling that day, I might get a fine or some time in jail. If prison was my punishment, it was more likely that I would be sent to Brandenburg where political prisoners were kept, while Peter would probably end up in Rudersdorf.

After prison, life would be very different. A convict couldn't return to his own town, sometimes for many years. The government provided mandatory job training during incarceration, and would find him work when he was released. It also provided an apartment and would keep him under surveillance for a period of time to monitor his success in readjustment. What the three of us had done might prove to be the end of everything. There was no going back, and we were

251

running out of time.

We sat quietly in my car, just letting the wind blow through the open windows.

"I know what you're thinking," Uwe said at last. It was impossible for me to hide anything from him anymore. "Don't forget our plans. Don't forget everything we've worked so hard to plan."

It must have appeared that I hadn't heard at all.

"He could have blamed me, you know. He could have let Seifert know that you were there, too."

"Sure," Uwe said, "but he didn't, and it isn't over yet. In fact, the bad trouble is just getting started. We can't afford to get any deeper into this than we already are." Uwe looked intently into my eyes for a long moment. "I told you, I know what you're thinking, but trying to bring him along could destroy us. Carsten, we might get killed even if things go just as we planned! Another variable at this point …"

It had finally been said, so I began the debate.

"If two could make it over the Wall, why not three?"

"Why not?" Uwe shook his head over and over, as though I had proposed a trip to the moon. "We've planned this for years, and now we have to go! Vacation is almost over for both of us, and there's no time to change anything. Suppose he gets a little drunk and tells someone? Suppose the cops or the Stasi are watching him now? What if he doesn't want to go and just turns us in with the idea of getting a lighter sentence? Think about what you're saying!"

"I know, but I can't get the thought out of my mind. It just feels like the right thing to do."

For a while, three or four minutes, we sat in silence, then Uwe spoke.

"You're crazy, and we'll probably die on the Wall. Tell me how you're going to ask him."

I was excited!

"If there's a trial, I might get jail, but more likely it'll be a fine and one last warning from the judge. They might not even find out about you at all. But Peter is finished now. They're going to throw everything at him! His life is over forever." I drew my right index finger across my throat. "Getting out could be the chance for him to start over."

He nodded. "Since you're serious about this, you need to think it through. Just what are you going to say? You can't just walk up and say, 'How would you like to escape over the Wall tomorrow, Peter?'"

"Of course not, and before I do anything, I'll let you know. You are half owner of all of our plans anyway, and I'm not going to do anything without your complete agreement."

"I'll think about it. We both have to think about it," he said. "You can't talk to him too soon, but you can't know how he'll take it either. He is as much a risk as the Grenztruppe and their machine guns."

"I'll see if I can feel him out first. You know, what would he think about escaping if he could, that sort of thing."

Uwe's face filled with earnest concentration.

"This will be it for us. We'll never have another chance, and if anything at all goes wrong ..."

About a week went by and we stayed almost invisible, trying not to draw any attention to ourselves.


Peter had decorated his house with some extraordinary ornaments. A large mattress lay in the living room instead of the bedroom. Long ago, he had decided that it was better to sleep there so he could watch TV or listen to his stereo without having to get out of bed. That was, of course, before he smashed my Fiat and the State sold his stereo to help pay for repairs. He had bought a second-hand one since then, but he complained that it wasn't equal to the original. One inexpensive metal floor type and one table-top lamp lighted the room mostly from one side, casting long shadows on the wall. Once there had been a ceiling fixture, but he had removed it and a pair of boxing gloves now hung on the dangling rusty chain. The centerpiece of this abode was the human skull he had somehow acquired several years before. It wore sunglasses, an American army fatigue hat, and clinched a cigarette in its untiring jaw. One wall was adorned with a meter-high poster advertising a well-known West

German cigarette, WEST. 'Let's go West,' read the caption.

I stood in front of the TV and inspected the skull from up close.

"Is this real?"

"Of course it's real." He feigned offense. "Besides, where do you think you could get a good copy of anything in this town."

"Where did it come from?"

"That was years ago, Carsten. Some of my friends helped me dig it up."

I gulped audibly, but he continued.

"I've been thinking. Do you see a resemblance between the skull and anyone you know?"

Squinting at the skull again, I shook my head slowly. The gaping nasal orifice and dry eye sockets didn't bring back any familiar faces at all.

"Reminds me of Seifert," he said.

"Come to think of it, you're right."

"That's what we'll call him, then. Seifert!" He studied the object, then tenderly brushed dust from the cheek bone. "This one has a better complexion, I think."

"What about the boxing gloves?"

"I don't use them anymore." He smiled and smacked his left palm with his right fist. "This works better anyway." Then his face revealed a new depth of his feelings. "I liked boxing, but they threw me out of the club when I was 16."

"How come?"

"I hurt a few people. Those gloves only look soft. You can really rattle a man's brain if you can hit." He sighed and looked away. "I had a few fights after the workouts, too." Peter stood and stretched. "Make yourself at home. I'm going to take a shower."

"Are you going somewhere?"

"No. I always do that when I get home from work, so I won't have to in the morning. That way I can sleep late."

As he left the room, my mouth felt dry, like I was in trouble or having to give answers to a policeman for breaking some law. Now was the time to talk about the escape, but how was I supposed to do it? What if I had misjudged him? What if he told the police? It was impossible to know beforehand what would happen. I had been wrong before about people's intentions.

The stereo thunked 'Rough Boys' by the American rock band ZZ Top, and my throat began to constrict. I was about to reveal my most private secret, my most closely held hope, my dearest life-sustaining dream, and it wasn't at all like I imagined it would be.

Fifteen minutes later, Peter returned from the shower and flopped carelessly in the overstuffed chair. He poured a cup of coffee. Hot and black. No surprise there.

"How was your day?" I said. "Anything in the mail?"

"From the cops? No, nothing." He shook his head and looked away at the wall. "I wish I could leave it all behind," he said. "The police, my past, everything." Then he shifted and grew even more serious. "I remember Budapest on vacation." His tense features softened. "It was great to be there even though it was crawling with Russians. The Hungarians are a lot more free than we are. It's something in their blood maybe. Even the Russian army can't break them."

Just a little further and it would be my turn to speak. I had to say it just right, then even if he did tell someone, I couldn't be accused of trying to persuade him.

He laughed, but not about anything funny. It was more of a short, bitter explosion of breath.

"I even thought about trying to cross over the Hungarian border, you know. ..." His voice died.

I nodded. The music seemed to fade in and out as Peter spoke. Familiar melodies, none of which seemed to fit the occasion.

"Too risky. I didn't speak Hungarian and I had a bunch of luggage. The Hungarians don't go out of their way to help Germans too much, anyway. Then I thought about trying the Wall, but there have been a lot of people killed on it, and I didn't want to end up as just another unlucky corpse."

"What if there was a way?" I said softly.

He closed his eyes and shook his head slightly, as though trying to shut out the thought.

"It would have to be a very good way. Some of the people

who are shot on the Wall don't die. The Grenztruppen drag them away. They just get crippled forever and sent to prison on top of it all."

"But what if there was a really good way?"

He looked at me oddly, as though he did not understand the question.

"If it was foolproof, I'd do it, but otherwise it would be better to try and exist here than get shot in the back by some dumb guard. Carsten, nothing is foolproof!"

It was time.

"Perhaps I know a way," I said.

He stared and everything stopped for an instant, like in a photograph.

"How is that possible?"

It was necessary to pull him in a little closer before putting the whole thing on the table.

"You know," I said, "it seems to me that you don't have much of a future here no matter what happens about this problem with Mario."

His mouth twitched in acknowledgement.

"This time the judge is going to give it to you, isn't he?" Slight nod. Otherwise, no movement. Maybe not even breathing. "When you get out, your reputation will be even worse."

He was concentrating, taking in every word and pondering it. Now I could go for it.

"Peter, you're my friend and I feel down in my heart that I can really trust you. If you could get out of East Germany, you could start everything over. No more gang of tough guys, no more tearing up the bars, no more police looking for an excuse to arrest you. No past at all. Just a future. There'd be hope for you to make your life into something you could really be proud of."

His voice came, but almost in a whisper.

"Once I applied for permission to start my own business, a little auto body shop. The government wouldn't even take the application." There was a new light in his face. "I'm a good welder, and I can fix anything. That would work if I just had a chance."

"Get me a pencil and paper," I said. "Here's how it's going to go."

The drawing came easily after two years of preparation. I had sketched the walls, wire, and other details a hundred times. Sometimes just hovering in the background, it was always in my thoughts. I could close my eyes and see every centimeter of the area where we planned to go over. I could have done the pictures in my sleep.

Peter sat very still as though any sudden movement might cause the opportunity to fly away like a frightened bird. Ladders, supports, ditches, patrol schedules all came forth from my memory like a fondly remembered poem.

Peter's face clouded. Doubt? Yes, it was doubt all right, but that made sense, too. Who wouldn't have some doubts when a young man who was an enemy only a few days before suddenly offered to save your life by helping you escape? An error in judgment could result in machine gun bullets shredding your body. Only an idiot wouldn't have doubts, and Peter Zimmermann was no idiot.

"Go through it again," he said finally. "Maybe we could actually make it, but I'm not going anywhere unless I can see it first."

"Are you ready now?"

"Now?" A microsecond's hesitation, then, "Let's go!"

As we drove to pick Uwe up, my mind was racing. We were fully committed now, and when we went for this reconnaissance, nothing could go wrong. A flat tire in the wrong place, being stopped by a random police patrol could put them on immediate alert, and it would be all over. If the authorities saw Peter, Uwe, and me together, we'd have no chance.

We arrived at Christel's apartment at 11:00 p.m., and I rang the buzzer. Uwe didn't know that we were coming. No answer. Knock. Ring again. Nothing.

"What's the problem?" Peter didn't like waiting.

"I'll have to whistle, I guess." Since we were kids, Uwe had heard my special whistle from time to time. He would know that it was me and answer the door for sure. I let it go, and the shrill tone echoed like a dying scream down the silent streets.

"The whole town had to hear that," Peter whispered harshly.

Fingers in my mouth, I repeated the painfully loud noise. Muffled thumps, footfalls on the stairs. Uwe opened the door and greeted me. Looking at Peter, then me, he simply raised his eyebrows.

"Yes, I told him everything," I said. "Now we have to show him."

Uwe nodded, then reappeared two minutes later, pulling on his shirt and pants.

We drove to within two blocks of the frontier area, and I stopped on Berliner Strasse and let them out on the shadowy corner.

"I'll be back."

Driving slowly up and down the street twice, I saw nothing moving. No guards in the bushes, no one smoking a final cigarette on the front porch. Not even a light in Koch's window. Back to the corner.

"Uwe, you go through Detlef's yard like always. Peter, get in the car and lie down on the floor in the back." My heart was racing, and it seemed as though my insides had turned to jelly. I wondered why I was still afraid even though I had done this so many times before. No matter how I fought, the fear came just like the first time. Uwe was waiting in the backyard as I slipped Peter out of the car.

"All right. One of us goes with Peter to the Wall, and the other is lookout."

"I'll take Peter," Uwe said.

"Then I'll walk slowly down the street like I'm getting some air. Go through Jerke's yard, but don't get the chickens stirred up."

"What's the signal if someone's coming?"

"I'll whistle."

Peter spoke in a sharp whisper.

"You're crazy. Whoever heard that would know you were signaling someone, and you'd wake up the whole neighborhood."

Uwe's grin showed even in the deep shadows. We had used the signal before.

"No, I'll whistle a tune. Do you know Hank Williams' 'I'm So Lonesome I Could Cry'?"

I heard Peter's muted guffaw.

"Let's go," he said.

Uwe and I had been to the Wall so many times, it was just another evening walk. I scuffed my feet, raising small drifting puffs of dust in the street, and in two minutes they were back. Even Peter was breathless with excitement.

"I know we can do it," he said. "It doesn't look bad at all, and I'm definitely with you!"

Uwe melted away into the shadows, and I hid Peter again on the floor of the car. We pulled out of my yard and drove slowly up the street.

"Here are the new rules," I said. "No more drinking, and not a hint, not a suggestion of this to anyone." The back seat was silent, but I knew that he had heard every word. "No trouble of any kind with anyone! You have to concentrate everything on getting ready."

"What do I have to do?" his voice was muffled, and half-drowned by the whine of the two-cycle engine.

"You'll need white clothes as camouflage for when we get between the walls, but we'll get them for you."

He replied something that I couldn't understand over the road noise, and I thought for a moment how ridiculous it must look for me to be talking over my shoulder to what appeared to be an empty back seat. I had to laugh.

Uwe was waiting on the corner.

Peter sat upright in the seat and we drove at a normal speed, but somehow the night had taken on a new feel. The summer breeze wafted the two-cycle smell of the car to somewhere else and blew in a refreshing arc across our faces. It tousled our hair and washed our faces with its delicate touch. How good it felt to be alive, to have a strong beating heart, to have strength, to believe in tomorrow, to have precious hope even more strongly than before.

"You need to go through your personal papers," I told Peter. "Remove anything you don't want the Stasi to confiscate. Find someone you trust to keep them, or throw them away. If you

give them to someone, you have to make a believable excuse!"
His attention was at maximum. "Figure out a way to give away
anything you don't want the Stasi to carry off, because that's
what they'll do when they search your house. If they can't find
anyone to buy your stuff, they'll just keep it themselves. They'll
interrogate anyone whose name they find at your place, so throw
away anything that might get anyone else in trouble."

"What will we be taking along?"

"Your Ausweis and just a little money."

"Why the identity card?"

"It's important to be able to prove who we are. Otherwise
maybe they'll think we are spies."

"What size clothes do you wear?" Uwe said.

Peter told him.

"We'll be sure to get you something the guards will find hard
to see."

In the rear-view mirror, I could see Peter slouch into a
relaxed position.

"Life is so strange," he said. "A few days ago, all I could
imagine was prison with the walls and the guards. I've heard all
the stories about what they do to each other in there, and I
would have had to fight a lot." His face was almost serene,
painted with the radiance of peace. "Now I can look forward to
a real life. I can be alive."

The Pneumant tires rumbled a rough bass vibration, and the
light from the instrument panels cast an unearthly glow on our
faces. The cool night flowed in through the open windows. It
tasted of freedom.

"Thank you both," he said. "Thanks for taking the risk of
showing this to me. Only true friends would share such a
beautiful secret." His voice faded and was lost in the vehicle
noise.

I wondered when the last time was that Peter Zimmermann
had told anyone thanks. We dropped Peter at his house, and
Uwe settled comfortably in the seat as I drove him home.

"I'll spend a lot of time with him so he doesn't get into
trouble," I said.

"I just hope he doesn't get drunk and start trouble," Uwe

said. "But one thing about all this is really good. You and I have been over the plan so many times that I couldn't tell anymore if we had missed some important detail. He believes it will work, and that helps my confidence." He slapped me lightly on the arm. "It's a good plan, Carsten. We're really going to make it!"

In the ensuing days, the only way to keep Peter in sight was to hang around with him, so we drove to Staaken on impulse, hoping to find some diversion. The dance hall was absolutely bursting, so no additional people were being admitted. The intermittent cacophony of voices and music seeped through the walls. We loitered outside the door next to a line 30 people long.

"We may as well go. It's totally jammed," I said.

Peter shook his head negatively and waved his hands in protest.

"I have connections. They'll let us in."

As he pressed toward the door, a tall, burly man stepped out of the line and into his path, extended his hand and placed it squarely into Peter's face, stopping his advance.

Peter stiffened, and took one step back.

"Don't put your hands on me again," he said.

My heart stopped and normal thoughts were frozen in an instant of panic. There was nothing I could do to help Peter. He was less than two meters tall, while this man was much taller and at least twenty kilos heavier. His arms were thick with muscles, and he peered dimly through schnapps-glazed eyes. Thick lips parted in a guttural laugh, and fine white teeth gleamed in the blinking neon. His hand whipped out again, pushing into Peter's face.

I was surprised at Peter's seeming lack of reaction, but noted how he shifted stance and stepped sideways so the flashing sign was no longer in his eyes. Was he going to challenge this Neanderthal giant?

"If you do that again, it's going to happen to you," he said simply.

Bleary eyes glanced cunningly at the nearby gawkers. He was a showman putting on an impromptu performance for his admirers, making ready for a well-rehearsed play. A confident laugh rolled forth, and the hand reached out again.

Swiftly, more swiftly than I had ever imagined possible, in an amazing blur of muscle and bone, Peter's fist snapped forth and jolted the leering face twice. There was only the faintest sound, a sort of thunk, then the man just collapsed.

Peter stepped up to the still form, bent slightly down and spoke in a loud voice.

"I told you it was going to happen!"

More people turned to point and stare.

I grabbed him by the arm and pulled.

"Let's get out of here. The next thing you know there'll be police and they'll haul you in."

He followed my gesturing hand toward the parking lot.

"I told him it was going to happen."

"Come on!"

"Oh don't worry," he said, "it happens all the time here. No one thinks anything about an idiot getting knocked cold. I'll bet he doesn't even know what happened when he wakes up."

Our gait grew more jaunty with every step, and we were both laughing by the time I wheeled the Trabant out onto the highway.

Peter's mood abruptly subsided and his eyes narrowed in concentration.

"It's going to be like this for the rest of my life if I have to stay here. If I can't start over, I may as well be dead."

For a while we drove in silence, then the thump, bump, rumble told the story. Flat tire. The station on F-5 was only a quarter mile away, so I pulled in, parked the car and checked the boot for the jack. No jack. I asked an attendant. No luck there either.

"What do you mean, no jack?" Peter asked.

"I just don't have one. Neither does the Tankstelle."

"That's a great combination, a car and a filling station both without a jack." Peter got out and stood surveying the rear of the car. "Get the tire tool and spare," he said.

I opened the boot, retrieved the items and turned in time to see Peter stoop down and slowly, without any show, grasp the bumper behind the wheel and stand up. Slowly, steadily the body rose, then axle, then the wheel was clear.

I worked as quickly as possible as Peter stood there, holding my car in his hands, and showing nothing more than a little extra concentration. He wasn't even sweating.

The attendants gawked and grinned, and I set a new record for changing a spare.

At my signal, he set the car gently back to the pavement.

"I need to wash my hands," he said.


Friday morning, I knocked on Kubicki's door. Ulf was at work, but that was all right because I wanted to speak to his mother, Annelies, privately.

We sat in her living room.

"I just wanted to stop by and thank you for all the help you have given me over the years. During some hard times when I needed some good advice, you were always there."

She knew me well, having heard my complaints and sorrows as a friend for the past five years. She sat in her favorite chair, worn into a comfortable, accommodating shape. Annelies knew that something was going on with me, but she couldn't imagine what it was.

"I never really gave up my wish to go to America," I said.

"Whatever you do, Carsten, I wish you the best in life."

Looking around the room, I drank of its familiarity. Photographs of each family member smiled from their wooden frames. They were all my friends, and since I couldn't take them when I left, I had to be sure that proper goodbyes were spoken. I wished to somehow absorb the essence of that friendly place until it was engraved upon the foundations of my spirit. I was leaving, but part of me could never really go. Like everyone who really lives life, I had come to a point where I had to move along, to choose between leaving behind people and places I loved, or crawl into a hole and become blind to what I would become. I was being torn apart inside. Perhaps if I concentrated hard enough, if I fully opened the passages of my memory, I could later reach back and touch these places. I scanned the room again, trying to pull every possible detail into my heart.

Frau Kubicki hugged me, and I left asking her to give Ulf

my best regards. She stood framed in the doorway, waving goodbye as though I was going on a trip.

That afternoon, Uwe and I drove to Rangsdorf for a last visit with Lutz Bobzien.

"What's wrong with you?" he asked. "You look pale. Are you sick or something?"

"Tired. It's been a long week and I've stayed up too late."

"Well, you're on vacation and you ought to be happy."

I smiled, but it fooled no one. We were close friends and he knew that something was amiss no matter what I said. Lutz had helped me to understand life, and had, like an older brother, taught me about moderation. "You have to learn," he once said, "that it's all right to challenge, and to question, but you have to do it in a way that doesn't always offend people. There are many things wrong with our society, but there are a lot of good people here too, and you can't get the two mixed up." The three of us drove to the theater so he could check to be sure it had been cleaned that afternoon. The conversation was artificial and strained. I struggled, trying to behave normally while bearing the sadness of parting, and he struggled empathetically, watching me hurt, but not knowing how to help because I could not allow him to understand. Returning from the brief ride, I placed a box on the table and pointed.

"For you," I said simply.

Opening it, he straightened suddenly and stared at me with frank disbelief.

"I can't believe this. You're giving me all of your Elvis slides? All of them?"

"Sure," I said. "You're one of the best friends I have ever had. I just wanted you to know how much I appreciate everything you've done for me."

"You don't like Elvis anymore?"

"It's not that way at all. Like I said, I just wanted …"

"That can't be," he said. "Are you going to die or something?"

I tried to laugh, but an odd croaking sound fell out.

"I have never done anything for you," he said. "We're just friends, just the best of friends."

Uwe shuffled his feet nervously and excused himself to go outside.

Lutz and I had a friendship that was marked by complete honesty. When we had first met, he had taken the time to look beyond my temper and restless nature and observe that there was a little boy trying desperately to grow up. One day, he had simply told me that if I didn't get hold of myself, I would be forever knocking my head against life and getting nothing but a hard time back for my efforts. He told me to slow down and not get so excited about things.

"There is plenty of time for everything, Carsten. You just have to let things come in their own way at their own time."

Perhaps he was thinking of his own brother, Harald, whose social rebellion had culminated in an attempted escape across a rural stretch of the border into West Germany. He was captured and served two hard years in prison before the West German government decided to ransom him with a cash payment. Lutz knew of my desire to go to America, and of my adventures with the government watchdogs, and he had reinforced my sagging spirits when the relationship with Yvonne came to its sharp demise. He helped me survive the sorrows of life, do the possible, and dream the impossible, so one day it too could be done as well. Lutz had helped me believe in myself as a whole person. I owed him, but I felt that there was no way to pay.

We sat in his living room, watching a pirated video of "Smokey and the Bandit."

I agreed verbally, but thought how nice it would have been to actually jump the Berlin Wall.

"That's the kind of car you need, Carsten," he said. "If you really want it, maybe someday there will be a way."

Then Uwe and I made excuses about having other places to go. Our hands met in a firm shake.

"Goodbye Lutz. I'll be seeing you."

He stood at the window on the upper floor and waved goodbye like every other time. But I knew one way or another, it was the last time.

Uwe and I went back to Peter's house and tried to settle down, waiting for the friendly darkness, and hoping for rain.

Peter was waiting, and eagerly opened the package of clothing we had brought. Without speaking, he hurried into the next room, and emerged a minute later wearing the new items.

"Looks good to me," Peter said. "These are just fine." He brushed the sleeve of his white wind breaker and smoothed the denim pants. "Very stylish for the occasion. Do you think we'll start a fashion trend?"

It might have been the time for a joke under different circumstances, but the issue was deadly serious. If the border troops didn't see us immediately, chances would be much better that we would live to tell about it later.

"I think it'll work just right. You'll blend in with the wall completely," I said. This was certainly not the time for reconsiderations, but I couldn't help but wonder just how effective the camouflage would be when we got into the lighted area. I shook the thought off and tried to focus. Peter was saying something.

"Now for my surprise," Peter said. "I knew that you liked pickles, Carsten, so I got a little jar." He opened a box and removed a four-liter glass container.

We chuckled, but the humor was only a reflexive response. Under other circumstances, I might have enjoyed the challenge, but now neither my stomach nor my mind were in the mood. My insides were becoming unsettled, like I had eaten something spoiled.

Peter opened the jar and seized a big one like it was a prize fish.

"Come on. You can't take anything when you go over, and if we leave these, the Stasi will just eat them." The pickle disappeared in two vigorous chomps behind Peter's straight white teeth. He belched vigorously. "We don't want those pigs to eat our food do we?"

I took one and bit. The smell and taste were familiar, but there was something missing. It looked like a pickle, but my taste buds were not sending the information I expected. Instead, there was an odd dryness of mouth, an unusual and unpleasant flavor, like unbrushed teeth. I was tasting my own fear.

The sun finally crawled beneath the horizon, but every

moment was elongated into creeping eternity. Once an hour, I walked outside and looked desperately upward into the heavens. Only the brightest, strongest stars had enough light to show through the ever-present glow from the border lights. The sky was clear, so horribly clean and clear. It even seemed as though there was less than a normal amount of auto smog. Like a farmer in the midst of a drought, I wanted it to rain. It had to rain. Our need was such a tiny thing. Only one half-hour of good downpour would be enough. Surely in such a great universe, a small thing like rain was not too much. Was there not some power who could grant our request?

Still, it was only Friday, and there were two more days left. Surely it would rain at least once. I came back inside and looked at Uwe.

"The sky looks clear, but there's always a chance something will show later. If that doesn't work, there's always tomorrow."

Uwe stirred and shook his head slightly.

"Tomorrow is Saturday, then Sunday, the last day." He paused to let the words sink in. "Sunday is not just the last day we can go for now. It's the last day forever."

He was right of course. We had waited too long, planned too much, and made too many irreversible decisions to turn back now. We were committed, one way or the other.

I heard Peter's throat gulp as he drained the coffee cup, and the taste of the sour pickle faded in my own mouth as I swallowed involuntarily. Knowing something in the mind is not the same as savoring its reality. The night of our first attempt, during the rain, Uwe and I had rushed madly to assemble the ladders. There had been no time to think, only time to do. This was very different, and my taste for all nourishment was now completely gone. How, I wondered, could men condemned to die even think about a last meal?

Peter turned the TV on; a West German announcer was reading the news. His words jumbled in my mind. Whatever he was saying didn't make sense; it was tangled, meaningless, like a foreign language. My imagination was locked on the Wall, the glittering barbs and broken shards of glass, the glistening copper alarm wire, the mass and bulk of the structure itself. Was I crazy? Was this action insane? We were at least alive, but when we went over the Wall, that could all change in a few seconds. Unbidden, a vision of Mowes' leering face came into my mind. There he was again, pushing the paper toward me, but this time he was laughing, laughing as I withered to dust.

I was trapped. We were all trapped inside a country where human beings existed to serve the government, where they could never grow up to fill the measure of their creation because the government had their lives so neatly planned. We could all live a perfect life if we would just do as we were told.

I involuntarily revisited the visceral feeling when Mowes took my coerced recantation in his hands and neatly arranged and clipped the paper so none of the edges would overlap. It was better to risk everything than to live as a half-formed puppet.

I took a deep breath and stepped back outside to clear my head, and my mind reached out to touch the mood of the night.

The breeze ruffled the fruit trees, then pushed lightly through hutches where rabbits slept in their friendly clumps of tender softness. It stirred Jerke's shirts, which his wife had forgotten the day before on the clothes line. It then moved on, picking up the corrupted essence of cigarette smoke and stale urine from the Siedlereck tavern, and bid a gentle good evening to the animals in their terminal accommodations at the nearby chicken and pig farms.

Laden with these mysterious essences, like a new fragrance from Paris, it swirled and danced in the night, slipping through the bronze-surfaced guard tower windows where the true extent of my country's depravity was displayed to the world. There it must have stopped, pinned to the Wall itself, tangled in the sharpened barbs, feebly struggling with its dying twitch to pass by, to flow across the earth as a breeze should. The air around me was stagnant, palpable like a physical weight pressing upon my consciousness until I couldn't escape its crushing embrace. Just a mile away, above all my little fears, loomed the craning necks of distant deadly floodlights, rolling back the natural darkness, illuminating the strip of hostile ground that symbolized a greater darkness, a vacuum of spirit. My body sagged, every muscle and bone aching with dark depression.

I was cold inside, feeling the essence of death itself. We had to have rain, but I could see that there would be none.

We would wait at least one more day.

Saturday morning faded in from sticky-mouthed unconsciousness. Stiff joints, standing up, walking with an unsteady straight-legged gait, fumbling with the toothbrush, trying to hurry so I could use the bathroom. The sallow face in the cloudy mirror was shocking with its red-rimmed eyes and stubbled dirty look. Not from drinking or smoking, but deformed by the crushing weight of mental fatigue that lay inexorably upon the foundations of my very being.

Eleven in the morning. That was good. At least we had slept late. But we were nevertheless aware of every moment, every infinitesimal tick of the watch. Time had become our mortal enemy, a gnawing cancer chewing our will into little pieces, devouring them, rotting our courage. We wanted to rush the day, to waste it in the most rapid and distracting manner. There was nothing more to consider. Nothing more to plan or discuss. All of our meager assets were in place except for the rain and the darkness. For those, we would have to wait, and it was the waiting that became more and more intolerable.

"How about some food?" said Peter. "I'll cook."

Eggs and toast. We filled our stomachs out of habit, not hunger.

After 20 minutes of sitting and staring at each other, we realized that we had to do something or we would quickly go crazy. We piled into my Trabant and drove. The streets were all familiar. The little car bumbled down the best thoroughfare in town, Strasse der Jugend, past the Apotheke where Mom bought medicine when anyone in the family was sick. I couldn't remember the name of the woman clerk I used to see there. Would all of my memories fade and slip away? Would my past evaporate, leaving me without any point of reference in the world? Who would I be if I left my home and family? It was all too painful to dwell on. Would anyone remember my name if my life were ended by a copper-jacketed Russian bullet? Would anyone remember me if I went to prison?

I heard that the West Germans left tiny crosses to mark

places on the Wall where people were killed trying to escape. At least there might be some kind of memorial. Who else would remember? Frau Taschner would look at Vivien and say, "I told you he was no good. Now see what's happened to him!" Lutz would remember. Frau Kubicki, Jurgen, and Gabi would remember. Mom, Dad, and Roberto would remember, but there would be no memorial except in their hearts. The state would wash my blood off the concrete and pretend that I never existed. But that didn't matter anymore. Nothing mattered except our desperation, darkness, and the hope of rain.

Bergman's Eisdiele store was on the left. Ice cream was popular in the summer, but there were many times when they ran out of flavors, and we had to settle for vanilla or whatever they had on hand. Haus der Dame, where Mom worked. She had risen early for the last 12 years and ridden her Diamant bicycle to work in good weather and bad. Handling the latest women's fashions made her twice as popular with the local ladies. If we hadn't lived in the frontier area, how many close friends might we have had visiting for Sunday cookouts? There was the low concrete building where I held my first job — Radio Fernsehtechnik; I could see Herr Doktor's car parked in its specially reserved spot. Past the radio and TV store where I first saw Yvonne.

It was strange how that particular memory now meant so little, how it had been so roughly displaced in the face of a rising sickness inside. A right turn took us down Post Strasse for a mile, then right again onto Hansa Strasse past the Intershop, where the favored few stopped to shop clutching their hoarded wads of Western currency. Passing Koch Strasse, I didn't turn right because that would have carried us past the city jail, and we didn't want to be reminded that it even existed. On the left was Lenin's monument, the concrete head with the stern gray visage looking bravely to some distant horizon, while the birds deposited white fecal streaks to accentuate its features. When we three were gone, there would be no statues to us. Right onto Spandauer Strasse completed a rough square as we passed the Gebaude Wirtschaft, where Dad worked. I shifted gears reflexively, remembering the time Dad took me to work to meet his friends, thinking how the men always greeted him as they arrived in the morning for work. Whether arriving on bicycles or a fuming, lurching brown bus, they would speak and pass an early-morning acknowledgment as they reported for their daily assignment. Here and there on the streets, I saw a nod or wave from a familiar face passing as in a dream.

Our own intermittent comments mixed with the distracting vibration of the car, and the kilometers rolled by, minutes creeping into interminable hours. We stopped for an occasional soft drink and packaged snacks to help fill the void that usually would have been occupied by animated conversation. Then the sky began to darken noticeably, and I pushed the car back toward Staaken. It wasn't cloudy, and still much too early to think about going back to Peter's.

"I'm really tired of riding," Uwe said. "Isn't there someplace where we can go and stretch, get some exercise?"

Peter suggested a fair in Staaken, and we grunted agreement.

I parked the car along a crowded street, and we slipped easily into a shifting clot of people moving toward the center of activity. Familiar faces emerged from the murmuring, flowing mass of good-humored humanity. Small-town Germans love to get together to eat, drink and buy things, and though there was never anything new to buy at the fairs, the food was always good.

"This might be a good Volksfest," Peter said.

"Hello, Carsten."

On of my acquaintances from high school. I acknowledged his existence with the faintest of facial expressions.

He stared.

"Are you feeling all right?" he said. "You don't look ..."

"Sure, sure," I said without looking at him. We kept walking and he fell behind.

Three swaggering young men emerged from the crowd and approached, clutching beer bottles, their faces blank with inherent vacuosity and alcohol.

"Hey, Peter, what's new in your life? Painted any houses lately?" Laughter and mutual congratulations at the cleverness

271

of the joke.

"Not today," Peter said. His face was completely without expression, like a store mannequin.

"Buy us a schnapps."

No reaction at all from Peter. It was as though he had not heard, and we kept walking.

The three looked Uwe and I over as though we had forgotten to wear clothes, suspicious at our presence. Were we ruining Peter's reputation? They frowned in disappointed puzzlement and stood dumbly as we picked our way steadily through the crowd. Then they were gone, swallowed by a new phalanx of browsers.

Drifting in and out of the improvised booths, we smelled familiar foods as they sizzled in a pan or waited in a nest of powdered sugar for someone with an irresistible habit to pass close enough for the aromas to do their work. There was the inevitable glass blower. Mom would have liked some of the figures. There was no point in buying souvenirs, but we purchased a few delicacies and ate as we walked. I looked at the bratwurst and wondered why I had even bought it. A reflex probably. Going out usually meant eating out. The food had taste, but our tongues were not picking it up. Nourishment of the body has no meaning when your insides are filled with a vision of your own doom.

Summer night slipped gently into place, and it was obvious that there would be no rain. No clouds now meant no rain later. The cold heaviness grew inside, and my legs felt rubbery. People swirled around in pursuit of things that for us no longer held any meaning. We were drifting on the surface of the town like jellyfish in search of a friendly tide. We climbed back into the car and drove the two kilometers back to Falkensee in almost complete silence.

"Where to?" I asked no one in particular. Uwe shifted in the seat, trying to get comfortable, but said nothing.

"How about stopping by the Finkenkrug Disco?" Peter said.

I didn't answer, but stepped on the gas. Why not?

It was a nice club considering the size of our town. Plenty of colored lights, Western records and tapes, and more Western pop music than was officially allowed. If they were going to be successful, they had to break the law. Regulations required that a certain number of East Bloc selections be played and that Western records couldn't make up a majority of the music. The problem with that was that young people by far preferred the Western music, and the club management was always on the edge of either offending its clientele or the government. In the long run, the tastes of the customers were a greater influence than the dogmatic laws governing public display of artistic works.

We paid at the door and stood, hands in our pockets like lost children. Another familiar face appeared.

"Well, well, Uwe," Bernd said. His voice was loud and grating as usual. This old school chum had moved to East Berlin nine months ago and was back for a visit. He was nothing more than a casual acquaintance, and Uwe didn't even remember his last name. What luck!

"It's been almost a year. How are you? Where are you working?"

Uwe shrugged and looked away without answering.

Bernd continued, oblivious to Uwe's lack of response.

"How's your project, you know, going to America?"

There must be an immutable law inscribed on one of the pillars of the universe guaranteeing that whenever someone is about to say something embarrassing about you, no matter how noisy the crowd, a moment of silence will occur at the exact instant the remark is spoken so everyone around can hear. Several people nearby heard Bernd's question and heads were beginning to turn, eyes beginning to recognize, to inspect us.

Bernd prattled on.

"Uwe," I whispered sharply, "do something with him! Talk to him, distract him, but shut him up! One idiot like that can get the wrong people interested in us again." This was the worst possible luck. I felt sick again, insides like water, barely controlling my own bodily functions.

Uwe took Bernd aside and after a short conversation rejoined Peter and me. Bernd wandered aimlessly away in search of other conversational opportunities.

"What did you tell him?" Peter asked.

"I said we were leaving and I'd see him some other time."

"For this we paid two marks apiece? Who wants to get shoved around by 150 people?" Peter said. "Let's get out of here, this is too much for me tonight."

As we drove back to Peter's, I reflected on the evening. So many faces had displayed amazement when they saw the three of us together. For a whole year, Uwe and I had not associated publicly, and now suddenly we appeared again and Peter Zimmermann was with us, or were we with him? I could see their questions, see their lips moving, buzzing the newest tidbit of information into ear after ear. Uwe and I would have been enough to start the questions again, but the three of us guaranteed prime-time exposure on the Falkensee gossip channel.

We couldn't just stay indoors and wait another full day. The police or the Stasi could hardly be expected to hear about our open association before Monday, and even then, it would take a few more days for them to decide whether we were worth watching again or not. By then, we would have already succeeded or failed.

Again I looked to the sky, searching for some sign of hope, but there was nothing but a few stars. On a clear evening when everything was just right, I could see some of the major constellations, but not this night. In the distance, there was only the glow from the border. My friends moved in slow, labored motions, faces pale and grim, mouths in perpetual grimace. If things went much further, depression might utterly overtake our hearts, and who knew what effect that could have. Would we lose what little nerve we had managed to gather?

"Fix some coffee, Peter," I said. "We're staying up."

Television programming was distracting for a while, then we watched music videos on a West German channel until 3:45 a.m., when the last of the hit parade was finished. They were both asleep on the mattress in the middle of the floor, and my eyes were tired and heavy. In a final confused gesture of desperation, I stepped over my sleeping friends and out into the night. Not a cloud.

Our depression deepened to new low level of gut-numbing agony.

Tomorrow was Sunday.

Rain or no rain, no matter what happened, no matter how we felt, we would have to go on Sunday.

Sunday in East Germany was different from the other days. Stores were closed, and traffic was almost nonexistent on the narrow streets.

Wisps of aromatic smoke were beginning to rise intermittently among the houses as early risers started their barbecue grills, preparing for ritual visits of family or friends later in the day. Dogs barked, and birds flitted through the cool morning air. For the most part, the people of Europe's Garden City rolled over for a few more minutes of sleep.

Eleven o'clock in the morning. Almost to the minute, the same time I had awakened on two previous mornings. It was as though there had been no night at all, as though we had been beaten senseless and half-slept the fitful slumber of the condemned. Tired eyes burned and itched. Light was painful. Every limb and muscle was stiff and reluctant to obey my fuzzy brain. Both Peter and Uwe lay awake and, like me, tried to find some way to move about without discomfort. My mouth tasted like old coffee and unbrushed teeth. Our shirts and pants were wrinkled and shabby. Sleeping on a park bench would have left us just as presentable.

"I'll make us something to eat," Peter said to no one in particular. His voice was flat, toneless, without inflection.

Uwe stirred but said nothing.

"How about if we buy it," I suggested. "We still have some East German marks, and they won't be any good where we're going." That would be true no matter how things turned out. I wondered if they got the double meaning.

Murmured agreement, then a sullen silence as we put on clean clothes.

I asked, "Where can we go?" It didn't really matter, but was asked as a reflex.

Uwe spoke.

"My favorite place is Speisestubchen, in Schoenwalde."

It was a privately operated restaurant noted for excellent food and service. "I hardly ever had the money to eat there before," he said. "It's funny that we should get to go now."

"All right," Peter said, "we can combine breakfast and lunch. The other places around here have food that tastes like what we ate at the high school cafeteria."

I stuck out my tongue, and my companions noted the attempt at humor. No one laughed. We had some money to spend, but more importantly, we had time to spend. We wanted to consume it, to have it fly swiftly into the night.

The restaurant staff eyed us with interest after we had been seated. We tried to look normal, but it was simply impossible. Both Peter and Uwe looked like they had the flu, sallow and listless, and they assessed me tentatively, no doubt thinking that I appeared the same. We surveyed the menus for a moment, then ordered three of the same dish.

The appetizer was fried chicken in some kind of sauce with melted cheese with a French name. Then Rinderbraten — steak — for the main course. The meat was tender, but I chewed and chewed. Hardly any taste. Adding salt did nothing. It was my taste buds that were out of order. I chewed more, then tried to swallow, but it stuck halfway down. I saw Peter and Uwe struggling with the food, too. In particular, Peter looked out of place as he carefully cut the meat with the fancy knife. His T-shirt was dark blue, stretched tight by his muscular chest; across the front in large white letters were the words 'BAD BOYS.'

Silently, I reflected that it might have been an artistic touch, perhaps even real bravado if we had all worn the same shirts, but I kept the comment to myself. The thought was too insignificant.

"Is everything all right?" the waitress asked. "Is the food to your liking?" She carried a soft white hand towel daintily in her hands.

"Yes," I said, "just fine." I wasn't convincing, and she moved away still wearing a worried expression.

We had somehow managed to eat most of the food.

"I can't stand sitting still anymore," I said. "Let's get out of here." No one else spoke, but we moved our chairs away from the table in unison.

"Please come back," the waitress said.

"Look," said Uwe, "they have a guest book. Maybe we should sign and leave a last message."

I saw Peter look at the book, but we trudged outside without pausing.

A 15-mark tip! I could see the surprise on the waitress's face. After watching us pick at the finely prepared meal, she probably wondered if we'd leave anything at all. Her enthusiastic exclamations of thanks followed us all the way to the door.

As we pulled away from the curb, I wondered what time it was, then decided that it didn't matter. It was still light, so once again we took to the road with the Trabant's inescapable exhaust noises reverberating in our ears. Kilometers clicked by, consumed by the aimless wandering of our wheels. Spikes of radio noise, music, the predictable canned enthusiasm of the AFN disc jockey competed with the racket of the motor and body.

The Trabant was a cheaply made car that was supposed to be the workers' answer to cheap personal transportation. The body of the little machine was constructed of a kind of plasticized material, laminated, coated, and pressed into fenders, roof, and hood. Its special features included a gravity-feed fuel system, which you had to remember to turn off when the engine was shut down in order to prevent the carburetor from flooding. The spark plugs fouled regularly due to the oil-gas mixture, and the body was guaranteed to disintegrate into a thousand irretrievable pieces even in the slightest accident. It was the last of my cars, the seventh, and almost as rough as my old Lada, the first one I had ever owned. Dad had a Trabant. I remembered the day he brought it home. He had waited over ten years to get the machine. Two months later, I had my first car. The neighbors, particularly Koch, appeared openly amazed and envious as I drove down our gravel-lined road. Why should I, a wet-nosed child, own something that they had to wait years for? Where had I gotten the money for that anyway? While their sons and daughters bought motorbikes in high school, I road my bicycle. They laughed at me as I pedaled past their groups of parked machines.

The money I didn't spend on motorbikes went into savings until that day so long ago at the used car lot in East Berlin. It was easy to understand if anyone cared to think a little. Life is filled with choices, and mine had carried me to a place where independence was the most important thing of all. Long ago, I willingly paid the price for a measure of freedom, and if everything went as planned, I was about to do it again.

On the left was Friedhof Falkensee, the local cemetery. Uwe spoke.

"Do you remember the time we were coming back from East Berlin and we were just passing the Friedhof here? AFN started playing 'She and I' by Alabama and you said, 'I bet we can get all the way to my house before the song is over.'" He paused, savoring the thought. "We must have been going 70 through town, and we made it! That Lada was really fast! We didn't worry so much back then, did we?"

His smile made me smile, too. It seemed forever since anything had felt as good as that smile. It was warm with the glow of foolish childhood remembered from a day when the only fear from speeding was an accident or traffic ticket. Today there would be no speeding. I didn't dare attract attention.

Passing the old Oberschule classrooms and soccer field, we turned onto Henningsdorfer Strasse and slowed as Yvonne's house came into sight. Two of her mother's breeding stock of highland terriers were in the front yard. I blew the tinny-sounding horn as we were abreast of the house, and both dogs turned toward the noise. No one else was visible.

Winding around, we passed Bergman again. I pulled in and made a slow circle of the concrete parking lot, stopped the car, and we got out to stretch. A few young people were there, and they nodded a greeting, but they were all younger. Overnight, it seemed that we didn't belong anymore. They seemed like children, and I felt as though we had suddenly been displaced by the rising generation. They occupied our gathering place as though they had a deed. Just a week or two earlier, Uwe and I had discussed growing older and inventoried our stock of memories. We had a lot of fun, romanced the girls of our languid town, went to fun places with fun people, but even then we knew that it was almost over one way or the other.

Many of our high school friends had gotten married, moved away, or gone to work or into the army. Many of them already had children of their own. Our classmates were going under one by one, letting go of their childhood dreams, slipping into the stagnant meandering stream of our country's culture. Their future was blending into the tomorrow imagined for them by a small group of men in government offices. That group governed the economy and men's lives the same way, within the framework of central planning and reflected in the perpetual mirror of Marxism.

It wasn't so odd that they denied the existence of God. As long as they were in charge, there was no room for another one.

So many hopes, so many spoken and unspoken dreams died without a struggle, without so much as a whimper, and it was time for us to move on or join the ranks of the dead and dying. We held onto our memories for one last wandering.

Peter spoke.

"Everybody is probably at the Volkshaus in Staaken. Let's go see what's happening."

Perhaps another buzzing crowd would be a little relief. It had been no good to linger in the restaurant, and now it was no longer any good to stay in the car just burning gasoline and stopping to go to the bathroom.

There was a crowd at the dance hall. Not bad for 5:30 in the afternoon. The night was creeping on its way, and the young people were streaming in like moths toward a bright light. As far as nightlife was concerned, there were only a few places in Falkensee worth visiting. Siedlereck tavern, near my house, was the worst. It was known for fights and loud entertainment, and the regular police watched it closely. Siedlereck's problems were related to broken noses and cuts on the face from fists. No one dared to use any kind of weapon other than a chair leg or a stick found in the ditch. The penalty for carrying weapons made their possession a risk for only the most calculating or foolhardy. This crowd looked fairly civilized, and since the day was mostly over, it couldn't hurt to stop awhile.

"Hey, Peter!" A group of his regular associates hailed him with a cacophonous greeting. Two approached after surveying Uwe and me with obvious surprise. Then they ignored us and focused on him. "Have a drink. It's never too early for beer!"

Peter said nothing. His pupils were very wide and glassy, as though he was in shock.

Then it hit them. Something was very different, very wrong with their old comrade. "Are you sick? You look awful," one said.

Another spoke with conviction.

"Have a smoke and something to drink and you'll be all right in a few minutes." More laughter.

"No, I don't want anything right now." He turned to me and spoke quietly so no one else could hear. "Let's sit down. My legs won't support me." His hand reached out to touch the table like an old man trying to sit without falling. Uwe and I sat, too.

Peter's friends shuffled away still acting amazed and a waitress appeared.

"Beer," said Peter.

"ASCO cola," I said.

"Cola," Uwe said.

The ASCO was watery as usual. I had always hated it, but maybe it would settle my stomach. It was wet and cold, so I sipped.

"Does anyone beside me have shaky knees?"

Peter and Uwe both nodded.

As we drank, the people stared. They made no effort to disguise their curiosity. An electrician I knew from Plastikwerk approached, paused, then withdrew as I waved him away without even a greeting. What a sight it must have been, the two young men who had been arrested for visiting the American Embassy having a drink with the young man who had broken more bones in anger than anyone else in town.

Yet as we sat together, we were wooden and lifeless, like pale death itself. We wanted nothing from our friends, but didn't speak to each other. The music played, the people danced, drank and made their propositions in the corners of the room, but around our table lay a shroud of deadly silence as tangible as fog on an autumn morning.

The stress was too much for me.

"I can't stand this anymore. Do you mind if we go?"

It seemed that the walls were closing in, and the stares of the people were almost palpable. They might as well have been handling me, touching my clothing. I felt like every one of them had guessed what we were going to do, and that they would run and tell as soon as we left.

We paid for the drinks and shuffled uncertainly through the door, our every movement observed and cataloged by a hundred interested eyes. Behind us, Peter's glass of beer was more than three-quarters full, hardly touched at all. The soft drinks were likewise nearly full. Some spectators sifted through their minds, wondering what they knew about each of us; others simply reacted like mindless amoeba tickled by a new stimuli. These twitched and wiggled with delight. Here was a new story to tell at work tomorrow!

It was only 6:30 p.m. We drove.

"How much money does everyone have?" Uwe asked. "If there's enough money left, we could go back to Speisestubchen." He paused and added the rest in a lowered voice barely audible above the motor. "Who knows when we'll get a good meal again."

I looked across the seat at Peter. He shrugged and stared straight ahead.

The staff at the restaurant was visibly surprised. Perhaps we were going to make it our permanent home? The waitress seated us at the same table as before and hovered nearby, the prospect of a large tip lighting her plain features. We ate a small meal mostly in silence, and elicited the same puzzled looks as we had that morning. When the food was gone, we sat for a moment and discussed what to do next. Peter called for the check and we paid, leaving the rest of our East German marks on the table. The tip was a good one, and the waitress was beside herself.

"Come back soon, anytime," she said.

We nodded and trudged outside.

Uwe said, "If we ever get to come back, I hope this place is still here. Their food is really great."

How amazing, I thought, that he can still be so spontaneous. Then we were out the door and standing on the restaurant's front step.

Precious darkness had arrived at last. At 9:30 p.m., we drove back toward Falkensee, and I stopped for the last time at the gas station on F-5 where so many important things had happened.

Gasoline gurgled into the ten-liter tank, and I remembered the afternoon five years ago, at age seventeen, when I met the Americans there who were refueling an enormous motor home. It was almost as large as one of our city buses, and I was amazed. Passing through our country on one leg of a European tour, they were friendly and open, answering my questions and asking a few of their own.

"How do you feel about the Russians?" said the lady.

I laughed. "They're here, but no one will miss them if they go. They have to stay in separate compounds most of the time so they won't get into trouble. I hate them."

"Hate? Really?"

"Well, just look at it this way. On the West side, at least the American Army gives something to the economy. Here, the Russian soldiers' money is no good, and they have a bad reputation for getting drunk and starting trouble if they wander around on their own. All they do is take from us and, in return, supply our government with weapons to use against us. They aren't allowed to mix with us much. No decent German has Russian Army friends."

"What about America? Do you know much about us?"

"Where are you from?" I asked.

"Kenosha," she replied. "That's in the state of Wisconsin. The capital is Madison. It's bordered by Lake Superior and Lake Michigan." I was going to tell her that I had known that since geography class in fifth grade, but reconsidered. I wondered how she would do on a German geography quiz, but didn't ask. No point in embarrassing them.

Her eyebrows arched in appreciation.

As we talked more, a picture of America's soul acquired shape and depth. These were open people, with an almost child-like interest in Europe. To them, the world was an object of fascination, and they wanted to touch it all, to have their picture taken with it like they did with fuzzy, benign animals in a petting zoo. They were basically unaware of oppression as a way of life, and could only relate to it in the abstract.

"I have always wanted to go to America," I told them.

"That would be great. You could visit us, and we could show you around."

Perhaps they were just being polite. Surely they knew that I could not simply buy a ticket. Surely they understood that they were inside the zoo, and that the animals could not just leave when they wanted.

Then the gas tanks were full and the motor home started again. They were leaving.

"Perhaps we could exchange letters?" I was hopeful.

"Of course."

Addresses were written and, in the months that followed, they kept their promise. They answered my letters, then after a long time, I ran out of things to ask about and the friendship became dormant. Even so, I retained my impression of the people of America, seen through the sample I had taken that day so long ago at the gas station of F-5.

The tank was full and I paid the attendant.

"You don't see many of those," Peter said, pointing to a green Chevrolet Impala with West Berlin license plates cruising past the station. American cars were very rare on the east side. "See you later, perhaps," he said toward its receding tail lights.

Perhaps we would. Perhaps the plan would work as we had designed it. Perhaps we wouldn't be seen as we went over. Perhaps nothing would go wrong. Perhaps it would rain. I looked again into the sky. Just stars. No, it wasn't going to rain, and the sickness of fear was rising to flood level this time. Would it overcome me? Would my thoughts congeal and prevent going through with the escape? I was swept by an icy chill and forced my mind off the subject.

"We'll drive slowly now, so no one will notice, and we won't push our luck. It's time to go to my house." I started the engine.

Their faces changed almost immediately. I could see a difference in Peter and Uwe, and assumed that I too had begun to revive. For the past three days, we had moved about like pale robots, going through the motions of normal life, jerking at small sounds, staring without seeing, waiting for the terror to come nigh. Now it was time to behold the face of death.

Once again, the yellow-green of the instruments painted our faces with sickly shadow, but now it was different. Even though the sky was still full of stars, it no longer mattered. I could once again feel my inner being and could see life in the reanimated expressions of my friends. Action was the only antidote for our paralytic fear, and now we could actually begin our enterprise for real.

Eleven-thirty at night. Lights on in a few houses. No traffic on the street. Monday had almost arrived, and the quiet people of Falkensee planned to greet it with snoring. No street lights. Homes quiet. The last of Sunday's darkness covered the neighborhood like a child's favorite blanket.

After dropping Peter and Uwe temporarily on the corner of Berliner Strasse, I wheeled the rattling Trabant up and down the narrow lanes. Calvin Strasse, Zwingli Strasse, Pestalozzi Strasse. No one, nothing on the roads, no one on the porches, no one taking a walk after a fight with his wife. My neighborhood wore its normal quiet shroud. I stopped to pick Peter up, and watched Uwe fade into the shadows, heading into Detlef Jasmund's yard for the last time. First gear, shift, the burbling sputtering engine hesitated, second gear up to about 40 k.p.h. The little car had served me well, the last in a long line. Yes, I had owned seven cars since I was eighteen. They were important because of the mobility that came with them, but no car could take us where we needed to go now. I became suddenly conscious of the steering wheel's plastic texture. I would never feel that again, would I?

I spoke over my shoulder to Peter hiding under the blanket in the back.

"I know one thing for sure. I won't be taking you out of here again."

No reply.

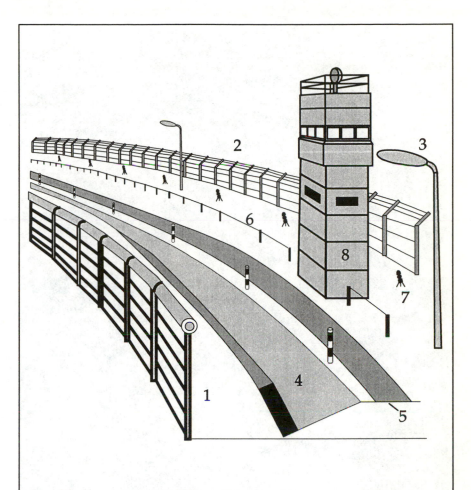

DIAGRAM OF THE WALL IN ITS MOST DEVELOPED FORM

1. Twelve-foot concrete wall with piping on top
2. Inner wall with tripwire
3. Lighting
4. Anti-vechicle trench
5. Guard patrol road
6. Dog track guide wire
7. Alarms
8. Observation tower

Guards cart off Peter Fechter, shot during his escape attempt
shortly after the Wall was erected

# CHAPTER NINE

Fear is only a word until it comes to visit you. Now it fastened itself upon my body like a strangling vine, like deadly sucking tentacles, holding me close in its cold embrace. Once again I became numb, hands and feet working like distant wooden appendages, driving the little car with programmed motion, devoid of any sensation. I had become automatic, mechanical like the machines I used to repair at Polymath.

Then we came to my parents home. It appeared suddenly in the yellow sweep of the headlights. Stop. Switch off. Set brake so it wouldn't roll. How foolish. The yard was flat; it couldn't possibly move on its own. Turn off the fuel valve. It was all reflexive. Be sure to close windows in case it rained. But it was not going to rain. I was thinking again. The gnawing surge of terror moved again like an awful blossom within, blotting out my very consciousness. I had to get control if we were to continue. Looking both ways, up and down the street, I saw nothing. Complete silence. No lights even in Koch's house. There would be plenty of lights soon.

"O.K., let's go," I said.

Peter slid sideways from the door and ran at a low crouch into the deep black next to the house where Uwe was already waiting. At the front door, I let myself in quietly. Our white escape clothes were there in the bag exactly as I had left them. Mortal terror was really alive now, charging around inside, screaming, tearing, filling my mind with writhing nothing, blocking everything but heartbeat. The harsh, sharp breathing was mine, but I didn't dare show fear. To do so in front of my comrades would be to weaken them. Their insides also must have been leaden, but if we could keep up appearances a few minutes longer it would be all right. We could fool ourselves into functioning just enough to save our lives. When action began, the plan would automatically take over, and there would be no need to think anymore.

"I have a few things more to do in the house," I said. "Back in a minute."

"We'll get the ladders ready," Uwe whispered. The shadows changed, grass rustled, and they were gone around the corner toward Dad's tool shed.

Standing in the living room, I felt like an intruder, yet the room was as familiar as my favorite sweater. I turned my head slowly, absorbing the essence of the only home I had ever known. To the right, the kitchen where Mom spent so much time cooking for the rest of us, even after a long day at work. Even when young, I understood how hard that must have been. "It will be ready soon," she would say. "Wash your hands and get ready to sit down." Brushing back the blonde hair where it drifted into her eyes, she'd wipe beads of perspiration away from her smooth forehead. At the table, Dad would praise the food and she would smile and shift in her chair. I could almost hear the voices. Roberto would complain about some vegetable, and whine the way I used to. Dad would acclaim the dessert, knowing how hard it was to get the spices and special ingredients. That was where Mom's connections came in handy. Women who wanted something special from the clothing store would gladly do her a favor by picking up some extra condiments through their own connections. That was the way it worked everywhere. One hand washed the other. After the meal was over, she would return to the kitchen and dishes. Pots were cleaned and tucked away like children put down for the night.

To the right, my brother's room was silent. He was visiting his grandparents in Schoenwalde. What would his friends in school have to say about me in the West? Would they insult him, or ask in awe how I did it? Would he try to defend my painful choice or retreat in bewildered silence? Would his teachers watch him through narrowed eyes? Would he get a personal interview from the Stasi?

A few days earlier, I saw Roberto on one of my sporadic appearances at home. His thoughtful comments caught my interest and evolved into a surprisingly deep conversation about the subtleties of life.

"There's this girl at school," he said. "She's really smart, and good-looking, too." He motioned with his hands in the air, indicating the universal sign language for the feminine body shape. "I'm not sure if she likes me or not." He stopped and smiled shyly.

He was really beginning to grow up. At 15, Roberto was discovering the opposite sex, and like me many years before, wondering exactly what to do with his feelings.

"Does she look at you a lot?" I asked.

"Well, sometimes. Yes, I think so. She smiled at me Friday, but when I said hello to her after lunch, she acted like she was busy and didn't want to talk. It's confusing."

I related some of my earliest experiences when Heike Puttnins and I would take walks at Falkensee lake with Uncle Reinhold's dog, Blackie, straining at the leash, dragging us from tree to tree. "She never even said she liked me," I told him. "You just have to be patient and be sure that the girl knows that you think she is pretty, smart or whatever."

"Then what?"

"What do you mean, then what?"

"Well, how do you know if she wants to go out? I'm afraid that I'll ask her to go to the movie and she'll say no."

"I guarantee that'll happen sometimes, but don't let it bother you. If you never ask, you never know."

Our 15 minutes together covered other important segments of life. He was wondering about what he would do for a living after school was finished. He admired Dad a lot, especially the way Dad could fix things, and the way people looked up to him because of his kind personality.

"What can I become?" he asked.

This one was more difficult than the questions about girls. Roberto didn't yet understand that he would have to be more lucky than anything else if he were to be happy after choosing a career. In less than a year, he'd have to sign some kind of training agreement that would narrow his choices for the rest of his life. The only way out after that was to become a renegade like me and swim upstream forever, like a salmon trying to get home for the last time, but maybe never finding the right river. A lot of them died on that desperate journey.

"What would you really like to do? That's what you have to decide."

He mumbled a few possibilities.

Involuntarily, I relived the anger that suddenly flooded my memory from the time when I struggled with my own situation. This business of mandatory career planning while still in junior high was criminal! How could any child be expected to make those kinds of choices? Adults of 25 barely knew what they wanted, but by then, it was much too late.

I saw my brother's childhood being stolen and remembered the theft of my own. Men were not machines that had to fit into neat little mountings in a factory somewhere. They were entitled to test, to try, to make mistakes, to try again, and even fail again. I remembered the voice on the early-morning radio program from West Berlin that I listened to as a young child. They rang the Liberty Bell, and the announcer read a short passage. The words were powerful, reaching into the deepest parts of my heart with phrases like "all men are created equal" and "they are endowed by their creator with inalienable rights, including life, liberty, and the pursuit of happiness."

I stood in the hallway and slowly regained control. Roberto would have to do the best he could with what he was going to become. My way would probably not be his way, and he had to find the value of life for himself. Following blindly down my path would only bring a greater tragedy.

I swallowed hard and turned my back on his silent room.

To the left, across from the kitchen, was the family room, where we had spent so much time together, where Dad would relax watching soccer games. In later years, I took off in search of my own life and paid little attention to him, but even when I wasn't interested in his wisdom, I couldn't help but absorb his steady outlook.

"It's good to have a family, Carsten. My happiest times are

spent here with you, Roberto, and Mom." When he came home in the evening, almost always after working overtime, the distinctive, building buzz of his Trabant would announce his approach at the corner of Calvin Strasse and Zwingli Strasse, momentarily rising, then falling as he wheeled into the yard. Dad's car was the cleanest in Falkensee, kept like a valued prize, as though he owed some special allegiance. He would groom it like it was a family dog, carefully washing the fragile body. If there was ever a beautiful Trabant, it was the one that belonged to Dad. He was grateful to finally get it after years of waiting, and took extra special care to keep it in perfect condition. When I got my old Lada, he was impressed and happy.

"Take good care of it, son, and it will take good care of you," he said when I was washing the wreck one afternoon. No matter that it was in the throes of terminal oxidation, he was elated that I could have some of the better things in life without waiting as long as he.

The dim light softened the tiny glass figurines and cut-glass dishes on Mom's armoire. Sometimes, when the afternoon sun fell just right, it would strike the crystal cuts and fragment into a thousand parts. Then for a quarter of an hour, the bands of color would move with exquisite slowness across the walls. I was sometimes so fascinated that I would stand close to them trying to catch every special detail before the moving sun changed position and wiped the spectacle away.

My parents' room was quiet. I listened intently, hoping that my parents wouldn't awaken and find me there. They wouldn't be surprised because my comings and goings were irregular anyway, but I didn't want them awake since they might somehow see us outside and thereby become accomplices in the crime of escape.

It was hard to think of leaving as a criminal act. We would take nothing except our own clothing, a little money, and our dreams of freedom. Perhaps, in a way, it was a crime, because we were stealing a part of East Germany's tomorrow. We were tiny parts of that promise, and multiplied times a thousand or tens of thousands, our act would bleed the country until it was feeble and helpless, unable to carry on even the normal daily tasks. But then, we were not stealing anything from the government, because our futures were our own. Even though we had been told of our obligations since the earliest years, we three, at least, understood that the government didn't own us. We were free men in our hearts, and it was time to validate these aspirations with our own blood, if necessary.

Slowly, carefully I tiptoed up the stairs. In my own room for the last time, I struggled to slow my racing mind. It seemed that here were a thousand details to remember. Surely there was still some loose end. Nothing whatsoever could remain behind that could suggest that anyone had prior knowledge of the escape. To help someone leave the country illegally was worse than to do it yourself. My parents didn't need to be left holding evidence that would validate that accusation. It was enough that they must face the harassment that was sure to come. It only took a few minutes to write the predated contract noting that I sold my Trabant to my father for 4,000 marks. I didn't know if it would pass the Stasi's inspection, but if I left nothing at all, the automobile would surely be confiscated. Dad would find the note and realize my intentions.

My bed was still made, shoes in their usual place, no dirty clothes on the floor. Mom was always happy when the room was neat. Socks were rolled and neatly stored in the wardrobe that served as my closet. Everything was in its place.

As I stood in the doorway, the Elvis poster caught my attention. I had just celebrated my 14th birthday, signifying my arrival into adulthood. The party was a family celebration where gifts were given, and I had my first shave with a straight razor at the hand of Uncle Reinhold. Mom had asked what I really wanted, and I had joked about an Elvis poster, knowing that it was impossible to obtain one in our country. A few days later, Mom said, "You're looking a little ragged around the ears again. Go by Jutta's and she will trim your hair." Even though I had gotten a haircut only a few days before, I visited the hair stylist as Mom suggested. To my complete amazement, she presented me with a cardboard tube containing the poster. I hugged her so tightly that she groaned. Mom had asked her to get an older relative, who could travel freely to the West, to pick it up in the other Berlin. Roberto wasn't interested in Elvis, but perhaps he could trade it to someone. There was no need for that part of my will to be written.

Then there was the room itself. So many days had been spent here. Uwe might as well have called it his. I recalled when we decided to remodel the room, and stayed up five nights in a row until three in the morning painting, wall papering, and rearranging the furniture. Uwe and I had to go to work each day, but the fatigue was nothing compared to the satisfaction after the job was done. From the beginning of our friendship, Uwe was welcomed by my family, and after my parents realized how bad his home life was, he was treated with special kindness. Our home was his home, any time for any reason. It was almost like having another brother who came to visit periodically instead of living in. Mom always asked how he was doing and whether he was eating right, whether he was hungry or was getting enough sleep, just like his own mother should have done. She was aware that his visits were escapes from an impossible situation and that even though he suffered greatly at the hands of his step-father, he still had feelings of love for his mother.

Uwe came to us in friendship and to recuperate from the latest traumas. After a few days, he would go back home to await the next storm of drunken anger. Uwe's mother and step-father developed a strong dislike for my parents, probably out of shame that they mistreated their son so much and the whole neighborhood knew it. Even at their house on Pestalozzi Strasse, they would hear the alarms and the gunfire tonight. Would they wonder whose back was in the Kalashnikov sights? Would they wonder whose life was in the balance? If they knew that it was their son, would they even get out of bed?

A final check in the attic confirmed that the new stereo I had purchased for my parents was still in its hiding place. Soon, Mom would find my note with the cryptic reference to the attic and Dad would go up to look. Other than that, I left nothing to connect me to ownership of that device still in its original box. They both liked music, and it was the best I could get on our side of the Wall.

I slipped on a pair of jeans beneath my white escape clothes.

If we made it, I'd at least have a change of pants.

Now I could feel everything beginning to close in. The longer I stayed in the room, the heavier my heart became. Turning off the light, I closed the door without a sound and left that part of life in neatly organized darkness. If I didn't leave immediately, I'd be paralyzed by the pain inside.

Reverting to the mental list I had carried for so long, I made one last stop in the kitchen. Each detail, one by one scrolled through my mind. Yes, it was all done. Car contract on the table. Goodbye note next to the contract. The note was simple.

> *Whatever is going to happen, I want all of you to know that I love you very much. Even if you don't understand now, there will be a time when you will.*
>
> *Forever yours,*
> *Carsten.*
>
> *P.S. I cannot live only in my dreams anymore.*

Those few words lifted the emotional load and now I could function without distraction. The task was at hand and I tiptoed from the front door.

"Where have you been?" Peter said. His whisper seemed so loud.

"I had things to take care of." I patted my own back pocket. "Does everybody have his Ausweis?" Our ID cards would at least prove our identity to the West Germans, and if we were captured, the DDR couldn't charge us with the additional crime of failing to carry them.

"This is the last thing and you have to remember it," I said. "Each of us is carrying 100 West German marks so we won't be going into freedom empty-handed. If we're captured, you must eat the money quickly so they won't discover it. If we're caught possessing it, we could get an extra two years in jail for smuggling Western currency."

Uwe made a chewing gesture and smacked his lips. He was going to do just fine.

"Let's get moving."

Out onto Zwingli Strasse for my last walk. Stomach heaving, body quivering with uncontrollable tremors, lips too dry to whistle the look-out warning even if Erich Honecker himself were coming.

Look both ways twice. Nothing. No movements. No lights in any neighbor's house, quiet along the Wall itself. Jerke's house loomed like a silent mountain in the familiar darkness. Uwe at a run carrying the ladders, sliding like a pale ghost across the lawn and into Jerke's yard. Each of his steps raised small puffs of dust, but somehow made no sound. It looked unnatural, like a poorly focused scene on television. Carefully walking between the house and the chicken coop, then setting the ladders on the ground, he stopped, listened, turned in a full circle to be sure we were still alone, then motioned for Peter and me. We darted past the sleeping chickens and stood next to him in the shadows, hearts pounding so loudly we could scarcely hear fighting the cold gnawing looseness of our bowels.

There was no need for conversation as we hefted the ladders and slipped on tiptoe around the small wire enclosure and shed. A slip could cause a cackling feathered frenzy, and that might bring a sleepy Jerke out to see what was going on. If he turned his porch light on and looked to the south, he would have an unobstructed view of the three of us, but thanks to Jerke's obsessive interest in keeping his yard clean, there was nothing to trip over. Once past the chicken house, we hugged the Wall itself but were completely exposed should someone come down the street. From any other angle, we were obscured by some structure or vegetation.

Normal thought was impossible. My ears were reverberating from my own crashing pulse. My heart was wriggling inside my chest cavity as though trying to escape my body. I had walked this way many times in practice, and a thousand times in my dreams, but nothing could have prepared me for the avalanche of terror that buried my consciousness. It was good that my feet knew the way because my brain was nearly useless.

The place we had chosen to cross was five meters south of the chicken coop, but before we could erect the ladders, we had to know the exact location of the patrols. Since they were irregularly scheduled, that meant we'd have to wait until one actually passed. Even then, there was no guarantee that the guards would not turn unpredictably and come back within a few moments. If that happened, we'd certainly be discovered.

Standing with backs pressed against the Wall, I willed myself invisible. My breathing, short tortured gasps roaring like surf in my ears. At every odd sound, every imagined thud and thump, every chirping cricket or distant barking dog, I twitched like a frog dissected on a laboratory table. We were fixed, pinned like specimens to the awful Wall, waiting for the coming of those who would kill us if they could, waiting to make our fearful passage in the noisy wake of our would-be destroyer.

The towers hovered on the periphery of my vision, but I dared not raise my eyes to behold them directly. To look upon them was to gaze into the face of death itself. With all the energy of my heart I prayed, "Lord, if you are really there, please help us to make it!" The words never left my lips, but a quiet reassurance settled around my mind and soothed my heart, enabling me to continue. Against our backs, the Wall was cold, like a tombstone, unyielding, impregnable, an immense monument of concrete and interlaced steel thrown up to memorialize the determination of men to control their brothers. We waited, would-be chameleons clinging to a concrete leaf, and my mind replayed all that I had gone through to arrive at this point. Life scrolled by a blur of faces, feelings, names and situations. The past had its price, one which I had been willing to pay. Now was the payoff, but I would never know of its real value until I collected in full.

The noise began as a distant hum, steadily increasing in pitch and volume. As the motorcycle drew closer, its exhaust echoed and reverberated in an odd way, resonating, flattening in a distorted dopplar, then resonating again as its position changed slightly within the enclosure. Daggers of light jabbed through the cracks between the slabs, and I could have easily put my eye to one of them and watched the cyclist pass. The urge to look was almost overpowering, but I didn't turn. It would have been insane to look and risk losing control altogether.

In a few moments, a matter of seconds, I'd be getting a better look anyway.

"Don't look," I said out loud to Peter and Uwe. The words sounded distant. Was that hoarse whisper really my own voice? I was nearly gagging from fear.

The motorcycle passed three meters away and moved southward at an undiminished speed along its asphalt path.

I looked toward Uwe. His face was all in shadow except for his nose, which was illuminated like a pale check mark by the light spilling over the Wall.

"We'll make it," he said.

Hearing that was exactly what I needed. On my signal we stepped away from the Wall and erected the first ladder and its odd appendages. With C-clamps to hold the struts in place, the ladder braced solidly against the Wall, yet the top was held far enough off the wire to avoid the overhanging alarm strands. If any part of our bodies or clothing even brushed an alarm wire, everything would be over, and if discovered at this point, we'd have no chance to run for it.

When the ladder was up, Peter and I stepped back to the Wall and flattened ourselves against it. Uwe took the second ladder in his right hand and climbed quickly to the topmost rung. Balancing there, he reached his left foot into the air just above the alarm wires and planted it upon the broken glass embedded in the 15-centimeter-wide top of the Wall itself. Legs spread across the wires, he had to lean awkwardly inward and down to place the second ladder gently on the ground and lean it against the inside of the Wall. As his weight shifted and the three-meter ladder wavered in his right hand, Uwe's left leg, the one still braced on the outside ladder, drew ever closer to the top alarm wire. Five centimeters, three centimeters. Then I could see hardly any space at all. My eyes grew wide with horror. Surely he was going to touch it, and there was nothing that I could do.

Any voiced warning might be a fatal distraction. For a long moment he stood there, arm quivering with the strain, balanced in that impossible position just a fraction from terminal destruction, then at last he straightened. I thought a sigh passed his lips. Then in one smooth movement, he brought his outside leg over the wire and disappeared down the other ladder inside the Wall. I moved quickly into the dazzling open. Like a knife, the light slashed away the safety of our comfortable darkness. The wire was above me, then in front, then beneath as I hopped easily across the shiny strands. Glass fragments embedded in the Wall tore at my tennis shoes, then I was down on the ground. Stepping to the side and pressing against the Wall to minimize exposure to the towers, I was struck by the utter silence of that place. As we were shivering in the darkness outside the Wall, I had been aware of some noises, the muted but still present background sounds of a living neighborhood. But only one-half meter away, in the carefully groomed desolation between the barriers, was complete deadness.

It was as though a lid had been pressed over the whole area, shutting out the very air and trapping even the muted sounds of our shallow, fearful breath. Nothing could have prepared me for the terror that seized my heart as I stood in that arena trying to blend into the Wall itself. My body was starving for air, and there was none for my lungs to take in. The stories we had heard were all true. The Grenztruppe saw to it that nothing whatsoever remained alive between the walls. Everything, every blade of grass, every weed, every spider web was systematically eradicated.

The troops went tirelessly about that daily task with the meticulous dedication of monks keeping some sterile cloistered cemetery. Spade, herbicide, and bare hands did their work; the brown-suited legione even groomed the bare dirt, raking long neat lines so foot prints would show if anyone strayed there by design or chance. It was like descending into an open tomb on some kind of a foolish dare, then trying to clamber out again before the grave diggers could come and cover us up. People on both sides of the Wall called it "Todesstreifen." The dead zone.

An instant after I touched the ground, I was aware of Peter on the ladder behind me, another second and he was down. For one-half second, our lives were suspended between existence and oblivion. Vital functions all but ceased, and my neck seemed somehow locked, frozen straight ahead so as not to dare a look at the towers of doom behind us. I heard someone's harsh breath, possibly my own.

No one gave a signal, but we all jerked away from the first wall at the same instant like horses instinctively bolting the starting gate at the races. Dancing an impossible chop-step ballet over the first two alarm wires, we raced in a mindless frenzy into the shallow end of the wedge-shaped anti-vehicle ditch. The momentum of our flight gave enough leverage for us to hand-vault out of the deep end of the trench. Peter and I cleared the ditch still at a run, and in my peripheral vision I saw Uwe slightly behind, carrying the second ladder with an odd pumping motion as he ran. Jumping the second set of wires, we avoided setting off the location alarm indicators.

As we sprinted the last 25 meters, I was conscious only of a primal necessity to run, like a hunted animal bursting to scream, but petrified to panting silence, knowing that the executioner was following, but too frightened to look back. My own footsteps were muffled hollow floppings ringing with dull echoes between the barriers. Breath came in painful gasps and the outer wall loomed before us only meters away.

With a sharp slap, Uwe threw the ladder against the second wall and stepped quickly to the right. According to the plan, I was to go over first.

There it was before me, the last ladder, crafted by Uwe's sure hands, rungs spaced to the calculated interval of a frightened man's stride. Painted white, piece by essential piece, it had been smuggled into my father's shed without his ever suspecting. Those scraps of wood and screws were the final bridge to life from this place of death. It was now the only exit from this jurisdiction of death that had been the last stop for many men stronger and smarter than we.

The wooden pathway reached into the night sky, to the top of the Wall, to the end of my time in the cage, to the beginning of my life-sustaining dream. A few steps and my feet would carry me into the future that I had risked everything to possess.

But I couldn't move at all. Like a stunned ox, I froze one step from the ladder and stared, unable to even reach out and touch it with my hands.

Behind, in the sterile earth, I heard the scrape of shoes and Peter's voice punched through the paralytic haze gathered in the middle of my mind.

"Wir schaffen es!" he shouted. The words echoed and rang in my ears. "We will make it!" In the same instant, he reached from behind, gripping me at the waist like a father helping his child onto a playground swing, picked me up like a toy and set me on the third rung.

The movement was enough to trigger my reflexes and I ran up, up. From somewhere, as though very far away, came a strange popping, angry buzzing, of concrete, and chips of something hard struck my face. We had avoided all of the alarm devices, but now the soldiers had seen us and opened fire.

There was the top, the large smooth tube on the summit of the Wall. I flung myself onto it, sliding across the slippery mold, and threw my body uncaring into the friendly blackness below.

I did not fear the fall, nor did I feel the impact as I crashed disoriented into the tangled vines four meters below. Reflexively, I thrashed about attempting to stand, then the forms of my friends scraped over and dropped crunching into the bushes practically together.

I could hear the gunfire more distinctly. They were still shooting. Maybe it made them feel better. It was semi-automatic mode, and coming from the south tower. Then a great commotion commenced in the area we had just left. Noise rose up and blossomed, a cacophony of voices, vehicle sounds, banging and slamming doors. Tearing at the vines around us, we regained our feet and instinctively ran, but in our wild dash for the high ground on the West Berlin street a new noise followed. It was our own laughter, wild and abandoned, like school children at the beach, intoxicated by the miracle of survival, filled with boundless energy and explosions of half-shouted, babbled sentences.

And then we were on the pavement, the ground where for years I had watched the West German buses turn around at the end of their route, the place where I had aimed my little arrow so long ago, seeking an unknown friend.

Overshadowed by the huge apartment building and illuminated by the benevolent street light, we hugged and laughed, shook hands and shouted over and over with exhilaration. Looking back from the high ground, we could see flashing lights between the walls, blue, red, blue, red, and somewhere the ragged warble of a police siren. It could wail forever and we wouldn't care. Uwe looked at me, tears filling his eyes, and we embraced again. Peter yelled something back toward the Wall and snapped his right arm upward, middle finger extended in the age-old gesture of contempt. Above us in the apartment building, lights began to flick on here and there as the West Berlin citizens awakened to the spectacle of an East German W-50 truck full of soldiers racing down between the walls followed by a couple of motorcycles. We watched for a few moments, and then it didn't matter anymore. The guards had their own problems now, and we had made it.

We were free.

In the light of the mercury vapor street lamp, we looked each other over.

Peter pointed to my clothes.

"You look awful!"

He was right. They were stained black where I had slithered through the mold on top of the Wall.

"Me? How about you? Both of you need a bath."

Uwe grabbed my arm, then Peter's.

"We did it. We're free." In his eyes was an energy I had seen only a few times before.

"They didn't kill us!" Peter was shouting. "They're lousy shots!"

More hysterical laughter.

"Wait. Wait." I had to yell to be heard over their celebration. "Breathe the air."

They sucked great lungs full.

"Do you understand?" I was waving my arms, sweeping great circles. "It smells different here? The air is even better."

More laughter and slaps on shoulders.

"Let's go find some human beings," Uwe said, "a policeman

or something."

The sounds of men shouting and racing vehicle motors between the walls faded away behind us, and we began to walk down the street.

Lights approached and we waved our arms. The car slowed.

"Hey," I said, "we just escaped from East Germany."

The driver muttered a Turkish obscenity and accelerated down the street.

Another half mile seemed like nothing. More lights. A city bus. We waved and shouted.

The plump driver opened the door and studied our dirty clothes. Drunks?

"We just came over the Wall," I told him, "escaped from the East side."

"No kidding," he said. His eyes narrowed and studied us for a moment. I held out the East German Ausweis with my picture on the inside cover. Then he was smiling, excited, animated. "That's great, congratulations!" Half turning, he called to his only two passengers in the rear of the brightly lighted vehicle. "These guys just escaped over the Wall." Then turning back to us, "Over the Wall, right?"

A young man and woman waved tentatively as if they had not clearly understood.

"Well, get on board," he said. His dark blue uniform with its shiny black buttons balanced the kaleidoscopic advertising signs that covered the walls. The interior was clean and neat, someone had taken good care of it. The driver laughed and gestured. What was he saying?

"Do you smoke?"

A pack of Marlboros was thrust forward. Cowboys and campfires. I had seen it in magazines. Now we were in the middle of it all.

"Ja, ja," Peter said.

Uwe grinned and took one, too.

"I never saw you smoke," I said to Uwe.

He shrugged and stuck it in his mouth.

The driver's lighter clinked open and ignited both cigarettes. Uwe inhaled and began to cough immediately, but his smile didn't fade. Smoke gathered and swirled as he sucked on the white paper tube. More coughing as he was looking around for somewhere to throw it. The driver understood his groping and pointed to the ashtray. Out it went.

The driver began asking questions. How did we do this and that, did they shoot, was anyone else with us?

"I think we need to go see the police," I said. We needed to get on someone's official records so the West German authorities could be aware as soon as possible.

"Oh sure," he said. "I can get them on the radio." He keyed a microphone and began to converse with the police operator. In a moment he signed off and replaced the microphone in its metal cradle. "They'll meet us at Rathaus Spandau," he said. "Only a few kilometers. No charge for the ride."

We took seats and the bus lurched forward with a diesel roar. The trees, signs and cars on the paved streets flowed by the windows as we gawked like aliens taking in the sights of a new planet. It was really happening. We were alive. It wasn't one of my dreams. We had really come over and we were on a West Berlin bus driving down a West Berlin street. I was a living sponge involuntarily soaking up everything around us. The newness and freshness of everything was exhilarating. I felt neither hot nor cold, not hungry, not tired, not scared, not anything but free. At that moment, the whole world and all of its possibilities were before us. All we had to do was reach out and grasp them.

The driver looked at us in his vast rear-view mirror.

"Where are you guys from?"

"Falkensee," Peter said.

"We planned this a long time," Uwe said. "A long, long time! I can't believe that we really did it."

The bus hissed to a stop and the door swung open.

"Rathaus," the driver said.

The green and white BMW was parked next to the curb, and two uniformed officers were leaning casually on the fender. They straightened and smiled.

The bus driver waved like a grandfather sending loved ones off on a trip.

"Good luck with everything," he said. "I'm glad you made it!" The two young people in the back of the bus never moved from their seat, but they also began to wave.

The bus groaned away in its cloud of fumes, and one of the policemen offered his hand. I had never seen that before.

"Welcome to West Berlin," he said. The smile and relaxed posture told me that he meant it. It was so strange to see one of them acting so cordial while he was on duty. Still, this wasn't really "one of them" that I was used to. He didn't call his partner by the familiar "Genosse" that East German Polizei used to differentiate their caste from the common citizen.

"Get in and we'll go to the station." We all shook hands and loaded into the car, laughing like clowns in a circus.

"Nice." Peter fingered the upholstery. "The police even have good cars here."

I was struggling with conflicting feelings. All my life, the police had been present, in control, openly asserting their power. Now I shivered with instinctive fear, but my rational mind told me that these men were benevolent. As friendly and open as family, they could have been taxi drivers or tour guides, except for the guns. Ahead was a crowd of uniforms clustered around the entrance to the police station. They were tall, short, wearing the bright green of motorcycle officers, street clothes of shirt-sleeved detectives, green jackets and badges of regular patrolmen, mixed groups of women, men, and a couple of steely-eyed dogs. All smiling and waving. I couldn't help but smile, too, then the shivers returned.

"Welcome to the West, congratulations!" The voices were warm and genuine. Someone applauded. They seemed happy to see us.

We grinned and waved back. In a swirl of excited voices, we were escorted into the station break room. Tables, chairs, bulletin boards full of dangling official notices. Coke machine. Stale with the film of cigarette smoke and coffee. Faces crowded around like a huddle at an American football game.

"You guys hungry?"

Hands reached for us, to shake hands or to touch our windbreakers, like some lately arrived sacred objects.

The background was filled with the frequency-distorted crackle of the patrol car radios coming over the dispatch monitor.

"Have some cheese," someone said. A hand thrust from the wall of officers and pressed a fat piece into my hands.

"How about something to drink?" Then came the Cokes. Real Coca-Cola, not inferior imitations. We slurped the fluid and I tried to recall the last time I had tasted a good soft drink. Uwe and I exchanged glances. No doubt he was recalling the few times when I was able to obtain Coca-Cola. Drinking it had been a major cultural event and we had savored its bouquet as though it was the finest of wines. Peter slugged a fizzy mouthful then moved his neck around trying to belch silently.

A tall officer offered a wrapped sandwich.

"Take this if you like Schnitzel. I don't need anything more to eat anyway." He patted his thick midriff. Laughter.

Our full mouths made the story telling more difficult, but we munched more out of gratitude than real hunger. The faces pressed closer and questions came in flurries.

"How did you do it?"

"Where did you come over?"

"Did they shoot at you?"

The last query was echoed several times.

Peter answered. "Yes, but they aren't very good are they?" Laughter.

"How much did they shoot? When did they see you?"

I swallowed a mouthful of Schnitzel sandwich.

"I don't think they really saw us until we made the second wall. There wasn't time to do much."

A detective spoke. "You can bet that the tower guards are wishing they had followed you across the Wall." Murmured agreement. Everyone understood that the guards had already been arrested by their own officers and were under tough interrogation.

"Does anyone need to see our ID?" I asked. Their level of interest was amazing. It was completely focused on us as human beings; we were more than just an interruption in their late-night routine. They really cared.

A tall, hefty uniformed sergeant blinked, straightened, and

West German newspaper articles about the escape — August 4, 1987

Carsten Kaaz, Uwe George and Peter Zimmermann in West
Berlin, the evening after the escape — August 4, 1987

Carsten Kaaz, Uwe George and Peter Zimmermann at the
Deutsch-Amerikanisches Volksfest in West Berlin,
one week after the escape — August, 1987

Carsten and Peter eating McDonald's French fries
on second day after escape

Carsten Kaaz

at the

refugee compound

in West Berlin,

after

the escape

— August, 1987

shook his head as though he had just been reminded of business. "I guess so. This really isn't a police problem, but I'll make copies for our report." He collected the papers and headed away to the copier.

Unbelievable. These were not the kind of police I had known all my life. I imagined that my parents might have invited some of these to Sunday barbecue. They were just another part of the society, not some caste above it. More food was thrust from the surrounding crowd and the mood settled. We told an abbreviated version of the plan and our actual escape. They leaned comfortably on the table and nodded in appreciation when I explained our white clothes camouflage and how we blended in with the Wall.

"Maybe they'll have to find another color for the Wall now," someone said.

Another voice. "The people will just dye their clothes." More smiles and subdued laughter.

"What about your families?"

"We left it all behind. Everything," I said. Heads nodded in solemn understanding.

A sergeant spoke. "It's getting late. We better get you to the refugee center at Marienfeld."

Five-thirty in the morning was late to them I supposed. Perhaps their shift changed at 6:00 a.m. Hands reached forth, pressing money into ours and the group dissolved into small bundles heading off to their routines. Good luck wishes.

"What do you think about this?" Peter said. "I've seen a lot of police, but these are the friendliest. They actually seem to like us. They even like each other!"

It was like being in the movies when the camera switches to a lens showing everything in soft focus. The police radio sputtered and whistled its slang-abbreviated imperatives and my mind was filled with the wonder and incongruity of our situation. We were treated like honored guests, and no one had asked anything of us. No one probed us for secret information, and our identity had not even been challenged. We'd been greeted as friends in a police station, a place that had formerly been known only as a house of fear and pain. Even among the trappings of force and authority, even among these men and women who carried guns, there was a visible foundation of human decency. I marveled for a moment until more events overtook us. Then it was time to get moving again.

We sat like children on a school field trip, enthralled by early-morning Berlin, as the police bus picked its way through traffic. The windows were covered with wire mesh, but we had no sensation of being imprisoned. Gray dawn brushed the buildings, revealing shadowed doorways among the slashing, blinking neon. In Falkensee, the town would be stretching one final reluctant time before Monday morning began in earnest, but here was a city that vibrated with the eternal electricity of irrepressible humanity.

From the nightclubs with their gaudy titillating solicitations to the skyscrapers shimmering in their glass and chromium sheaths, the place was alive. Buildings craned their concrete necks into the low-hanging clouds and lights winked on here and there as the rhythm of the neon night was replaced by the pulse beat of the business day. The green bus stopped and started, turned and paused, and the face of West Berlin unfolded. Streams of humanity trickled forth from buildings, headed for important destinations; knots and gaggles of preoccupied men and women came from the U-bahn exits clutching briefcases and parcels with early-morning enthusiasm. Peter, Uwe and I didn't speak for a long time. They were trying, as I, to grasp the reality of our new situation while fathoming their own new feelings. For a solid hour, the three of us could only exchange smiles and point at this or that wonder. We were full of the excitement of our new home, and even though we had been awake for nearly twenty-four hours, it was unthinkable to be tired.

The address was Marienfelder Allee at Stegerwaldweg. The refugee complex was an enclosed, single-story, rectangular compound that received everyone who entered West Berlin under refugee status. It was constructed to provide shelter for individuals or families, a place for debriefing, orientation, and physical security while the process of resettlement was commenced. Access was strictly controlled, but it was no jail.

"Welcome to the center," said the neatly dressed young man.

"Please complete these forms as much as possible. We need to have this information so you can receive benefits from the government."

Of course, there were forms. Lots of them. Name. Place, date of birth. Parents' names. Former home address. On and on. Who could remember all of that? Turn over the East German identity papers. I felt somehow incomplete without the Ausweis that had been my constant companion since I was 14. The young man answered our infrequent questions and looked up from time to time to be sure we were moving along with the forms. Our feet shuffled in the fluffy carpet.

At 8:00 a.m., a woman entered briskly and walked directly into the office marked "Director." A few minutes later, we were invited in.

"I am Frau Materne, the center director. I understand that you came over the Wall together?"

Of medium height, firm build, neatly groomed, Materne carried herself with an air of acknowledged authority, not the monolithic, dispassionate, commanding presence that I had seen on official faces all of my life. It clung to her naturally like a friendly, worn sweat shirt. She was businesslike, but not all business; more like a concerned citizen, perhaps a social worker.

"It took all of us to do it," I said. "Uwe made the ladders, and Peter provided special assistance at just the right moment when we were crossing over."

They both smiled in acknowledgement.

"That's really amazing. Usually when there are larger groups, someone doesn't make it. I can't remember the last time that three came together." She looked at each of us in turn, studying our appearance. "You're really lucky. Were you injured in any way?"

"No."

More general questions, then she got down to details.

"Here's how things are. You are free men now. You can come and go as you wish, and no one's going to tell you what to do. That's going to take some adjustment, and for a while it will seem really strange." She opened a file folder and scanned the contents. You already have maps of the compound, so we can

312

save a discussion of that for later if you have questions. Right now, you have to start collecting your thoughts because over the next couple of weeks you'll have to make some very important decisions about your future."

The future! My future had been getting over the Wall without being shot in the back. My future had been escape. My future had already happened, and now I had to refocus everything. This wasn't going to be easy, but as of that moment, my future was even better than I had dreamed.

"You have to register with the police just like any other West German citizen, and one of our doctors will give each of you a physical exam." She leaned forward on her elbows and spoke softly. "After you have finished with the bureaucratic garbage, you'll have to deal with the press."

I was stunned.

"The press?" It sounded almost like a threat.

Materne looked surprised, then a small laugh escaped.

"They already know that you are here, but this is one of the few places in Berlin where they can't come. They're like a bunch of hungry sharks when they smell a good story." Her fingers stirred a batch of message notes on the desk. "There have already been 20 calls."

"From who?" I asked.

She named one after another, some newspapers whose names I recognized, and other unknown titles.

"The last bunch are the tabloids. You know, two-headed babies, aliens from outer space, that kind of garbage. My advice is for you to stay away from the trash and sign an agreement with one that's reputable. The other ones will put all kinds of words in your mouths, and you don't need that." She made careful eye contact with each of us. "You have an opportunity to make some money with the press, so don't sell yourselves too cheaply. Don't let them rip you off."

Uwe and Peter looked at me, reflecting my own perplexity. We'd have to figure out how to handle this new opportunity. I had no idea how much our experience was worth, but it was definitely not like selling a used car.

"Which is the best?" I asked.

"I can't tell you that," she replied, "I only suggest that you pick from the well-known names."

The conversation continued without me as I leaned back in the chair. Seven hours into our new life and we were already in the news. Soon our pictures would be in the papers. How would it feel? On the surface it seemed exciting, but I was sure that there was more to notoriety than just fun. Personal lives melt away before the camera lens. Fame steals life's common sweetness. That much I did know. We took the stack of message slips and discussed the names. After a few minutes, it was obvious that we'd have to take our chances to some degree, so we picked a familiar name.

At 2:30 p.m., we met the Bild representative to discuss an exclusive contract.

"Dieter Mahlow," he said. Hand extended. Stylish clothes. Firm handshake. Big friendly smile. Direct gaze sizing us up. Amusement when he noticed the "Bad Boys" logo on Peter's T-shirt.

I introduced everyone.

"Before we get started, let's talk about the contract."

"Sure, sure. How much do you want?"

We had already discussed the possibilities, so I ventured. "Well, we talked it over. What do you think about 500 marks?"

His eyebrows arched.

"Five hundred? I'll tell you what. My editor is a generous guy. I'm sure I could get you 600 apiece."

Apiece? I had meant 500 for the three of us. Back home 600 Deutschmarks would have been a small fortune. What a great beginning!

We boarded Dieter's spotless black Jeep Wrangler and drove back to the Spandau district to the point where we had come over.

"Look," Uwe said, "the vines are poison. That's why we're all itching."

We laughed about that, and Dieter made notes, then came 35mm photographs. Standing together, leaning on the Wall, pointing to the place where we slid across the tube, standing this way, that way. It all looked slick in the magazines, but it was a lot of confusion and waiting as the photographer scurried about with his light meter posing us like mannequins.

So there we were at our Wall again. I ran my hand across its gray surface. Rigid, inanimate, but sunlight-warm against my hand like a living thing, cracked and spalling concrete flakes in places. Unlike things that spring naturally from the earth, it was unchangeable and inflexible except in its crumbling. Like a mountain, it was wearing slowly away, its time measured perhaps in generations rather than the flickering, hurried days of men. It stood without apology for its blood stains, in silent defiance of men, even whole nations, who wanted it down, as the most prominent twentieth century historical marker commemorating the undying principle of slavery. Children would never bounce a ball against it in their sweaty, squealing games; its only friends would be the restless guards and neurotic attack dogs. The Wall had a life of its own, a deep morbidity, an ambiance rooted in sharp edges and the blood of despairing humankind. I shuddered and turned away.

More pictures. Camera angles had to be just right. Hold still. Very good. Very good! Just a few more.

Our position on the high ground gave a good view into our old neighborhood.

"Look," said Uwe, "there's somebody in Krippner's window."

It looked like my friend, Henrik.

We waved.

The face disappeared and returned in a moment with others. It was the whole family. We shouted and jumped up and down.

They waved back, then abruptly closed the window. They had probably just realized they were breaking a law by communicating across the border.

The guard towers stood without visible activity, the afternoon sun reflecting sullenly off their windows.

Then the pictures were all taken, and we rode away with Dieter.

It was time for television. Our stomachs were uneasy as Dieter drove us to our afternoon appointment at ZDF-TV. I asked the TV journalist for 100 marks apiece to do the story, and he acted insulted, but in a moment relented and confirmed the arrangement. After the brief taped interview, Dieter retrieved us for another session at Bild. We met in one of the dazzling offices, and midway through the discussion, we were interrupted by the clink of dishes as a formally dressed waiter wheeled in a serving cart loaded with food.

"We wanted you to know that we're sincerely glad to have you with us," Dieter said.

In all the excitement, we hadn't even thought of food. Now, we were as hungry as locusts.

We stuffed ourselves and muttered thanks with half-full mouths. It was our first real meal in nearly 12 hours. I savored a piece of celery as my taste buds renewed their normal function.

"Can I make a phone call?" I asked.

"Anywhere you want."

My parents were at work and there were telephones there. A call would confirm that we were all right. The connection clicked in and the ring tone began.

"Hello, Haus Der Dame." It was Mother's supervisor.

"Could I speak to Frau Kaaz, please?"

The voice hesitated. "Carsten, is that you?"

"Yes, yes, is my mother there?"

"Sure!" His voice was excited at first, then he cleared his throat judiciously. "Are you all right?"

"Yes, they didn't hit us at all. Can I speak …"

"Here she is."

It was Mother's voice, roughened by a flood of emotion. "Carsten?"

"I'm all right, Mom. Everything's fine."

She began to cry, great shuddering sobs.

"They are treating all of us very well. Please don't worry." I searched for something to say that made some sense. "Didn't you figure it could happen?"

"I knew that you hated it here, but I never dreamed that you'd do something like this." The crying subsided somewhat. "The gunfire woke your father. I was afraid it was you. I thought…" She began to cry again, then regained control. Every normal breath was a minor victory. "You wouldn't believe the trouble we have now. The Stasi came at 5:30 a.m. They had a pack of dogs and the street was full of ..."

The line went dead.

My hosts sat in polite silence, and I tried to dial the number again. Nothing doing. The East German operator would not even ring the number.

"They broke the connection," I said.

The Bild people shook their heads, but not out of surprise.

"How about me," said Uwe.

"Go ahead, anywhere you want."

Uwe's eyes darted back and forth like they always did before he told a joke. He dialed the number from memory, and the rest of us scooted closer so we could hear.

"Hello," he said, "guess who this is?"

"I have no idea," said the female voice. Sounded like an older woman.

"Didn't you watch the TV news tonight? Didn't you hear the radio? How about the latest news from Berlin?"

"News? What are you ... only that some people from Falkensee escaped from ... Uwe is that you? Is it really you? Where are you?"

He laughed and squirmed in the chair.

"Yes, Tante Elke, it's me. I'm in West Berlin now."

"Are you all right? You have to tell me everything!"

"I will, but right now I'm in the middle of a newspaper interview. I'll call soon, but you'll be able to read it, too." He hung up. "She wants me to visit her in Hamburg."

"How about you Herr Zimmermann?"

"There's no one for me to call, but thanks anyway."

Dieter nodded respectfully.

"It's not a problem. I have all the friends I need right here!" Peter said.

Later Dieter drove us to SFB-TV for an evening talk show.

We had all seen Hans Werner Kock's TV talk show over the years. Now we sat in the studio with make-up artists painting our faces like in a high school play.

"This makes me nervous," Uwe said.

"People back in Falkensee need to see that we are all right. I bet every TV in town will be on this channel, and who knows

317

what the Polizei and the Stasi have been saying." I said.

The lights came on and the questions followed. Pleasant but insistent. Probing. Why this, why that, how did we escape?

"It was just the three of us," I said. The unnatural dead black of the camera lens stared back as though seeking my innermost soul. "We planned it and did everything without anyone else knowing. If anyone back home gets in trouble for this, it will be because the government is trying to make it look like it has solved a big conspiracy." More questions about how we did it. Worry began to nag my mind even more. What would the Polizei and the Stasi do? Who would they arrest? Finally, Kock thanked us and the lights went off, fading to red glowing dots, then to darkened, cooling glass globes. After the handshakes and thank you's, a Mercedes taxi drove us back to the Marienfeld compound.

Our apartment had two bedrooms, but we pulled one of the beds into the other room so we could all sleep in the same area. It was 11:00 p.m. and we had been awake for more than 45 hours. Even though our minds were still ringing with excitement, our fatigued bodies were shutting down.

Lying in bed with the lights off, I couldn't resist the urge to talk, to draw out this most special feeling just a little longer.

"What a day," I said.

"What a day," Peter agreed.

"We really made it," Uwe said. "And that TV show was really something. We were on TV! I never thought I'd ever be on TV!"

"What did you like the most, Peter?" I asked.

Silence.

"I think he's out," Uwe said. "Let him sleep."

Peter began to snore.

Like so many times before, it was just Uwe and me trying to sort out life, talking things through, sharing the feelings of our hearts.

"Just one question, then," I said. "If we had to go back and do it again, what would we do differently?"

He was silent for a brief moment.

"Everything went exactly as we planned. Everything!"

"Yes, but what could we have done better, differently?"

Silence. Thinking again.

"I considered that today, and the answer is that we did everything right. I wouldn't change anything at all." He laughed. "That's really saying something for an important plan, isn't it? We did it perfectly and now we're free men!"

His words rolled over and over in my mind, somehow mingling with Peter's intermittent snoring. I thought about the noise Uwe's saw made while he was modifying our escape ladder. The snore was a sound from eternity, a primal rhythm of the earth, a common thread of experience understood by all men. Perhaps all living things understood snoring. It was the rhythmic rasp of security. There had to be peace when a person could snore and not worry about who might hear it.

In another moment, Uwe's deeper breathing signaled his sleep as well. Now there was no reason to stay awake, except to savor life for another moment. For the second time in two days, there was no tomorrow, no yesterday, only the now. I was alive and my beating heart was setting its own rhythm. I was no longer simply floating upon a stagnant pond, but had leaped desperately upon the madly whirling tide of a whole new world. I was at the doorstep of life, bursting with questions about who and what I might become.

The thing that Uwe, Peter, and I had done was good.

Men ought to be free! We had staked our lives on that belief, and realizing that, for a moment I experienced an exhilaration beyond expression.

The AFN broadcasts had repeated those words years before. They seemed such elementary truths. I was afraid, too, for now my destiny was in my hands alone.

No more complaining about how a backward society held me down. I had paid the entrance price to the house of freedom and an infinity of possibilities lay ahead. The darkness of that room was comforting, and I slipped gently into sleep.


We went everywhere together, and people on the street recognized us.

319

In the record store, "Aren't you the three guys who escaped over the Wall a few days ago?" The attendant came out from behind the counter.

"Yeah."

"How can I help you? Come on and I'll find whatever you want." Other shoppers greeted us as we pawed through the disks.

Ten encounters later we were wondering how to cut our story down a little. Retelling it twice an hour was getting tedious.

On the way out of the U-bahn, the old woman stood as if waiting for someone. Her plain, dark dress made her look even older and more wrinkled.

She eyed us without subtlety.

"I recognize you. You were on TV the other night. Escaped from the East side. It's not often three make it together."

Our nods confirmed her understanding.

"Welcome to West Germany," she said. "You'll have to work hard, but you can make it if you want to." She rummaged and dug in her purse, pushing nameless folded papers ahead of her searching fingers. Then the weathered hand came forth clutching three five-mark coins. "Take this. You'll need a little extra to get started."

"Thanks, but we already have money," I said. "You don't have to do that."

Her shoulders straightened, and her face took on an angular look full of intense indignation. Then up came her hand, wagging an arthritic finger.

"If you're going to become one of us, you have to understand that people care about you. If you can't go along with that, you'll never get the spirit of freedom. Don't you have any manners?"

I apologized.

"We just want to be sure that you have enough for yourself."

"You're a nice young man, but let me tell you something." Her eyes looked away and a thoughtful expression came to her features. "I have survived two wars. There were times when shoe leather looked good enough to eat, and there was many a month when no one dared to let their dog or cat go outside.

If I wanted to keep my own little dog, I had to share my piece of bread with him." She leaned closer to be sure that we heard everything her raspy voice was saying. "I can take care of myself just fine. Probably better than you right now." Her hand reached out again, the weathered palm turning upward revealing the coins.

We each took one and thanked her.

Employment offers came from all over West Germany, and every time we ventured on the street together we were recognized and asked to tell the escape story again. After being interviewed by the French, West German, British, and American intelligence services, we began to examine our long-term possibilities. Peter found work in Berlin, deciding to stay because he liked the pace of the city. Uwe and I decided to take his aunt Elke's offer to stay in Hamburg. Four-and-a-half months later, Uwe and I returned to Berlin where I worked at Fernsehdienst Hennemann repairing VCRs and CD players until early afternoon. In the evenings I refurbished amplifiers and worked in a guitar shop for an emigré American, Leonard Lott. Making extra money and having something to spend it on was a new and pleasant experience. Later, I was able to start a small business selling changeable neon signs.

Life was going in the right direction, but things took a different turn one evening as I stood in front of the door to my apartment foyer fumbling for the door key.

"You are Carsten Kaaz," the man said. He appeared from the busy street and was standing slightly behind and to my left. His words did not form a question, and their tone had an uncomfortable familiarity, an undercurrent of command. Mowes, our police district head in Falkensee, always spoke in that tone. The Stasi in East Berlin had spoken in that tone. The keys rattled involuntarily in my quivering fingers, and my insides went to water.

"I'm a friend of your family," he continued. "I'd like you to come with me."

"No!" I said. Fear washed over me as in a horrible nightmare.

His hand reached out to grasp me firmly by the left arm.

That touch unleashed a flood of remembrance. The men who arrested Uwe and me after our visit to the American Embassy two years ago had taken me by the arm in exactly the same way. I knew instinctively what was standing next to me on this West Berlin street. He was about 40, dressed casually, indistinguishable from the numerous other people who even now walked unconcerned back and forth on the sidewalk only a few meters away. Beyond him, parked at the curb with someone sitting in the driver's seat, was a cream-colored Opel sedan. The passenger door swung open and the pressure of the man's grip increased on my arm as he pulled me toward the car.

"Let go of me!" He was 25 kilos heavier and obviously very strong. If there was going to be a fight, I'd get the worst of it.

At that moment, the apartment foyer door opened and one of my neighbors, a middle-aged woman, stepped abruptly into the doorway.

"What's going on here?" Her sharp demand snapped like a military command. For an instant, the man's concentration shifted, and I slipped from his grip, stepped quickly past her into the apartment lobby and slammed the door behind me. For a second, he stared through the glass, then turned, ran four steps to the car and jumped in as it accelerated away from the curb.

My neighbor said something, but I couldn't understand the words. I was trembling from fear and my mind was blank. From behind a locked door in my room, I called Leonard.

"Sounds like someone wanted to take you for a ride back east. I'll call the C.I.A. office." He later told me that the intelligence agency recommended that he contact the West German Bundespolizei. After the police heard the story, they dispatched two patrolmen who arrived 20 minutes later. They appeared unimpressed and filed a routine report after a cursory discussion.

Still upset, I called Horst Schumm, a Berliner who had himself smuggled many people from the east side until he was caught and imprisoned by the East Germans.

"They haven't given up the idea of you being a good Communist citizen," he said. "There's a way to fix this problem if you don't mind another small article in the Berliner

Morgenpost."

"Do whatever you can. I'm afraid to go outside now!" It was true. Even though I told myself that they wouldn't try again, I couldn't shake the feeling of being watched, stalked like an animal. Sleep came hard that night, and I awoke at the slightest unusual sound.

The paper ran a small column the next day, noting the incident on the police blotter as a possible attempted kidnaping and saying that I was happy in the West, and that I had a good job. Since I knew no military secrets and had no critical government job before defecting, my only value to the East was to somehow get me to recant my admiration of the West. That could only be accomplished by getting me back across the border to where I could be broken down and later made to publicly denounce the evil seduction of my life. The newspaper article was designed to publicly state my situation and negate the possible propaganda value of a forced repatriation. After that was done, my value to the East side was zero.

After a few weeks, I calmed down and life settled back into a predictable pattern. Things were really looking great. I lived in one of the most exciting cities in the world, had my own budding business, a nice apartment and money to spend. What more could any young man want?

I wanted America.

Uwe and I discussed the possibility of going.

"There's nothing to stop us now," I said. "No Wall, no Stasi, nothing but a few thousand kilometers of water and a tourist visa." Peter had never dreamed of the trip and was content to stay in Germany. It was just Uwe and me again.

"I have a complication," Uwe said. "It's impossible for me to get time off from work to go with you. I'll have to wait another two months."

We, who had been so inseparable, would have to choose. I could go now, or we would both have to wait another year before making the visit together. We decided that I'd follow through, and although I could see that it hurt Uwe's feelings, he made no protest.

On May 14, 1988, my Lufthansa flight left Berlin for

Chicago, where I had arranged to meet Gloria Torbati, one of the young people I had met while in East Berlin three years before. I sat on the 747 and tried to savor every moment of the experience. Idly, I scanned the pages of the Berliner Morgenpost, then an article seemed to leap from the page.

"Fourteen months' imprisonment for demand for freedom. Two East German citizens from Falkensee were sentenced to fourteen months by the Potsdam Court for putting a banner in the window of their home! 'We demand freedom and equal rights for everyone.' This statement violated paragraph 214 of the DDR penal code, interfering with government and civil order."

SEITE 10 – SONNABEND, 14. MAI 1988

## 14 Monate Haft für Forderung nach Freiheit

BM/dpa Berlin, 14. Mai

Zwei „DDR"-Bewohner sind vom Potsdamer Bezirksgericht zu 14 Monaten Haft verurteilt worden, weil sie mit einem Transparent im Fenster ihren Aussiedlungswunsch bekräftigen wollten.

Der 37jährige Detlef Kowalkowski und sein 32jähriger Schwager Bernd Schimanski hatten am 26. Februar ein Laken mit der Aufschrift „Wir fordern Freiheit und Gerechtigkeit für alle" an das Fenster der Wohnung von Schimanski in Falkensee in der Nähe von Ost-Berlin gehängt.

Die Strafen sind nach Paragraph 214 des „DDR"-Strafgesetzbuches wegen „Beeinträchtigung staatlicher oder gesellschaftlicher Tätigkeit" ausgesprochen worden.

My own hometown! Although I didn't know the individuals, it stirred my own pain again. I brooded over the incomprehensible mixture of pettiness and brutality. It wasn't necessary for the government to beat men black and blue to repress them. Yes, it sometimes happened that way, but more often the status quo was preserved by the relentless pressure to conform and now I knew more than ever that no one could realize a full measure of humanity unless daily life allowed a modicum of autonomy. I was free, but I felt guilty knowing that so many others still lived without hope. These brothers from Falkensee had paid the price of disrupting Ordnung, the principle of obedience to whatever is demanded by the society. Order must be preserved! Regulations must be followed! The state preferred tidy robots to rounded, whole persons. I tore the article from the page and stuffed it into my pocket, so I wouldn't forget the reality of my own past.

The aircraft lifted and jiggled in the rough air, and in a few hours, I could see the dark blur of America down below. We finally landed, and I actually felt lucky that I could walk down stairs instead of going through one of the tunnels.

The first step on American soil was glorious.

The week in Chicago visiting Gloria melted into a blur of new perspectives on everyday life. Then came Washington, D.C., as Christine Maugans introduced me to the Capitol.

"You know Carsten, I always imagined you as a southerner," she said. "I have some friends down that way that we can visit. Let's see how you like Atlanta."

It was late, 9:00 p.m., and the vast grassy expanse before the face of Georgia's Stone Mountain was covered with the lounging forms of a thousand people. Music began and the granite became animated in the excited jerks of a laser light show. For a long time, it was just great entertainment, but unexpectedly, the familiar music of my childhood floated across the reclining multitudes. As Elvis Presley's recorded voice sang "American Trilogy," I felt the same stirrings as long ago.

It had begun in the darkness of my room, when dreams were alive only in my own heart, when hope dangled by a tiny frayed thread over the pit of impossibility. There, I had dared to hope and gather my tiny store of courage for an impossible struggle against advancing darkness, a heavy thing, cunningly crafted to level and equalize the spirit, burying individuality under a coagulating shroud of mediocrity. The passionately sung syllables that I now heard were more than mere words from an entertainer. "To live and die in Dixie, … His truth is marching on. … All my trials, Lord, will soon be over." My heart, my whole being, filled with an inexpressible joy. Could this collection of unknowing disciples on the grassy ground comprehend the dream that played before them on the mountainside? Did their hearts nearly burst with a powerful, if only dimly understood love for this great unruly land? Would they be able to sort out the difference between what America stood for and what she really was, what they themselves really were? Did they even dare to guess how many hopes were interwoven within their own destiny, with the way they lived their lives from day to day?

The impression was singular, distinct and overpowering. It was as though after wandering in a foreign and hostile land, I had heard a half-remembered voice from a time before my own childhood. After a fearful and lonely night, the sun had finally risen, and I awoke to find that I had come back home. I knew that I had to seek after this America, distilling the essence of liberty, swimming against her swirling insecurity, and try to grasp with my mind, and then live, freedom. I wanted to grow up again, to refurbish my life in this most unique of all workshops, to fill the measure of my creation.

Adjusting was unimaginably demanding. Intermixed with my joy at this discovery was the realization that so few people comprehended the condition of spiritual slavery that gripped my country so powerfully. Even though I was 7,000 kilometers away, vestiges of that servitude clung to my every thought and action. Stopped for speeding in Atlanta, I began to tremble with fear when the policeman checked my license. Passing through the airport security checkpoints became an adventure in horror as remembrance of the spectral Stasi rose unbidden from my memory. It was going to take some time to unlearn fear of my government.

The phone rang late one night. The voice was familiar. But, who? …

"It's me, Jurgen!"

326

"Jurgen? Where are you? I heard that Gabi went to visit some relatives in West Berlin and never came back. I thought you had broken up."

Laughter.

"No, no. We had it planned. She walked over the border saying that she was going to see relatives, and a month later, I took the clothes on my back and went over the hard way."

"Where are you?"

"West Berlin! I'm free. We're free here together!"

I laughed and cried for joy. "How'd you do it?"

"There was another guy from work who got to be pretty close, and we decided to take the train." He paused, waiting for me to ask.

"What are you talking about?"

"The freight trains go beneath an elevated part of the road not far from my house, so I decided that we could jump onto one of them and hide until it crossed the border."

"How'd you know which one to get onto?"

"Only the best goes West, so we crawled out onto the edge of the bridge and stood directly over the tracks until coal cars came along. We knew that our best coal was sold to West Germany so we figured we'd eventually end up there if we could get on board. The instant I saw a coal car beneath, I jumped." He laughed, then an unusual silence descended. "I've never been so scared in my life. It was a five-meter drop to the coal and the train must have been going 100 k.p.h."

"Were you hurt?"

He laughed again. " I was so terrified I didn't feel a thing. I landed and fell backwards, then burrowed in like a rat so they couldn't see me at the border crossing. The dogs couldn't smell me for all the coal dust." More laughter. "I'm still coughing that crap up from my lungs. I nearly suffocated. One thing's very bad, though. The guy who went with me was so scared he didn't jump. When they learned what I had done, they tracked his scent with dogs and arrested him the next day at home."

"Tell me something, Jurgen. How does it feel to be free?"

He paused thoughtfully, "I'm still not sure. It doesn't seem natural." Then the voice brightened. "But none of that matters.

Carsten, if I had to die this minute, it was worth every risk and every fear to spend even a little time as a free man." The muted sound of a kiss came over the phone as his wife pressed near. "This is some club we belong to, my friend!"

I hung up, remembering my own first days of a new life, and felt very warm inside.

Then there were the dreams.

Somehow, I was on the street in front of my house in Falkensee, and they were after me. I ran and ran, but everywhere there was the Wall. I couldn't remember how I got back there, but I was trapped and they were coming for me again. With an involuntary cry, I jerked awake and lay gasping in a pool of my own sweat.

There was no way to erase the years of conditioned response. Time alone could dull that, but in order to exert some control over life, I resolved to raise my voice as a warning to anyone who would listen. I could cover the years of habitual subservience with future years of speaking out against the awful thing inside men that allows them to believe that imposing their will justifies any action as long as the "right" result is achieved.

This twisted corollary takes root irrespective of national boundaries, and knows no racial nor ethnic limit. The seeds bloom in ignorance of the simple fact that men can and ought to be much better than they are, and that they can be truly happy if they realize that they must consciously change their very nature. Without this metamorphosis, laws, political systems, and lofty ideals are impotent, because individuals refuse to sacrifice what they once were in order to improve themselves.

Iron Curtains are made in the heart, and can likewise only be broken down from there.

Those who make nations into prisons are still around. Like carrion flies, they live in every country, speak every language and have every color of skin and eyes. Details of their names and faces are inconsequential, because their intentions are the same.

In November 1989, what in most minds was considered an unlikely miracle actually occurred, and before anyone knew what to think, the Wall itself was gone, shattered and finally uprooted by the unleashed contempt and frustration of a whole generation. Once the people decided that death by bullets was no longer the worst fate, no walls could hold them back.

Mom and Dad came to visit my new home in Memphis, and after the hugs and kisses, the blurted news and earnest gazes, an expectant silence descended. My wife, Bethany, spoke no German, so she excused herself from the alien conversation and went into the kitchen.

Mother began to speak and I closed my eyes for an instant. We could have been sitting on the couch in their home at Number Four, Zwingli Strasse.

"How are you?" she asked. "You look tired. Are you eating enough? Are you getting enough sleep? Are you happy?"

"Yes," Dad asked, "are you really happy?"

Their lips spoke the words and through their eyes shown the same deep love I had known all of my life. But what they really meant was are you finally happy? After all of the tears and pain, turmoil and terror, did you find what you were after?

"I'm getting closer," I answered. "It was really hard, but I know that I did the right thing." My mouth searched for words to paint the colors of my heart. I was looking across a gulf at my parents. I wanted so much to cross it, even if only for a moment. "How are things at home?"

Dad smiled his kind, weary smile.

"I'm not sure how to answer that one. You wouldn't recognize it anymore. It's ..." his voice trailed away and he shook his head almost sadly, "all gone."

My voice came quickly, hurrying against the gathering silence.

"I talked to Peter on the phone a few weeks ago, and he says all the kids who used to show their red socks are laughing at the ones like us who left East Germany the hard way. He saw some of the ones who used to stick up for Communism in high school lined up at the West German banks to get their 100 marks for crossing over."

"I heard he went back with Yvonne," Mom said.

I shrugged. "Maybe they'll be happy." It really didn't matter.

"It was bad before, but now we have other worries. You can't tell how things will turn out. The political leaders shake hands and smile, but our businesses can't compete and they're closing down all over." She searched my eyes. "Is your life hard? Are you afraid for tomorrow?"

"We have to take care of ourselves here, Mom. The government isn't supposed to do everything. Sometimes I worry, but I still believe that if a man will only try, he'll make it."

Mom and Dad exchanged concerned glances, and in that instant I understood.

My reality had begun in the treehouse, playing a child's games with a wooden Winchester, but now that I had tasted both the dream and the substance of freedom, I was eager to eat the whole cake. My fears were of failure and not measuring up to what I believed man could become during his time on earth. The thought and the moment protracted, drawn out unnaturally as in a slow-motion film, but I really did understand! Was I touching the true essence of freedom?

I had thirsted after liberty until the urge had arced across my heart like lightning, forcing me to act. But for them, freedom had come to town unbidden, like a circus band awash with tumult and glitter, and they were still trying to figure out what to do with it. They had touched the romance of that ideal many times, but that white heat had not yet seared their souls.

Now, as in the past, they were still the foundation of their country, as fundamental to its future as the cobblestones of Spandauer Strasse. I had crossed the border in many ways that night so long ago, and now there was more than an ocean to separate them from the boy I used to be.

We finished our conversation and Dad asked when I would come to visit.

"They can't do anything to you now, son." He laughed. "I saw a kid flip the bird to a VOPO and he didn't even react. Most of them are like dogs now, jumping at every loud noise."

Bethany came back into the room, and I told Mom and Dad that we'd come in the spring.

"We don't have much room. You'd have to sleep on the couch because Roberto has your attic, but at least you'd be home for a while," Mom said.

We stood and I hugged her for a long time, listening to her

sniffle and feeling the sting of tears in my own eyes.

She knew that I was already home, my own home, and that Number Four, Zwingli Strasse was now only a former address.

It was raining when Bethany and I drove them to the airport and watched them fly away to a foreign land.

They had come to see my place of refuge, and now it was my turn. Sooner or later I would have to make the crossing again, and return to the place of my birth.

Carsten and Bethany Kaaz in Georgia — 1988

# CHAPTER TEN

America disappeared rearward into the haze, and soon the magnificent Atlantic cumulus began to creep beneath our wings.

Home.

On the phone, Mom had said that they were all so glad that I was coming.

Home.

The Wall was down, and the gruesome gang that had run the country for a generation was melting away, trying to hide in a fog of excuses. Honecker had disappeared into the Chilean Embassy in Russia. Stasi headquarters had been sacked by a mob of citizens demanding to see the once-secret records of their own surveillance over the past 40 years.

Home.

Not the home I once knew.

Mom and Dad had said that toward the end they went anywhere they wanted without fear, even to political gatherings. They recounted how the trucks and the men had finally come to tear the Wall down, and how the barbed wire had been so hard to manage, how the work gang had struggled and cursed as the springy wire tangled around their arms, cutting them in a hundred places. But taking the Wall down wasn't just another job to them, like putting it up had been so many years ago. They bled from the sharpened steel barbs, but their faces were smiling. These were no party men, but conscripts, ordinary people culled from the population and forced to wear the dusky green uniform of the Volks Armee. They hated the wire like everyone else, and now there was no need to hide it anymore. They sang as they sweated and bled.

After an eternity of flight, we descended over patchwork fields, angular buildings, gray on gray concrete spiked with jutting, brilliant reflections. Lower, arching across Berlin's upturned face, dots moved, becoming toy-sized cars, and tiny trees emerged from the featureless green swatches.

Nearby bumps and whines as doors opened, extending finely machined metal and molded rubber into the slashing slipstream, invisible restraints of deceleration as wing flaps whined forth and changed the airfoil's shape.

Up came our destination, the gray, black-streaked patch of waiting concrete, and my mind began to race. What was I feeling? My wife, Bethany, touched my hand lightly and held on as the earth rushed toward us. Then we were down.

The aisle filled quickly with a sluggish knot of exhausted people, moving, stretching, hyper-extending sore, cramped limbs, complaining in a hundred diverse tongues, groaning in universal commonality of discomfort.

Moving through the press of bodies at customs, we spotted Mom and Dad in the sea of searching faces.

Hugs, squeals of delight, kisses for both of us from both of them, then into Dad's West German Opel Kadett picking our way through the crowded Berlin streets. South and east of the airport, we left the downtown behind and cruised through residential suburbs. A thousand insignificant comments from everyone helped to pass the minutes, then a few more turns and we pulled over to the curb.

"Well," Dad said. "Does this look familiar?"

It was the high-rise apartment that I had seen every day as a child, the place where the West German buses turned around.

It was the field of the happy children and their kites where my little arrow had failed to fly.

I was stunned speechless by the tranquil beauty of the spot. Where the Wall had once stood was now an infinite expanse of tender new grass. I had watched TV as the Wall was attacked and taken down, but even the incredulity of those events hadn't prepared me for standing on the sight of a virtual park where the 'dead zone' had once cut the landscape like an infected wound. To the right, dumbly surveying this scene of pastoral gentility, was an abandoned guard tower, covered as high as a man could reach on every side by brightly painted graffiti. The angular gun ports were tight-lipped, steel-rimmed in their brooding impotent silence, and relieved the otherwise featureless monolith. Swirls of painted, outrageous messages mocked the fading echoes of curses uttered by a generation of stolid guards. The heavy entrance door was carelessly ajar.

Not so long ago, its occupants had tried to kill me and my friends. Now I felt curiously detached. That night, I had been too terrified to even look at the windows. Choking on my own bile, I had hardly dared to breathe for fear that they would smell my terror and turn their pitiless eyes upon us quivering by the Wall. Now my eyes roved quickly over the structure, noting where a rock had smashed one of the window panes. I had never really been angry at the guards, because in a way it seemed they were as much victims as I had been. Their main problem was that many of them believed that they were doing right. How awful it must have been to have a heart so twisted as to think that killing people to keep them locked inside their own country was somehow doing them a service. What unspeakable evil it was that made men's hearts turn to such an awful purpose.

Now the tower was different, a lot like an acquaintance's corpse. Whatever it had once been was because of what was inside, and now all that was gone. I turned away.

My throat tightened, lips suddenly dry, and I tried to speak. Not a sound.

Dad pulled the car back onto the street, and a few more minutes of travel brought us to the bakery on Spandauer Strasse. Mom went inside to buy bread, and as she returned, I stepped out onto the pavement. In a way, everything was the same, houses, yards, even the frontier warning signs. Nothing had changed. But in my mind it was as though it was all a movie, one in which I could only watch myself moving about, devoid of sensation, without sound or smell, a two-dimensional caricature superimposed upon a painted landscape. They had left the frontier signs in place. I wondered if it was some sort of reminder, but decided that such a thing was impossible. For most people, it was too soon to worry about remembering.

For now, they wanted only to forget. They would soon remove the signs and try to pretend that they had never existed. The paint was faded and peeling, and no one cared except me. Somewhere deep inside was the urge to preserve the thing, to have it embalmed as a kind of ghastly trophy. The thought rolled and turned in my mind. Should I try to take it home, maybe put it up in my front yard?

Frau Giede, the baker's wife, stepped onto the street and smiled at me as she wiped her hands on her apron.

"Well, the Ami is back! Welcome home, traveler!"

Something came from my mouth, a mumbled thanks perhaps, but the words were brittle on my trembling lips.

Tears began to flow and I scuffed my feet, walking as though in a dream away from Frau Giede. Seeing my state, she waved once more and retired to the bakery, casting a last compassionate look.

Up to the corner, bearing left toward the bus turnaround on Berliner Strasse, I saw the Siedlereck bar, and even though it was mid-afternoon, the drunks had already begun to gather for their daily session. One battered Trabant and an old Moskvich in the parking lot signaled that the establishment had retained its former low social standing. Faint music and echoes of guttural, ignorant laughter floated on the afternoon air.

And so my feet moved, step by wooden step, animating my form like a defective, leaking automaton. Here and there, a familiar face appeared on a porch or in a yard, but each one, after a greeting, comprehended something of my emotional disarray and respectfully retired.

An automobile engine muttered, then Dad's car drove slowly past and turned onto Zwingli Strasse. I walked alone.

"I can't believe it," I said to myself.

The few tears had become a torrent. Not a noisy kind of grief, it was a nameless irrepressible upwelling from the deepest roots of my soul. Vision blurred until my eyes were useless for anything but grief. Resisting was pointless, so I just walked and cried, having no focus for the grief until I saw it up ahead.

It was a street sign, the one marked Zwingli Strasse, tilted twenty degrees to the left, sagging like an old tree waiting to feel the earth's all-absorbing embrace.

Zwingli Strasse, its ornate iron post half-obscured by bushes, enameled black letters on a white background, reddish spots of rust intruding like incipient pox. For all of my life, there had never been so much as a weed near it.

Zwingli Strasse, the place where I began to be what I had at last become.

Ahead was the figure of a tall young man standing in the middle of the road, hands on his hips. His expression was unreadable. Perhaps he was unsure what to say or do.

Little Roberto was now three centimeters taller than I, and he hugged me so fiercely I could hardly breathe.

"I can't believe I'm back," I croaked.

"It's gonna be all right," he said smiling. "Come on in."

"I can't just yet. I have to pull myself together first. Let me walk down the street a little further." He nodded respectfully, retreating a few meters, and I breathed more deeply and regularly for several more steps.

"Carsten, come inside!" Mom called. It was the same voice that had summoned me to dinner so many times before, and yet I felt utterly alien. The last time I had stood there I had carried my father's ladder to challenge the Wall. I waved acknowledgement to Mom, then continued down the street, breathing deeply and trying to regain composure. Jerke still had his barnyard, but the house needed painting. There on the left was the Krippner place. No sign of anyone.

To the left was the Haan home, and there was someone out front.

My hand raised and wagged feebly, teeth showing, cheeks flexing in what I hoped would be interpreted as a smile.

"Carsten? Is that you? Is it possible?" said Frau Haan.

She came down from the porch, showing the biggest grin I had ever seen on her usually conservative face.

"Wonderful," she said, "it's wonderful to see you. You look great! America must agree with you. Tell us everything! What kind of job do you have? We heard that there are many unemployed over there."

Her warm enthusiasm made it impossible for me to be angry,

but I began to stammer, trying to answer the torrent of questions.

"Hello, Carsten!" It was Frau Schirmer calling from her front porch, across the street. "I heard you were coming. Welcome home!"

After a moment of conversation, my neighbors realized that I was not my usual self, and after offering more handshakes and good wishes, they respectfully moved away, allowing my walk to resume.

Zwingli Strasse simply stopped like it always had, only this time there was no tower, no fence, no walls, just more tender new grass. I was unable to assimilate the discontinuities that assaulted my pounding heart, so I slowly retraced my steps and stepped through the gate of my parents' home.

We sat in the living room surrounded by the warm swirls of the hardwood paneling. Mom's tiny figurines paused in their eternal glass dances, waiting for the sunlight to divide in their bodies and paint the walls for a few glorious moments. Sporadic questions, long appraising looks and awkward silences followed each other in a random jumble. We behaved oddly, with a sort of formality at first, wanting to make sense, wanting to talk and touch, yet hardly knowing where to begin. Their faces were strangely new, and I labored trying to match each line and expression with the memories. Bethany sat politely, attempting to find something to occupy her attention as German conversation swirled around her.

We stayed up talking that night until incapacitated by fatigue. Then, as Bethany stumbled down the hall to brush her teeth, Roberto sneaked up behind me, and caught my neck in a playful headlock.

"Day after tomorrow is going to be something, Carsten! Everyone's coming to the party. Everyone! It'll be the biggest thing to happen on Zwingli since the night you went over the Wall. Mom invited some of your friends, and within 24 hours the whole town knew about it. One of Mom's friends went shopping in Berlin and heard two old ladies talking about it on the bus. Everybody remembers our hometown hero. Everybody remembers the night that three made it together!"

I muttered thanks, excused myself abruptly and made for the bed. In the moment before succumbing to the irresistible wave of sleep, I stared hard into the darkness. It took a moment to verify the inventory, but they were all there, all the names and faces, triumphs and tragedies of a time that would never be again. In 48 hours, I would meet my memories again, and they would see me, judge me. What did they think I had become? Would they accept me again? My heart ached at the possibility of rejection, but even that fear wasn't sufficient to further postpone a deep and dreamless sleep.

By the time Bethany and I awoke, it was late the next morning. Slouching down the hall, rubbing gritty eyes, I tried to reconcile the smell of Dad's barbecued chicken with the stale taste that was everywhere in my mouth. The aroma resurrected more images from the past. How many weekends had begun with the smell of barbecue? The same familiar face peered back at me from the bathroom mirror. How many times had I seen it just so? Framing it was the same ceramic wall tile. That same rack had held my damp towel since I was old enough to remember. All of these things were in their places, but there was still something wrong. As I was trying to remember if jetlag could cause memory loss, the realization came.

Everything was perfectly in order in my parents' home, even to the color of the walls. I didn't belong. I was the thing out of place, and no amount of rearranging could change that.

I had some catching up to do, so I walked over to Kubicki's house to see if Ulf and his parents were home.

After the standard questions about life in the West, they began to ask the hard ones.

"How about it?" Annelies said in a kind tone. "The Wall's down, and the frontier signs are nothing but a historical curiosity. Was it worth it? Is living over there what you thought it would be?"

I answered quickly, "Better than I had hoped."

"All right then, tell us about it."

"Where do I start?"

"Happiness," Annelies said. "No matter what, you have to be happy!"

"Yes, I'm very happy! I have a great wife, a good job, nice home. We try to enjoy life together." That was true, but it was also a standard response. I tried to explain further. "It's almost impossible to describe things in a way that's going to make sense. In America, we're surrounded by possibilities. Everywhere there are choices! The pace is astounding, but I never knew that life could have so many choices. At first it was intoxicating! It seems more normal now, but it really takes some getting used to."

She smiled, and Ulf pressed his lips together as he always had when analyzing something important.

"Things are all right with you aren't they?" I asked him.

"I'm not complaining. I have a job when a third of our neighbors are out of work, and my parents were lucky enough to own their home. No ex-landlord is going to show up one day and throw them out," he said.

"What about the future?"

"Whose future? Mine or Germany's?"

"Yours first," I said.

"Mine is going better than I had hoped, but Germany's is another matter entirely."

It was as if the last five years had been peeled away and other days flooded forth to fill my consciousness. Ulf had always been studious and thoughtful. If a problem was presented, he would lock on and pursue until an answer was extracted.

"You remember the days of the Wall, and how slow everything was? How we all griped about the static society?"

I nodded as his face took on a special intensity.

"What you see these days is the calm before a terrible storm. People are afraid, and when they're afraid they often do stupid things."

"What do they fear?" I asked.

"Hunger, pain, being cold, all the normal things that people dread, but something special to Germans bothers them more than anything else." He waited for a moment, letting the silence gather my full attention. "We thrive in an atmosphere of rationality and order, but it's crumbling away every day."

I considered it and knew that he was right.

"But that's not just true for Germans. Everyone wants life to

Carsten Kaaz with his Karate instructor, Atlanta — 1989

Uwe George and Carsten Kaaz in
Memphis, Tennessee — 1994

have some predictability so they can live from day to day," I said.

"Have you seen the signs, 'Ich nicht verstehen, Ich bin Deutsch?'"

I had. They were commonly found on car bumpers. "I don't understand, I'm German" meant that the Germans were tired of going into a store to buy something and being addressed in a foreign language. They wanted to hear their own tongue spoken on the street corners and in the U-Bahn. They saw jobs being taken by more and more foreign guest workers, and they were afraid that theirs would be next. Some of their fears seemed validated, as marginal positions on the lower pay scales were gobbled up by newcomers from every point on the compass.

"Like I said, they do stupid things." He leaned closer, lowering his voice as though to speak a secret. "What do you think is different now from when you were here the last time?"

"Everything as far as I can see."

"Not really so very much. We've been let out of the cage, but a lot of us don't know quite what to do about it. Our Russian masters left us quite a few things to remember them by."

"Such as?"

"When they knew they were being shipped out, they sold everything they could steal from each other and their own army." He snickered, "They hawked their automatic rifles and pistols complete with ammunition. Grenades? You want grenades? I could get you some in a half-hour, and I'm just an ordinary man, not a gun runner. I hear that if you have the money you could pick up some of those shoulder-launched anti-aircraft missiles, too."

Suddenly, I felt a chill.

"Look at it this way. Take people who have never been allowed to make decisions, disrupt their society, take away most of the controls, strip away their security, the 'Ordnung' that they used to curse but also depended on, and then throw in unemployment, add some different-looking foreigners, and so many firearms that nobody can even count them all. Then mix well, adding liberal amounts of human weakness and prejudice." His eyes bored into mine with an intensity I had never before seen. "It's coming apart, Carsten. It's unraveling here and there, and the politicians are still making their speeches. They say this or that will fix things, but it isn't true. Germany's going to be a very unpleasant place to live until we get this sorted out. This generation of slaves won't be able to handle their freedom. They want all the nice material things and to be able to speak their minds and criticize, but too many are so afraid of failing, or being out on the street. Those are the kind that'll be begging someone to take over and run their lives again soon. They want all the benefits without any of the responsibilities."

I shook my head. "I don't know."

"It doesn't end at that. It's the rest of Europe, too. Maybe the whole world." His voice trailed off and he looked up and away in the direction of downtown Berlin. "If only we had more courage sooner. It's criminal to keep people caged up. It ruins their ability to make good judgments. Now when they have freedom, they run from obligations. When things get hard, they're quick to trade insecurity for what looks like safety, and once the deal is done, there's no going back, because their new masters own them. Using freedom wisely takes a lot of practice, and we haven't had much of that at all. Maybe it takes generations to learn how to handle it responsibly. The old East side is like a kid with a new bicycle who has just discovered that he can ride wherever he wants because Mom and Dad can't watch him every minute. There are bound to be some awful things come of this before we get it right."

"We just have to work for things that are good. Work together. Not give up," I said vaguely. My heart felt like it would sink to the earth. "Was all of this for nothing?"

"No," he said quickly, "but there aren't many that really understand what we've won." He smiled and I saw my childhood friend turn suddenly old as he continued those fearful predictions. "Freedom is worth any price you have to pay. I was really glad when you three made it over the Wall. I thought that no matter what they did, even if they were to find you and kill you, they'd never make you a slave again. It felt good to think that, and in that way I wished I'd gone with you. Not because I was so unhappy, but just to make the point that no man should ever be a slave."

Neither of us spoke for a long moment, then I ventured, "This means a lot to me, you know. You're still a great friend."

"Thanks, but you have a real problem."

"What's that?"

"Well you're the one who has to go out and tell everyone about this freedom business. These are very dangerous times. We're so wrapped up in trying to be successful, we can't see the danger."

I considered the words.

"Maybe you can help wake people up, get their attention or something. If we go under, that might start something terrible here in Europe. You'll do that won't you, for all of us?"

"Sure."

Ulf's wife appeared at his side, walking gingerly, the way a pregnant woman moves when she's thinking of her baby.

"Have you fixed all the world's problems?" she asked him.

He laughed and passed the question to me with a look.

"I think we covered it all," I said. "He's given me an assignment, so I'll have to get busy and not let him down."

"Remember!" he said.

I nodded and he said good night, helping his wife carefully across the brickwork floor.

The sun rose upon the day of the party.

I saw Herr Jerke parting the living room curtains. In years past, I had thought nothing of his persistent curiosity, but Mom had told me that he as much as admitted to being an informer after Stasi headquarters was rifled and so many files made public. He could watch all he wanted now. He could see who my friends were and write them down if he wanted. He was nothing now that his masters had gone away. That thought felt quite comfortable and it served to counterbalance the primitive urge to smash his face. How many lives had been spoiled by his prying eyes and scribbling pencil?

Lutz probably knew as much about what made me go as any friend I ever had. He showed up two hours early so we'd have time to talk. We stood out in the yard near Mom's garden spot and exchanged stories.

"I lost the theater when the former owner returned after the

Wall came down. He wanted it back, but he didn't want it to be a theater anymore."

"Can't we go by just for old time's sake?"

He looked away. "You don't want to do that."

"I don't want to see a movie, just sit down in one of the chairs and remember."

"You don't understand, my friend. It's a corpse. It's dead, stripped to the bone, paneling ripped out, screen torn down. It's nothing but a hulk." He shuffled his feet and shook his head. "Jeanette works in the best restaurant in Rangsdorf. At least one of us has a job."

"What about prospects for you?"

He smiled that easy, open smile. "I've never been unemployed in my life, but it's not so bad. I worked hard for years, so I look at this like a vacation. Something will turn up."

"It would be great to have you visit us in Memphis," I said. "Maybe you and Jeanette could get married there. Wouldn't that be something?"

He considered my comment silently.

"What are you driving these days?" I asked.

"They call it a Pontiac Phoenix."

I whistled. "Parts are pretty hard to get, aren't they?"

"Almost impossible. Notice that I said 'almost.' Connections still count for something, and I have a few." He pressed his lips tightly together and nodded affirmatively. "I got it from a guy in Berlin a few months ago, partly because it's in good shape, and partly because it reminds me of America."

"That's an expensive souvenir."

"More than just a memento," he said firmly. "I could have bought a good Mercedes or BMW, but neither one would remind me of freedom. That's why I got the Pontiac; because it reminds me of America, and America reminds me that there's still hope in this life."

"Aren't you happy here?"

"That's a relative thing, Carsten. I'll tell you this for sure, and I know you can understand what I'm about to say. We have something great here in Germany, but the government still runs everything. Sure, I'm glad the Wall is down, and I'm happy that

I don't have to worry about police informers or being reported for showing the wrong kind of movies. But they never take your training wheels off over here. The government has its hand on your shoulder from the first breath until they plant you in the ground. For me, the idea of America is like riding a motorcycle. It's dangerous and unpredictable, but so exhilarating that you don't care. Once you go there, you're never the same again."

"It sure isn't perfect!"

"Sure," he said. "Sure there are problems — a lot of serious ones. But there's nowhere else I know of that has a better chance of solving them than America. They know more about handling freedom than anyone else."

The clock's hands moved and the rest of my past began to assemble, parking their cars on the street in front of the house.

The patio filled with both friends and curious neighbors who stopped by to say hello. Some came to renew our friendship, and some came to see my American wife and find something to gossip about. Whatever the reason, I didn't care.

One by one, I took certain guests aside for a brief walk in the yard, away from the others.

Peter Zimmermann sipped his beer and met my eyes with a strong, confident gaze. He had truly started over and was an independent insurance broker, employing two salesmen. He lived well, and liked the way things had developed.

"It's funny, you know," he said.

"What?"

"The way things turned out. It was unthinkable that we'd ever become friends, much less hatch a plan and make it over the Wall. Then when we did, we had no idea what to do next."

I laughed. It was true. Escape was the object, and at first we didn't care what followed.

"Getting out was the thing. Leaving it all behind forever, and then it was strange watching the rest of them get it for free," he said. "At first the whole thing was unbelievable. It was a cosmic event, like a comet or something. Anyway, my new life is great, but it still seems strange, like there's something missing."

"Is what we feel the same to us as what they feel?" I asked.

Peter's eyes moved quickly, reflecting a kaleidoscope of

thoughts.

"I was assigned to a city work gang in the 1980s, and we were ordered to go cut down all the wild shrubbery in the frontier area on a very hot day."

"Where?"

"A lot of places. This area was one I think."

He might have been the one who had butchered my tree house. I made a mental note to tell him about that someday.

"We sweated our butts off, wrestling those chain saws and dragging brush until we were dead tired. Then they told us that we could take a break, and we sat in the shadow of the truck because we had already chopped up all the trees and all the shade was gone. I remember the breeze. It was the most perfect, beautiful thing in the world at that moment. It made all the sweat and dirt go away for a moment as it cooled me down." He smiled and narrowed his eyes for emphasis. "It can never be the same for them as for us. We paid full price for everything we have. We're the ones who risked it all and won. We'll never forget the cost! Freedom feels terrific, like the shadow of that truck and the breeze on a hot day." He paused. "We did it the hard way, but maybe that's the only way people learn about freedom. I wouldn't change a thing!"

"What about the rest of them? Our old friends, schoolmates?"

He laughed, then quickly grew serious.

"The party's over now, and they're left with reality. You know, I watched all the stuff on TV, and I wondered how it could be possible. I tried to imagine what had changed so much in just a few years, and I think I know."

I raised my eyebrows in inquiry.

"It's tough being a prisoner like we were, but it's even harder to be the jailer. The inmates have a never-ending desire to be free, but the men in the towers will finally lose the will to continue. The Russians went away when they got tired, that's all. They were tired of shooting people, tired of expending all that energy to supposedly protect us and getting nothing but contempt in return. They were tired of trying to scare us into cooperating, and there was nothing else to do but start shooting again. They thought it over and decided that it wasn't worth it any more, so they resigned." He stretched, and asked about freedom.

"It's different to different people," I said.

"You're stating the obvious."

"Maybe not. Look," I said, "living in America has really been an eye-opener. They've had liberty for 250 years, and they're still arguing about what it means. Some people think that the government ought to be everyone's father when they get into trouble, and others think that government ought to go away and never show itself. Then there's the in-between where most of the people just want to live from day to day and not be bothered."

"Like here."

"To some extent, but I think our traditions are a problem. Over the years, we've transferred a lot of responsibility for everyday life to the government. Americans are still debating whether or not that's a good idea. They don't expect as much from the government as we used to."

"We still expect a lot over here."

"Well, where are things headed?"

Peter rubbed his chin and took another long drink of beer. "That's a good question. One thing's for sure, we better get it under control in a hurry, because there are a lot of people who would just as soon see our government take everything over if it will bring order to society."

A silence descended, and we shuffled our feet.

"How's Yvonne doing?" I asked.

"Oh, she's all right," he said, "but it's nothing serious. We're more friends than anything else. She's changed some, maybe a little more mature."

Coming from some people, that remark would have been pretentious, but he really meant what he said. It was an assessment fairly given from a young man who had been hard at work catching up on real life as soon as he had cast off his chains.

"What about Uwe?" he asked.

"It's been a long time since I saw him. He was in Atlanta for a while, then he came back to Germany."

"I always wondered what he was thinking. He never really said much."

"One thing's for sure. If it hadn't been for him, I never would have been able to keep my dreams alive. He was the reason I made it to the Wall, and you were the reason I finally went over." I raised my glass of soft drink. "Here's to both of you, my best friends, my brothers in our struggle for freedom!"

Peter's face took on an unusually serious appearance.

"Yes," he said, "it took all of us to get the job done, didn't it. Yes, here's to Uwe, our blood brother in our struggle for freedom!" His half glass of beer disappeared in one gulp.

Vivien walked up behind me.

"Hello."

"It's good to see you," I said.

"Well?" She smiled, and we hugged.

I felt awkward, but we began to talk and the tension left. "I'm glad to see you. How are things?" I asked.

"Oh, fine. I'm working at Sanssouci in Potsdam."

"You must be in heaven surrounded by all that architecture."

"Yes, it's very nice."

She arranged her hair absentmindedly, as though by habit and not out of any real appreciation for how it looked. She was still very attractive, but something new had invaded those normally bright eyes.

Every few minutes, an aircraft flew over on its way to Tegel, so we'd smile and point up in the air, stopping the conversation until the noise died away. During those moments, I felt a growing sense that something was bothering her. Her glance was tentative and she looked away too often. Her eyes were clouded by a deep but silent sadness. Had she suffered some tragedy?

"We took some nice trips, didn't we?" she asked.

"Yes. I really liked Czechoslovakia the best."

"You were bored with the fountains and the endless statues."

"I never claimed to like statues that much," I said. "That wasn't why I went."

She smiled at the implied compliment.

The conversation was ridiculously artificial, and I couldn't stand it any longer.

"Are you all right, Vivien? I mean, is everything going well in your life?"

The frankness of the question caught her off guard, and I saw lines of despair etch into her young face.

"So many things have changed, it's hard to know which way to go or what to do."

"Married?"

"Me? No, not yet." A brave smile followed.

Mom had been right, then. Vivien was still living with Herr Porzich.

"What about art school? Are you … ?"

"No, I'm not. I have to work now that the government has changed. Maybe I'll get another chance. Actually, I'm lucky to have a job at all. There are so many unemployed."

"You'll get more opportunities. You're really talented."

"Thanks. Well, it's time to go see who else is here. See you later." She pasted a smile on her face, and headed for the patio crowd.

There were a thousand questions, more about life in America than my own circumstances, and as I moved from group to group, I felt a curious separation from these familiar people who were speaking my native tongue. Refilling glasses in the kitchen, I slipped into a reflective mode, and was standing still in the kitchen when Bethany touched me on the shoulder.

"Are you all right?"

"Oh, sure," I said. "No problem. I was just …"

"You were just trying to figure everything out, right?"

"Right, but I can't. I am trying to figure where I fit now that everything has changed."

"You weren't ready for this, were you?"

"I guess not," I said. "I don't think they were ready either."

"What do you mean?"

"When I left, I really left. I mean, I put everything and everyone in a little box in my heart, and closed the lid. I just don't feel home here anymore, my home is America now. Coming back to Mom, Dad, and Roberto wasn't so difficult, because they were always on my mind. These others, most of them anyway, went into my own private museum." I tapped my chest. "This one. The one where things can still live when I think they've gone forever."

"But here you are, and now they're back."

"This new society is a shock to them, and they're acting on the outside like they're happy, but on the inside, they're going full speed trying to figure out what to do. It's tearing them up, Bethany. Some of them don't even know it, but it's tearing them up. Gaining this much freedom was a shock to them all; they weren't prepared."

Vivien had been talking to Lutz for the last two hours, and now she approached to say goodbye.

"It was a nice party."

"Thanks. I'm glad you could come."

Intermittent laughter from the patio, random chunks of words and the clinking of party glasses filled the awful silence. I felt like a mourner at a funeral home, watching an old friend grieving. It made me sad to behold her pain. Then her eyes brimmed and spilled involuntary tears.

"Hans is waiting. I have to go."

"I'm really glad you could come," I said.

"Your wife is very pretty. Bethany isn't it? I've never heard that name before."

"It's from the Bible."

"Of course. You go to church now, too?"

"Yes. It means a lot to me."

"Well," she said finally, "I had to come and wish you good luck in everything. Keep following your dreams."

"You too."

She leaned over quickly and kissed my cheek, then turned away, walking quickly to the car. The door slammed and she was gone.

I watched until it turned the corner. Maybe she was searching for something to rekindle the determination that used to burn so brightly in her heart. Vivien was as lovely as ever, maybe more so after the passage of those few years. All but her eyes. Their awful emptiness haunted my thoughts even in the midst of the revelry. I had no idea if I had given encouragement or taken it away. Someone called my name from the patio and I walked slowly back.

Mom and Dad went to bed about midnight, and as the guests tired, they took their leave in small groups. Then they were gone, and the patio was again as it had always been, a quiet family place next to the family garden.


I returned to America and hosted various friends as they visited Memphis, taking special pleasure in showing Lutz around Graceland. I also stood as best man at his wedding to Jeanette.

On April 29, 1992, in the company of a hundred strangers who spoke the tongues of many lands, I repeated the precious words that confirmed my citizenship in the United States. Like countless others, washed to these shores by the tides of far-away trouble.

And thus my flight from fear ended. It was so simple as to be laughable, but on my own I would have never seen. From the beginning, I had thought that escaping was just for me, never comprehending that so many followed in their dreams.

If I could paint the fear that lingers in Europe, it would be a portrait dipped in bloody red and black. The men whose heels had rested for so long upon the neck of my nation did their work well. Their crime was not just building a wall, or killing innocents who challenged their rule. The depth of that evil was much greater than even they had hoped.

They were thieves of men's souls, cursed pirates of tomorrow who crippled a whole generation as surely as if they had shackled the legs of every newborn child with life-long iron manacles.

Freedom is a special recipe, and like any good stew, it takes a long time to make. My countrymen have had no practice at making the kind of choices that must be made if any people are to obtain and keep their freedom. They still have to learn how to balance personal responsibility with their own desires, how to tell a government that it need not do everything for them, and how to give of themselves to those in need without being commanded by an unthinking bureaucracy, grinding along in its rule-worn rut.

Do they have the time to learn these lessons before some calamity sweeps those good intentions away in a flood of expediency?

I do not know.

Here is what I do know.

I owe my fellow dreamers. The urge to freedom springs from sacred fires in the heart, and I must remain true to the dream; nurturing a living memory to those who tried and failed, adding a confirming approval to those who succeeded, contributing faith to those who are yet searching for the courage to begin their journey out of the night.

Hope is what I owe, and I will pay the debt in full.

# Promise of America

*To every man his chance*
*— to every man, regardless of his birth,*
*his shining, golden opportunity*
*— to every man the right to live,*
*to work, to be himself,*
*and to become whatever thing*
*his manhood*
*and his vision*
*can combine to make him*
*— this, seeker,*
*is the promise of America.*


*— Thomas Wolfe*

# Epilogue

Carsten Kaaz lives in Memphis, Tennessee with his wife Bethany and son Kyle. His parents, Fred and Barbara Kaaz, and his brother, Roberto, also live in Memphis.

Uwe George, Carsten's best friend, has also moved with his family to Memphis.

Peter Zimmermann still lives by himself in Berlin where he works as an independent insurance agent.

# Acknowledgements

I would like to thank my co-author, Mike Riemann and my editor, David Yawn, for many years of unwavering support and encouragement; Peter Zimmermann for trusting me with his life; Annelies Kubicki for believing in me, when hardly anyone else did; Ulf Kubicki for sharing many common interests; Henrik Krippner for countless hours of conversation; my elementary school teacher, Gudrun Kranert, for caring; Jessica Stille for her thoughtfulness; Rhonda Lee Brock, Gloria Torbati, Christine Maugans, and Kyle Peterson for helping me to keep my dream of freedom alive; John Penrod, Leonard Lott and Jurgen Gaertner for being my friends and confidants; Rodney McAnally for making me laugh; Roberto for being a good brother; Uncle Reiner Grossert for fixing my cars; Oma and Opa Grossert for their stories and delicious food; Oma and Opa Kaaz for being great grandparents; Oma Wanda for her love; Roger and Karen Avrit for their daughter; Mike and Ruth Anderson for helping me get my life started in America; Drs. John Ward and Terri Hyatt for taking care of me; Greg Hughey for his valuable opinions; the people at Guild Bindery Press, Randall Bedwell, Robbin Brent, Pat Patterson, Palmer Jones, Toby Lyon and Edward F. Williams, III; and all the girls I once loved ...

Carsten Kaaz
October 1994
Memphis, Tennesee